Rethinking Rights

The Eric Voegelin Institute Series in Political Philosophy

Other Books in the Series

Rethinking Rights

Historical, Political, and Philosophical Perspectives

Edited by
Bruce P. Frohnen and Kenneth L. Grasso

University of Missouri Press   Columbia and London

Copyright © 2009 by
The Curators of the University of Missouri
University of Missouri Press, Columbia, Missouri 65201
Printed and bound in the United States of America
All rights reserved
5 4 3 2 1   13 12 11 10 09

Cataloging-in-Publication information is available from the Library of Congress.
(cloth) ISBN 978-0-8262-1820-9
(paper) ISBN 978-0-8262-1831-5

This paper meets the requirements of the
American National Standard for Permanence of Paper
for Printed Library Materials, Z39.48, 1984.

Designer: Jennifer Cropp
Typesetter: BookComp, Inc.
Printer and Binder: Thomson-Shore, Inc.
Typefaces: Palatino, Sabon, and New Berolina

*Publication of this book has been assisted by a contribution from the Eric
Voegelin Institute, which gratefully acknowledges the generous support
provided for the series by the Earhart Foundation and the Sidney
Richards Moore Memorial Fund.*

Contents

Acknowledgments

Bruce Frohnen wishes to thank several research assistants who, over several years, helped in a number of projects that contributed to this volume and in particular to his contribution thereto: Matthew Bowman, Guy Conti, Brian Eck, Raymond McAuliffe, Sean Morris, Christopher Persaud, and Amy Ruark.

Both editors wish to express their appreciation to Beverly Jarrett, the two anonymous reviewers, and everyone at the University of Missouri Press as well as Professor Ellis Sandoz and the Eric Voegelin Institute. As always and in all things, we wish here to express our appreciation and love to our wives and children, and in particular our gratitude for the patience they displayed while we were working on this volume.

Rethinking Rights

Introduction

Rights in a Multicultural Age

Bruce P. Frohnen and Kenneth L. Grasso

The editors hereby present a collection of essays dealing with the subject of human rights from the perspectives of history, politics, and philosophy. We do so with the intention of throwing light on a social and political reality—rights—too often treated as a kind of god-term. Rights clearly have historical roots, are given meaning through political contexts and actions, and need to be understood in light of their place in the order of existence. But they increasingly have become mere rhetorical claims to good things over which individuals and groups conflict. Indeed, our understanding of rights seems dangerously disordered at a time of increased ideological and practical challenges.

We approach analysis of this situation with some trepidation, particularly given the sheer volume of literature on rights. We are comforted less by self-assurance concerning our own understanding of the topic than by the wisdom and scholarly acumen of those who have done us the honor of contributing to this volume. Most of the authors represented here have already made important contributions to the continuing debates concerning the origins, nature, and inherent purposes of rights. Herein the reader will find essays dealing with long-running arguments concerning when and how the language of rights developed a coherence and prominence sufficient to make itself heard in public discourse; how concrete rights developed in political, social, and economic contexts; how rights have been applied to and asserted by individuals, groups, and institutions; and how the manners in which we conceive of rights and of the person have related with one another to produce given types of society, with all their strengths and weaknesses.

We are aware that some readers will find the "program" of this volume—to reexamine our understanding of human rights by setting forth a more clear and accurate picture of their roots, development, intrinsic nature, and sociocultural effects—ill considered. Indeed, some recent authors have pointed out that Americans in particular "talk" too much about rights,[1] and others accuse liberal democracies of failing in their duty to spread and enforce the reality of rights to peoples and societies suffering from their concrete denial.[2] Genocide in Africa, terrorism centered in the Middle East, and systems of injustice rooted in race, class, and sex are brought to our attention as spurs to action rather than merely to more analysis.

But it is our contention that the very prevalence of rights talk—and rights thought—has rendered sustained consideration of what we mean by a *right,* and what rights mean for us, all but impossible. Rights arguments have devolved, particularly in regard to normative considerations. This is especially true in liberal democratic regimes—governments self-consciously built upon interlocking procedures and policies constituting a veritable system of rights. Yet, as a number of writers have noted, defenders of the liberal democratic rights regime in recent decades often have rejected any attempt at justifying, or even explicating, the principles upon which such a regime must be based.[3] This failure to defend liberal democratic principles seems to the editors tied intimately to a persistent failure on all sides to defend a full, reasonable conception of rights. Fortunately, in our view, rights, like many other good things, are not inherently tied to any one specific political regime or ideology, even one as old and respectable as liberal democracy.

We have asked scholars to rethink rights because they are so widely discussed and so poorly understood—and because they are at the center of

---

1. See for example Mary Ann Glendon, *Rights Talk: The Impoverishment of Political Discourse* (New York: Free Press, 1991).

2. William Bradford, "The Western European Union, Yugoslavia, and the (Dis)Integration of the EU, The New Sick Man of Europe," *Boston College International and Comparative Law Review* 24 (2000): 13–84. (Bradford complains about Western failure to act sooner in the Bosnia and Kosovo crises.)

3. David Walsh, *The Growth of the Liberal Soul* (Columbia: University of Missouri Press, 1997).

liberal democratic self-understanding at a time when liberal democracy's continued success threatens its own survival. At the core of public life in the post–cold war era lies a deep irony: at the time of its greatest triumph, liberal democracy faces a possibly fatal crisis. It faces a crisis in which, despite sustained attacks on its moral legitimacy, its greatest defenders refuse to give us reasons to value it, and in which the once-rousing story of its rise to power has become increasingly untenable. It is clear that liberal democracy, in spite of its apparent status as the sole ideology currently maintaining intellectual respectability, has lost its capacity to inspire.

For example, Western liberal democrats tend to believe that non-Western peoples uniformly yearn to build states and societies essentially like their own. But attempts to make over non-Western regimes, such as those in the Middle East, in the image of Western democracies have produced a backlash of ethnic, tribal, and religious fervor. And the rhetoric of liberal democracy, once used even by dictators in pursuit of legitimacy through the language, though not the reality, of individual rights and public consent, has been muted by calls for ethnically and religiously based rule. At home, liberal values of toleration and openness are being called into question as Western regimes become increasingly afraid of terrorists from the Islamic world—and among Islamic immigrants at home.

Underlying this increasing fear and agitation is uncertainty regarding just what liberal democracy is, and for what it stands. The institutional components of liberal democracy are known well enough: multiparty elections and judicial protection of individual rights are central. But for what good does such a set of arrangements stand? In particular, what common good does it seek to foster? The claim is that tolerance and openness to a variety of choices and styles of life show a respect for the autonomy of each individual's will, and that this is at the heart of liberal democracy.[4] Liberal democrats see the state as a tool to be used to protect individual rights, both from the state and from other loci of power, so as to enforce equal dignity, which they define as access to the choices needed to construct one's own lifestyle and identity. But the pursuit of authentic choice within a frame of immanence, in which the good is chosen by each self, buffered by its own rational constructs and even its own expressive interiority, is premised on, even as it furthers, a fracturing of any common good into niche goods relevant only to the self and, at times, its intimates.[5]

4. See for example Charles Taylor, *The Ethics of Authenticity* (Cambridge: Harvard University Press, 1992), 52.

5. We reference here the analysis of contemporary ethics constructed in Charles Taylor, *A Secular Age* (Cambridge: Harvard University Press, 2007).

The self-contradiction of the public decision to not choose any one way of life is shown by current strains within liberal democracies. The openness to which liberal democratic ideology lays claim has become increasingly difficult to maintain as the practical victories of Western nations bring more and more diverse cultures within its orbit. It is relatively easy to speak of freedom and toleration among comfortably post-Christian people in economically developed nations. But what of those who do not, in fact, think, act, or even look like prosperous, comfortably post-Christian people of northern European ancestry? Although they praise them for some of their customary forms of dress and cuisine, contemporary liberal democrats end up telling people from differing cultures that they have chosen the wrong values and that they must choose to behave like typical liberal democrats in their familial, religious, social, and political lives.

And rights? Rights have taken center stage in conflicts within liberal democracies. But they have done so not as the basis of principled compromise, allowing all sides to come together in respect for common beliefs and goals or even as the basis of principled mutual forbearance. Rather, they have served as sets of conflicting claims to power and autonomy. Shall rights include those of women to wear traditional Islamic garb in public schools? The right of one person to mock another's religion in public? The right to child marriage? Indeed, can any society, let alone one claiming tolerance of diverse viewpoints and lifestyles, survive the kinds of debates spawned by such fundamental disagreements over what is right?

Liberal democracy, as currently defined, is simply too thin a view of public life, resting on too thin a view of the person, politics, and the human good. In the end it cannot be defended as currently formulated. But this is no cause for despair, or for giving in to any form of arbitrary government. What *can* be defended—what *should* be defended—is constitutional, limited government respecting the inherent dignity of the person. This defense of institutions currently identified solely with liberal democracy does not require the rejection or devaluing of rights any more than it requires a liberal thinning of the common good. What it does require is that rights be grounded properly in a full view of the person's inherently social nature and proper goals, and in a vision of the proper nature and order of the common good, lesser goods, and the persons, groups, and institutions (including but not prioritizing the nation-state) making up society. Rights need not and should not be left undefended. But they need to be rethought in a manner that brings them back into accord with human nature and experience so that they may again serve the truly human good.

Liberal and Post-liberal Conflict

As liberal democracy has triumphed over its adversaries in the former Soviet Union and Eastern Europe, the supposed "end of history," not surprisingly, has failed to materialize. Now the standard conception seems to be of a "clash of civilizations" pitting Western, post-Christian civilization against some form of resurgent Islam.[6] And clearly there is something to this rather simplistic vision, as the barbaric acts of 9/11 attest. But the greatest threat to the hegemony of liberal democracy comes from internal weaknesses and inconsistencies—ones attributable in large part to a conflict of visions and norms, though not to simple ethnicity, as some have argued.[7]

Most Americans are familiar with some of the major conflicts among rights claims in our society today. The prototypically liberal statement, often ascribed to Oliver Wendell Holmes Jr. as well as John Stuart Mill, that "my right to swing my fist ends at the other man's nose" continues to be proven wrong even as it continues to encourage attempts to draw bright-line distinctions where none exist. There is a legal term for swinging one's fist just short of another person's nose: *assault,* that is, putting another person in rational fear of physical harm.[8] Yet the assertion of supposedly clear and absolute rights continues to create increasing conflict in our society: the right of workers to organize vs. the right of owners to control the terms under which their property shall be used; the right to free speech vs. the right to be free from invidious discrimination; the right to life vs. the right to control one's own body. These are only a few of the more obvious conflicts among rights in contemporary public discourse and practice.

Some have blamed such conflicts in large measure on the liberal democratic insistence that rights inhere solely in individuals. Purely individual rights, it can be argued, leave no room for recognition of competing social interests. And it is true that liberal rights generally are seen in individualistic terms. Today most liberals think of rights as inherently natural in the radical sense of being pre-social. And such assumptions go beyond the more traditional forms of universal naturalism summed up by R. H. Helmholz, according to whom modern natural rights are held "not simply

---

6. Samuel P. Huntington, *The Clash of Civilizations: Remaking of the World Order* (New York: Simon and Schuster, 1997).

7. Samuel P. Huntington, *Who We Are: The Challenges to America's National Identity* (New York: Simon and Schuster, 2004).

8. *Black's Law Dictionary,* 8th ed., s.v. *assault.*

because the government of the day concedes them to us. We hold them because we are human."[9]

John Rawls, arguably the most influential theorist of modern liberal democracy, goes so far as to demand that we hide our selves from ourselves. Imagining that we act behind a "veil of ignorance," we essentially must will ourselves to become ignorant of our talents and our very character so that we may idealize the proper, just form of society we should construct and defend. Thus the prototypical liberal self is an abstract maker of choices. This choice maker has rights that belong to it regardless of its membership in any particular group or category, and that trump all other considerations in that they are inviolable even in the face of potentially bad effects on the welfare of "everyone else."[10] Indeed, according to contemporary liberals, rights inherently relate only to individuals because only individuals can experience joy and sorrow, pleasure and pain, justice and injustice.[11]

This emphasis on individualistic rights has come into increasing conflict with the demands of people whose self-conceptions and personal choices conflict with liberal democratic assumptions. The argument, even among some calling themselves communitarians, has been put forward that the meaning of rights can and should be stretched to encompass demands arising from current views of diversification and multicultural justice.[12] In particular, we see efforts to accommodate the demands of people who define themselves in ways radically at odds with the abstract choice maker whom liberal rights protect, as well as to satisfy intellectuals harboring doubts regarding the moral status of the liberal democratic regime devoted to the vindication of these rights.

Liberal democratic regimes have eliminated or at least mitigated many injustices. Their deep, inherent reliance on and concurrence with the prime values of human dignity and objective truth have led these regimes to free individuals—women and members of various ethnic, racial, and religious groups in particular—from many of the burdens imposed by unthinking animus and pseudoscientific assumptions consigning them to subhuman status. But the manner in which liberal democracies have pursued these

---

9. R. H. Helmholz, "Natural Human Rights: The Perspective of the Ius Commune," *Catholic University Law Review* 52 (2003): 301–2.

10. John Rawls, *A Theory of Justice*, rev. ed. (Cambridge: Harvard University Press, 2005).

11. Robert Paul Wolff, "The Concept of Social Justice," in *From Contract to Community: Political Theory at the Crossroads*, ed. Fred Dallmayr, 65–68 (New York: M. Dekker, 1978).

12. Daniel Bell, *Communitarianism and Its Critics* (Oxford: Clarendon Press, 1993).

goods and the ever-thinner assumptions about human nature on which they rest have brought conflict, instability, and the atrophy of the social connections through which we live.

In legal terms, the movement in many instances has been toward ever-greater individual rights in a manner undermining even formerly central institutions and assumptions of liberal democratic society. Domestically, the desire to expand the realm and definition of rights has moved progressively toward including more and more activities and categories of activities into a realm of privacy marked off from public concern. Issues regarding homosexuality and marriage have been of particular note, here, with court decisions moving expressly in the direction of protecting homosexual conduct and social rights.[13] Particularly in the realm of more socially emphasized rights, this has meant that people of faith especially have seen their own rights, choices, and expectations limited by broadening definitions, for example, of marriage. The question has become urgent whether marriage, if defined to include any two persons (and only two? what of some cultures' recognition of the legitimacy of polygamy?) and if liable to unilateral breach by either party, with any subsequent battle over child custody expressly decided on grounds dismissive of any religious or moral concerns of either parent, any longer constitutes anything recognizable as marriage.

Equally problematic in their effects have been attempts to end all forms of invidious discrimination by regulating the conduct of nongovernmental groups. The liberal nation-state has taken on the role of policing lesser groups, from professional associations to all but the most explicitly private clubs, to prevent conduct violating individuals' rights to equal and open membership and participation. Thus individuals' rights increasingly receive vindication from the nation-state. The state may even be seen as vindicating the communitarian or multicultural rights demanded by thinkers like Charles Taylor, who see themselves as questioning liberal individualism. In Taylor's view, the "politics of recognition" are required as a support for individual human dignity. And this form of politics requires that the state construct the public sphere so as to recognize and support the claims of minority groups to full participation in all aspects of public life. Corollary to this, for Taylor, is the requirement that "partial groupings" be monitored by the state to ensure that they are fostering individual recognition according to the standards of the national "political

13. *Lawrence v. Texas,* 539 U.S. 558 (2003), *Goodridge v. Dep't of Public Health,* 440 Mass 309 (2003).

community." But participation in associations, and indeed the survival of a variety of associations, is increasingly endangered. The state in liberal democracy is becoming the arbiter of social life, an arbiter that is hostile toward the independent intermediary groups in which persons of all kinds once participated and in which oppressed groups once found community and protection.[14]

Moreover, legal doctrines are cutting people off from understandings of their relationships that go beyond economic self-interest. While antidiscrimination laws have served to end a number of bad practices and bad acts, in many cases they leave an "out" for bad actors—they can explain their conduct in economic terms.[15] Combined with the socially acidic demands of mass-market capitalism, the impetus toward state regulation is pushing people to act and even think of their actions as rooted in individual self-interest of the most narrow, economic variety.

Individual rights can be and have been stretched within liberal democracies. But this has been done at the cost of social life, and at the cost of increasing significantly the isolation of individuals and the empowerment of the state and market as bureaucratic mechanisms for producing economic prosperity and enforcing abstract rights. The result has been the reduction of social life and choice to movements along an individual-state-market grid. Social relations and social institutions—families; churches; towns; local professional, civic, and even recreational associations—are deconstructed through the calls of the market and the demands of the state. Families repeatedly move across the country, and even split up, in pursuit of success in the career market. Towns and cities sacrifice their character in pursuit of larger tax bases. The primordial liberal goal of liberating people from juridically imposed hierarchies that enforced severe restrictions on the opportunities of most people in favor of a privileged few has given way to a system of government-as-watchdog over all forms

14. This is the theme of Frohnen, "Liberation Jurisprudence: How Activist Courts Have Torn Family and Society Asunder," *Family Policy* (May–June 2001): 1–11. On the decline of group participation see Robert D. Putnam, *Bowling Alone: The Collapse and Revival of American Community* (New York: Simon and Schuster, 2000).

15. In *White v. HUD*, 475 F.3d 898 (7th Cir. 2007), the landlord was able to win at the trial level by claiming that she was unwilling to rent to a prospective tenant because she was unsure of the tenant's ability to pay the rent. The appeals court reversed because they thought that the landlord's actions indicated that she was discriminating against the tenant on the basis of familial status. The court did not, however, express any disapproval of the possibility that the landlord could refuse to rent to White, the tenant, after concluding that White's financial situation was precarious and therefore created a risk of nonpayment of the rent.

of association, balancing the good of individual freedom to associate against the potential harm of exclusionary practices limiting others' right to participate. The result is a system of law hostile to groups' control over their own membership and internal workings that undermines the formation and maintenance of meaningful, coherent groups with their own common goods and higher-order purposes.[16]

The obvious contemporary contrast to individual rights is group rights. Such rights—indeed, such entities conceived as real, with histories, purposes, and genuine rights of their own—seem not to exist for many contemporary liberal democrats. But liberal individualism has been challenged by the rise of an ideology of multiculturalism—according to which rights are meaningless if they do not produce public respect (or political recognition) for minority groups. Lawyers have been especially vigorous in criticizing theories of universal human rights for their very universality—a characteristic they believe renders rights hostile to the aspirations of groups defined by race, sex, and/or sexual orientation.[17] One legal academic has argued that he has lost faith in "traditional legal remedies" to race discrimination because "color blindness makes no sense in a society in which people, on the basis of group membership alone, have historically been, and continue to be, treated differently."[18]

Group rights may be seen specifically as the call for government distribution of goods to people according to their membership in particular categories. Liberal democrats of various stripes oppose these rights. Richard Epstein, for example, asserts that group rights constitute the rendering of "formal and explicit classifications into the fabric of the law"—a rendering Epstein deems inimical to liberty. Katherine Inglis Butler perhaps best captures the liberal view of liberal democracy as an ideology depending on the nation-state to mold the social and political order so as to vindicate liberal democratic rights and the liberal way of life. She condemns advocates of race-based distribution of voting rights, terming them "disturbingly

16. For contemporary arguments in this regard see Amy Gutmann, ed., *Freedom of Association* (Princeton: Princeton University Press, 1998). For a critique of current legal practice see Frohnen, "Liberation Jurisprudence."

17. See for example Catharine MacKinnon, *Women's Lives, Men's Laws* (Cambridge: Harvard University Press, Belknap Press, 2005), and Astrid A. M. Mattijssen and Charlene L. Smith, "Dutch Treats: The Lessons the U.S. Can Learn from How the Netherlands Protects Lesbians and Gays," *American University Journal of Gender and Law* 4 (1996): 303–33.

18. Edward Taylor, "A Primer on Critical Race Theory," *Journal of Blacks in Higher Education* 19 (1999): 122, 123.

oblivious to the potential for group rights to undercut our philosophical base and ultimately threaten the nation's existence."[19]

But the liberal democratic emphasis on purely individual rights has been breaking down in recent years. And there has been increasing recognition in our law of the need for some common standards of conduct that can, at times, limit the extent of individual rights. Thus we hear greater defense of environmental standards that limit individual uses of private property.[20] Indeed, arguably the courts have gone too far in limiting private-property rights by granting governments the right to take people's homes from them in order to give those homes to private developers who will demolish them to make way for their own projects, all on the grounds that the result will be greater economic prosperity for all.[21] We so little understand the nature and role of the group that taking a person's property and giving it to another person on the grounds that the second person will use the property in a more profitable manner now is considered a "public use" of private property.

Culture and Conflict in the International Arena

Perhaps in part as an outgrowth of the movement toward greater recognition of more broadly based rights, rights talk has taken to encompassing more groups, particularly those rooted in ethnicity and language. But the resulting multiculturalism thus far has produced more, not less, conflict. Particularly in the international arena, the notion of stretching our conception of human rights has brought significant conflict, both among proponents of liberal democratic rights and between individualist and multiculturalist rights proponents. On the one hand, the United Nations has acted to impose universalistic conceptions of rights on countries and cultures opposed to them. For example, the Committee on the Elimination of Discrimination against Women has issued a report arguing that "cultural and religious values cannot be allowed to undermine the universality of women's rights."[22] On the other hand, a number of academics have criti-

---

19. Richard A. Epstein, "Tuskegee Modern, or Group Rights under the Constitution," *Kentucky Law Journal* 80 (1992): 880–81; Katherine Inglis Butler, "Affirmative Racial Gerrymandering: Fair Representation for Minorities or a Dangerous Recognition of Group Rights?" *Rutgers Law Journal* 26 (1995): 595–624.

20. Ved P. Nanda, "Agriculture and the Polluter Pays Principle," *American Journal of Comparative Law* 54 (2006): 317–38.

21. *Kelo v. City of New London,* 126 S. Ct. 326 (2005).

22. U.N. Committee on the Elimination of Discrimination against Women, 18th Ses-

cized the very regime of international law as inherently discriminating against local cultures because it was designed from its beginnings to spread a colonialist, European code of conduct across the globe.[23]

During the cold war, United States foreign policy was aimed at a variety of goals, including the containment of communism, protection of strategic shipping lanes, and maintaining access to important minerals, as well as "promoting American values, notably human rights." Whatever one thinks of the validity of these goals, the first three have lost much of their salience since the close of that cold war, leaving America's liberal democratic ideology at the center of its foreign policy. With fear of Soviet communism now no longer a factor, American governments increasingly have acted on the basis of a self-identity deriving "from our dedication to the proposition 'that all men are created equal and endowed by their creator with certain unalienable rights.'" Thus, for example, Todd J. Moss sees at the center of the American foreign-policy establishment, including among African Americans in public life, a desire for "extending the Civil Rights movement" to Africa.[24]

The American desire to expand rights has been a destabilizing influence in the third world as it has demanded policies in keeping with its own liberal democratic ideals and preferences. At the root of the problem is the fact that liberal democracy, often denoted simply *democracy*, for Western liberals at least, "means more than elections." It rests on a specific kind of respect for individual and minority rights, as well as protection of the participatory, public role of opposition parties. As Moss points out, these institutions are "not well established in some parts of Africa." If the principles and institutions of liberal democracy are to be universal, they must be *made* universal. And this is a task of great magnitude. Thus Moss's question: "[I]s America really prepared to undertake a social engineering project so large as restructuring other nations and their cultural traits in order to match a desired liberal political order"?[25]

The problem arises, here, of the subjectivism at the root of liberal universalism. It seems self-contradictory to assert that while there is no universal moral code dictating a particular mode of life for all, there

---

sion, *Report on Indonesia,* prepared by Salma Khan, U.N. Doc. A/53/38 Rev. 1 (February 6, 1998).

23. See for example Frohnen, "Multicultural Rights? Natural Law and the Reconciliation of Universal Norms with Particular Cultures," *Catholic University Law Review* 52 (2002): 41, and citations therein.

24. Todd J. Moss, "U.S. Policy and Democratisation in Africa: The Limits of Liberal Universalism," *Journal of Modern African Studies* 33, no. 2 (1995): 193–94, 190, 198.

25. Ibid., 193.

nonetheless exists only one universally acceptable political structure, which alone has moral legitimacy.[26] Differing lifestyles would seem naturally to bring about differing social and political orders. Corollary to this point is Taylor's observation that "freedom and individual diversity can only flourish in a society where there is a general recognition of their worth."[27] What should be done, then, if most people in a given country do not recognize their worth, or at least not in a manner liberal democrats can understand?

The liberal democratic answer is that each individual must be free to choose the kind of society in which he or she will live. But what should be done if a majority of the people in a given country actually chooses a nonliberal government and society? Is one nonliberal electoral victory enough? Or must traditional societies be completely deconstructed and their members reeducated until they "choose" liberalism? And how much illiberalism is acceptable before reconstruction is necessary? Do we stop at the prevention of genocide (a goal Western liberal democracies thus far have failed to achieve)? Or are Western liberals obligated to push for truly liberal democracies throughout the world, regardless of the wishes of voting majorities?

Such questions have contributed to a movement away from liberal democratic assumptions in sub-Saharan Africa in particular. Here the reality of ethnic politics—that connections and sources of authority are rooted in extended familial, cultural, and linguistic ties rather than in public expressions of consent—for decades has undermined attempts to universalize liberal democratic values and institutions. Indeed, ethnic politics may be seen as the key to political strife in Africa. Ironically, moreover, the foothold of ethnic politics is only strengthened by imposition of the liberal nation-state on traditional, localist societies. Why so? Because the state has come to be seen by various ethnic groups as a means for distributing scarce goods and services.[28] The goal is capture of the state by one's ethnic group so that that group can monopolize the goods controlled by the state. The state in much of sub-Saharan Africa may be seen as more of a façade than a unifying center of power, coexisting with more powerful centers of authority rooted in kinship and patron-client relationships rather than abstract liberal democratic ideals of political consent.[29]

---

26. Ibid., 203.
27. Quoted ibid., 203.
28. E. Ike Udogu, "The Issue of Ethnicity and Democratization in Africa: Toward The Millennium," *Journal of Black Studies* 29, no. 6 (1999): 791, 793.
29. Moss, "U.S. Policy," 205.

The central importance of ethnic groups in sub-Saharan Africa has brought declarations of group rights and practical attempts to bind groups, qua groups, to nations. For example, Article 27 of the International Covenant on Civil and Political Rights states: "In those States in which ethnic, religious or linguistic minorities exist, persons belonging to such minorities shall not be denied the right, in community with other members of their group, to enjoy their own culture, to profess and practice their own religion, or to use their own language."[30] And the 1978 constitution of Nigeria decrees that "the state shall foster a feeling of belonging and of involvement among the various peoples of the Federation, to the end that loyalty to the nation shall over-ride sectional loyalties."[31]

As the Nigerian example shows, the very survival of the nation-state in sub-Saharan Africa is seen as depending on the reaching of an accommodation with deeper, more local loyalties. Thus military rulers in Nigeria have seen one of their chief tasks as that of securing increased tribal rights, especially through the creation of subnational governmental units.[32] Not surprisingly, sub-Saharan African governments value highly the reputation of respecting ethnic rights. Thus ethnic minorities in Botswana, perhaps the most successful state in sub-Saharan Africa in securing stability, peace, and prosperity, have sought to gain increased ethnic or group rights in part by threatening to harm the government's reputation in this area through complaints to the United Nations.[33]

Such demands for group rights have centered on the desire that the state support the use and public teaching of minority languages. They bespeak the power of Taylor's conceptualization of the politics of recognition. On this view one is not truly a citizen if one is stigmatized by the refusal of the majority to recognize the minority in public—in particular by fostering use of the minority language in state schools and other public realms.[34]

The struggle for recognition has been intense—but not solely as an end in itself. Sub-Saharan African regimes recognize the extreme dangers of ethnic politics to those controlling the apparatus of the nation-state. The nation-state being a Western import to the continent, imposed by colonial

---

30. Quoted in Richard Werbner, "Introduction: Challenging Minorities, Difference and Tribal Citizenship in Botswana," *Journal of Southern African Studies* 28, no. 4 (2002): 670.

31. Constitution of the Federal Republic of Nigeria, art. 15, cl. 4, quoted in Udogu, "The Issue of Ethnicity," 794.

32. Udogu, "The Issue of Ethnicity," 794.

33. Werbner, "Challenging Minorities," 672.

34. Ibid. This influence is quite specific. For discussion of the role of Taylor's ideas, see ibid., 679.

regimes, it has been defined essentially in opposition to more traditional, local systems of authority. *Tribes* may not in all cases be the correct term for these webs of authority. Nor is there consensus concerning what rights ought to be accorded them. Moreover, "tribal" groups have taken differing tacks in their relations with the nation-state—some choosing assimilation and others choosing to emphasize their differences from the majority and seek special status and rights.[35] But each has had its rights and its very nature changed by imposition of the nation-state.

The nation-state in sub-Saharan Africa has been built consciously as an alternative to more traditional, local associations. For example, Botswana began the postcolonial era with its political elites fostering a One Nation Consensus, according to which tribes would have to give way to a majority view, formulated at the political center, in terms of the use of language and distribution of control over land and mineral rights. Local and partial groups, including unions, were viewed as self-seeking, and the orthodoxy became one of assimilation that would cause tribes to fade away in favor of a centralized, liberal democratic nation-state.[36]

Again, Botswana has been relatively successful in its integration under a one-nation model. But its success and its particular bicameral system, empowering local tribal leaders as well as national parties, are all but unique in sub-Saharan Africa—a region replete with ethnic politics and violence. Some may choose to see this as a reflection of African character. One observer has claimed that, in Africa, political ethnicity arises from the expectations of the groups themselves, arguing that here

> the individual is seen as an embodiment of the tribe, consequently his fortunes are strongly identified with the fortune of the tribe. If he succeeds it is the tribe that has progressed, and if he fails it is the tribe that has suffered a setback. . . . [Thus], each time a high office goes to someone in the community his or her tribesmen jubilate openly, culminating finally in a delegation to the head of State to thank him for the appointment of their son or daughter to the high office.[37]

35. Ibid., 679–80, 675, 673. Werbner notes warnings in Botswana, the most peaceful of sub-Saharan African nations, that these politics may rise in that country and bring violence (679–80), and discusses the lack of consensus on what a tribe actually is, and what it should be called (675).

36. Ibid., 676.

37. J. D. Kandeh, "Politicization of Ethnic Identities in Sierra Leone," *African Studies Review* 35, no. 1 (1992): 81–99, as quoted in Udogu, "The Issue of Ethnicity," 798.

Not surprisingly, such jubilation may be seen as a taunt by other ethnic groups not so favored, and the result may be resentment and even violence.

But it is important to note the central role played by the nation-state in increasing the salience of ethnic ties to governmental power. Even in Rwanda and Burundi, nations in which mass murder and attempted genocide shocked most of the world, ethnicity was not the sole source of violence. The nation-state, with its capacity to control the distribution of goods and services, was central to the spiral of violence. The tribal distinctions between Hutu and Tutsi ethnic groups, which exist in Tanzania as well as in Rwanda and Burundi, are far less clear, impermeable, and concrete than press reports would indicate. Indeed, as Tony Walters has argued, "despite ethnic ideologies and academic debates to the contrary, 'ethnicity' is not the root cause of civil strife in Rwanda and Burundi." Rather, ethnic cleavages have been deepened and worsened by a variety of political and economic factors intimately related with the construction of modern nation-states in these countries.[38]

Particularly given sub-Saharan conditions of extreme scarcity of resources—with extreme poverty the norm and with actual starvation a real possibility—the construction of a centralized power structure with the capacity to deliver or deny goods and services to any or all groups increases exponentially the importance of political and military power. It makes it critically important for people to band together to gain as much control as possible over the distribution center (the state). And the most obvious, powerful, and ingrained basis of such solidarity is the ethnic group. Local, familial, and ethnic ties become more, not less, pronounced, as do latent and even new hostilities due to the link between political conflicts and huge differences in material well-being. Ironically, recognition of this problem has led political elites in some countries to opt for one-party states to dampen the possibility that multiparty democracy might lead to the rise of divisive and violent ethnic politics.[39]

Our point in rehearsing the tragedy of sub-Saharan Africa is not simply to condemn the nation-state, nor to recommend any particular "solution"—including any based in a specific form of ethnic politics. Rather, we wish to argue that the view of sub-Saharan Africa as an example of the unique difficulties of that region, rooted in over-reliance on ethnic ties and a failure to construct sufficiently efficient economic and political structures,

---

38. Tony Walters, "Tutsi Social Identity in Contemporary Africa," *Journal of African American Studies* 33, no. 2 (1995): 343–45.

39. Udogu, "The Issue of Ethnicity," 801, 800.

is rooted in a sad ignorance not just of sub-Saharan Africa, but of Western history. At least two analysts have pointed out that peaceful development in this region will require the spawning of a greater multiplicity of groups, not of an increasingly efficient and powerful central state. In particular, they argue for the formation of trans-ethnic groups outside the state that can build cross-ethnic loyalties to forge a civil society that is not rooted in politics or blood ties simply understood.[40]

Unfortunately, this seemingly obvious point—that the way to integrate cohesive, inward-looking groups into a wider society is through the fostering of associations that will cross ethnic lines without attacking the groups themselves—seems utterly foreign to analyses of the problems of "nation-building." It is foreign to such analyses because of the highly individualistic assumptions of liberal democratic analysts, assumptions rooted in a false vision of liberal society and of the very growth of liberty and human rights in the West. The self-made myth of liberal democracy's origins, deeply rooted in a skewed historical understanding of this most antihistorical ideology, has blinded liberal democrats to the social elements of human nature and human rights—roots as relevant to sub-Saharan Africa as to the West and, indeed, all the world. For the true, universal source of human rights is not an abstract vision of atomistic individuals, but rather a rich diversity of social connections and identities—a diversity on display in our own past.

The Problem of History

Defenders of liberal democracy and its rights argue that the systems they defend are truly universalistic—that they do not rely for their justification and instantiation on historical developments limited to one culture, set of cultures, race, or other category. In part, of course, this liberal construction was an understandable reaction to racialist theories of constitutional development, especially those rooted in ideas of "Germanic liberty."[41] Indeed, this is one advantage of the stripping away of social ties and considerations from abstract, universal rights claims. If the whole point of the exercise of idealizing a theory of justice is to strip away all the

---

40. J. R. Scarritt and W. Safran, "The Relationship of Ethnicity to Modernization and Democracy: A Restatement of the Issue," *International Studies Notes* 10, no. 2 (1983): 16–21, quoted in Udogu, "The Issue of Ethnicity," 804.

41. For a rehearsal of this literature see Brian Tierney, *Religion, Law, and the Growth of Constitutional Thought: 1150–1650* (Cambridge: Cambridge University Press, 1982), 4–6.

things that make one particular, then surely the theory itself is not particularistic, does not rest on only one, historically determined set of assumptions concerning the person and the social order?

As it turns out, of course, the abstract Rawlsian rights-bearer is the product of a very particular (Kantian) philosophical position and a very specific set of (liberal democratic) political and moral conceptions.[42] As it turns out, it is highly unusual (one might even say unnatural) to build a conception of the social order on a posited self that is as abstract and isolated as Rawls's. Few but liberal democrats would attempt such a feat, and even among liberal democrats the necessary self-evisceration is difficult to achieve and maintain. Thus liberal democratic authors must contend with the need for common assumptions and presuppositions in supporting rights regimes—especially those in favor of majority consent, toleration of minority opinion, and the primacy of rights accorded individuals deemed to be sovereign in the sphere of private conduct. As the commonality of these assumptions and presuppositions has come further and further into question, these authors have had to confront the very partiality of liberalism's own creation myth.

The myth of the abstract self has become increasingly untenable as its asocial assumptions regarding human nature and the social order have been called into question.[43] In effect, Rawlsian assumptions require a will to ignorance that cannot be maintained over time, particularly within a profession that has scholarly investigation as its reason for existence. Ironically, the result seems to be renewed interest in an earlier creation myth. This myth, premised on a particular reading of Western history, had been criticized by earlier scholars as too pat and too clearly ideological to stand up to liberalism's scientific methodology. Yet it remains powerful in scholarly and public discourse as the sole "reasonable" explanation for the growth of liberty.

In *The Whig Interpretation of History,* Herbert Butterfield criticized nineteenth-century Whig historians for taking their own chosen goods of progress, Protestantism and liberty, as universal goods toward which

---

42. John Rawls, *Political Liberalism* (New York: Columbia University Press, 1993). See also Walsh, *The Growth of the Liberal Soul.*

43. Alasdair MacIntyre, *After Virtue: A Study in Moral Theory* (Notre Dame, IN: University of Notre Dame Press, 1981). MacIntyre has been painted as a proponent of a more general communitarian critique of liberal individualism, but rejects that label as implying centralized political authority destructive of the face-to-face communities he finds essential to human flourishing. See his "Why I Am Not a Communitarian," in *After MacIntyre: Critical Perspectives on the Work of Alasdair MacIntyre,* ed. John Horton and Susan Mendus (Notre Dame, IN: University of Notre Dame Press, 1994).

historical events, through the efforts of Whig politicians in England, had moved. More generally, that work has been seen as a sustained critique of historians who essentially construct narratives of development through time so as to vindicate their personal political or philosophical positions. A historian who gives in to the impulse to use his or her own opinions regarding the political good as a prism through which to present persons, institutions, and events in a favorable or unfavorable (especially a "progressive" or retrograde) light is engaging in anachronism, distorting the truth of abridged historical experience that he or she is supposed to convey.[44]

Butterfield's answer to the problem of anachronistic history has its own problems. His call for noninterpretive history, focusing on specific statements of the concrete, the individual, and the particular, posits a neutral observer and a spontaneous achievement of meaning and order that are themselves ideological constructs. Facts do not spontaneously arrange themselves into meaningful order, and the belief that they can do so is a particularly Whiggish conceit, rooted in a simplistic empiricism. The historian in such an instance is called upon to empty himself, casting off personal interests, assumptions, and instinctive readings of emergent facts in a manner foreign to any methodology or craft, and impossible of performance.[45] Even Hume's *History of England,* with its studied eschewal of any causal or interpretive narrative, constructing history as "one damn thing after another," conveys an interpretive message—that of Hume's own philosophical skepticism.[46] It remains the case that one's reading of the past may be heavily dependent on the story one finds most congenial regarding one's own origins.

Whig history is very much alive, and it supports a very specific narrative of the rise of individual rights. This narrative often has been criticized in more recent years, in particular by postmodern and particularistic (for example, women's and "queer") historians concerned to show the role of oppression in the construction of contemporary society[47] and also by more communitarian-minded theorists, such as Taylor, who are concerned to argue for the motive force of an ethic at the root of modern culture. But the story's general outlines remain the same: Ancient thinkers—principally

44. Keith C. Sewell, "The 'Herbert Butterfield Problem' and Its Resolution," *Journal of the History of Ideas* 64, no. 4 (2003): 599–618.

45. Ibid., 600, 601.

46. David Hume, *History of England* (London: A. Millar, 1754).

47. For one critique of the drive to construct historical "projects" with uniform goals and assumptions, see James Schmidt, "What Enlightenment Project?" *Political Theory* 28, no. 6 (2000): 734–57.

Greeks and Romans, but to an extent also certain early Christians—
engaged in philosophical investigations concerning the nature of the person and the common good. These thinkers came to many interesting
conclusions, but failed to grasp the essential nature of freedom and, in particular, its intimate connection with the primacy of the individual. It was
not until the early modern era—variously defined in terms of the thought
of Machiavelli and Hobbes, the thought and practice of the Reformation,
or (often seen as building on these) the political philosophy of John
Locke—that freedom came into its own in Western history. With Locke's
explication of individual rights, and in particular his understanding of the
rights of property in oneself and one's labor, the ground was laid for ensu-
ing progress in terms of economic liberty, constitutional government, and
the rise of political consent.[48]

As Harold J. Berman has pointed out, such histories unthinkingly dismiss the contributions of premodern thought and practice, terming pre-
Reformation eras "medieval" and "feudal" as a means of indicating the
supposed darkness of any "age of faith."[49] Indeed, the rise of freedom generally is seen as part of another development in history—that of human
reason, exemplified by scientific analysis opposed to the superstitions of
faith-based societies. The culmination of this process is seen variously as
nineteenth-century liberal capitalism, American constitutionalism, or
post-Christian egalitarian individualism. But in each case the more highly
developed liberal democratic system is seen as a positive reaction to the
violence, oppression, and other evils of a worldview rooted in faith and
local, communalist loyalties degrading to the individual.[50] Whether defining themselves as politically liberal or politically conservative, writers in
the liberal democratic tradition tend to see the taming of religious viewpoints through liberal emphasis on science and the need to establish broad

48. For one example see John W. Danford, *Roots of Freedom: A Primer on Modern Liberty* (Wilmington, DE: ISI Books, 2000). For a classic statement of the Whig theory of history as applied to the United States, see Louis Hartz, *The Liberal Tradition in America: An
Interpretation of American Political Thought Since the Revolution* (New York: Harcourt
Brace, 1955).

49. Harold J. Berman, introduction to *Law and Revolution: The Formation of the Western Legal Tradition* (Cambridge: Harvard University Press, 1983). Berman dates modernity itself from the time of the development of the canon law, which he terms the first
modern legal system.

50. William Hard, "The Spirit of the Constitution," *Annals of the American Academy of
Political and Social Science* 195 (1936): 11, paints the spirit of the Constitution as the product of a change in attitude toward religion, or rather a rejection (through the Declaration of Independence) of its previously oppressive role in the lives of the American
people.

toleration and individual rights to secure public peace as being at the root of the good, modern liberal society.[51]

Some of those supporting the liberal democratic interpretation of history have seen themselves as critics of its results, especially in terms of individual rights. Michel Villey, for example, consistently argued that the older, Christian-based system of natural law understood the crucial term *ius*, which today is understood to mean either "justice" or "right," strictly in terms of what is just. What one was due, on this view, could not be captured by modern definitions of one's rights; it could be captured only by earlier ideas of what justice requires be done to, for, or by one. Later, modern thinkers, Villey argued, corrupted this understanding to mean what one has a right to do, and so produced modern subjectivism.[52]

A number of thinkers, especially of the so-called Straussian school of political theory, have consistently argued for a view of the birth of conceptions of natural rights in the work of Thomas Hobbes.[53] The view remains predominant, particularly in the field of political thought, that it was during the eighteenth century that individual rights truly flowered, though during the seventeenth century they first began to emerge into political and moral discourse. One clear reason for this view is the lack of discussion or even reading of important figures in the history of political thought during the so-called medieval era. As Brian Tierney has pointed out, "[I]n many general courses on the history of political thought, Aquinas provides the only stepping-stone between Augustine and the familiar world of Machiavelli and Hobbes and Locke." Yet, even among those with some knowledge of the sources, Tierney notes, the origin of natural-rights theories is traced to the Spanish Thomists of the early seventeenth century or, at its earliest, to the late medieval nominalists.[54]

51. James Q. Wilson, for example, argues that it was out of political necessity that rulers in the West established religious (and political) toleration. The fact of religious diversity, he argues, led rulers who sought the progress afforded by commerce and scientific investigation to insist that religious belief be cabined within a private sphere, thus ending the drive for oppression rooted in religious belief. "The Reform Islam Needs," *City Journal* 12, no. 4 (2002). That this vision is rooted in "Enlightenment" skepticism concerning the veracity and applicability of forms of understanding outside the reductive analysis of liberal scientific reason seems not to occur to Wilson. On the latter point see James Q. Wilson, *The Moral Sense* (New York: Maxwell MacMillan International, 1993), 244–45.

52. See Brian Tierney, "Natural Law and Natural Rights: Old Problems and Recent Approaches," *Review of Politics* 64 (2002): 391.

53. See the entry on Hobbes in Leo Strauss and Joseph Cropsey's *History of Political Philosophy* (Chicago: Rand McNally, 1963). For a concordant non-Straussian reading see Richard Tuck's volume *Hobbes* (New York: Oxford University Press, 1989).

54. Tierney, "Natural Law and Natural Rights," 406; Brian Tierney, "Religion and Rights: A Medieval Perspective," *Journal of Law and Religion* 5, no. 1 (1987): 165.

Thus the general view of the development of rights is that it occurred rather late, historically speaking.

More important, the development of individual rights is seen as tied intimately to the rejection of "supposedly sacred orders."[55] The rise of rights is seen as part and parcel of the destruction of inherited hierarchies, with their systems of inherited privilege and power (which is at least partly true), and also of rejection of the conviction that social order, itself necessary for liberty, requires a multiplicity of social groups with purposes, goods, and authority of their own (which is false). More generally, the rise of individual rights is seen as residing outside of, if not in direct opposition to, the tradition of natural law, with its emphasis on an ordered universe and the duty of the person to act in accordance with this order.

That history shows there to have been no dichotomy between natural law and rights has been the point of a substantial "strand of revisionist scholarship."[56] This scholarship has shown that natural rights did not enter public discourse suddenly in the eighteenth century, but rather grew over the centuries from very real, recognizable beginnings in the Decretalist literature of the twelfth century. One reason this growth and its beginnings have been overlooked is the modern prejudice against medieval communalism, and religious communalism in particular. The conviction that the Middle Ages were a time during which the dignity of the individual was not recognized, in which the sovereignty of individual choice and will were rejected, and, indeed, in which it is arguable that the individual (and thus individual rights) did not even exist, has permeated modern discourse.[57]

Here the modern prejudice against preexisting orders transcending the desires of individuals comes into play. The Straussian Michael Zuckert, for example, has argued that it is not possible to talk about a rights theory in premodern thought because natural law emphasizes duty, whereas "natural right" emphasizes the sovereignty of individual agents to do as they wish. According to Zuckert, natural law contains no sphere of personal autonomy within which the agent is considered to have full sovereignty to choose his or her course of action; thus this cannot be the realm of rights.[58]

---

55. Taylor, *Ethics of Authenticity*, 2.

56. Helmholz, "Natural Human Rights," 302. Helmholz refers in particular to the work of Tierney, his students, and his allies.

57. This is shown by the very need for Colin Morris's book *The Discovery of the Individual: 1050–1200* (New York: Harper and Row, 1972) setting out to claim that the individual person, as we know it, was coming into being during the Middle Ages.

58. Michael P. Zuckert, "Do Natural Rights Derive from Natural Law?" *Harvard Journal of Law and Public Policy* 20, no. 3 (1997): 716, quoted in Tierney, "Natural Law and Natural Rights," 395.

Tierney points out that Zuckert, among others, overlooks the realm of permissive rights allowed for in traditional natural law theory. Not discussed in St. Thomas Aquinas, but still of great importance to the Western natural-law tradition, permissive rights constitute a sphere of permissive conduct, within which the person is at liberty to make choices indifferent to the natural law. And this understanding is, itself, a natural-rights theory of significant importance within the natural-law tradition.[59] Natural law not only forbids some things and commands others, in still other areas of life it circumscribes a zone of licit behavior within which one might choose as one wishes. Development of this doctrine was of particular importance in the realm of property rights, wherein there were strong arguments on both sides of the question of whether religious precepts require or forbid private ownership. The resolution put forth by the twelfth-century Decretalists and developed by succeeding generations was that property resides within a realm of licit choice.[60]

Philip Hamburger makes the important clarification that these natural rights, as understood at least up to the time of the drafting of the United States Constitution, reside *within* natural law; that is, there are some choices that are not allowed even to one who is exercising a right. Free speech, for example, does not include the right to slander someone.[61] And the sphere of autonomy was recognized as substantive and real, even though the rights were "objective" in modern terms. That is, under the traditional natural law view, the sphere of licit behavior was one of prudence, within which one applied one's own reason, habit, and experience to determine how best to pursue a good, virtuous life. In modern liberal democratic terms, on the other hand, the sphere of rights is one of moral indifference or pure will, in which the individual's action is self-justifying and measured against no objective standard of goodness—limited only by its potential harm to others.[62]

It is not the case, then, that medieval thought and practice did not include and reflect substantive conceptions of natural rights. Nor were these rights purely "objective" in the sense of being mere derivatives of natural law duties. They encompassed a vast realm of prudence within an objective view of the good—action in accordance with the natural order of

---

59. Tierney, "Natural Law and Natural Rights," 400.

60. Ibid., 400–401.

61. Philip Hamburger, "Natural Law, Natural Rights, and American Constitutions," *Yale Law Journal* 102 (1993): 907.

62. See Romanus Cessario, OP, *Introduction to Moral Theology* (Washington, DC: Catholic University of America Press, 2001), 229–30.

the universe—to which people should and by nature would conform their conduct. Liberal democratic theories reject the view of the good, of the natural order of the universe, and in particular its roots in theistic conceptions, at the root of natural law. But it is wrong to claim that the limits imposed by natural law negate the reality of rights. Indeed, liberal democracy itself imposes limits on rights; these limits simply are not imposed by a coherent theory of the good. Instead they are imposed by political considerations (the maintenance of public peace, for example) and the philosophically underdefended assumption of individual sovereignty.

Individual in Community

Differences between natural law and liberal democratic conceptions of rights mostly have to do with views of the nature of the person and the person's relation to the social order. In the traditional natural law view, the person is seen as intrinsically social, gaining meaning and understanding from a variety of relationships in a multiplicity of morally authoritative groups, including family, church, guild, town, and other groups rooted in preexisting ties and current occupations and interests. For the modern liberal democrat, these loci of authority and meaning are at least potentially oppressive and so must be monitored and regulated by the nation-state to see that they do not interfere with individual autonomy.[63]

For liberal democrats, the world often seems one of individual *versus* community—in which the individual's flourishing requires that communities be brought to heel, if not broken up. Communitarian liberals have sought to modify this vision into one of individual *and* community—in which the individual gains real benefits from properly controlled communities. A natural law vision is closer to one of individual *in* community—that is, one in which the individual person is seen as social by nature, and naturally part of a variety of communities that both constitute the person's identity and encompass a variety of goods that no person can achieve alone. The natural law vision entails recognition that our communities are in the nature of our being, rather than external and accidental; that they result from a combination of duty, rational choice, emotional attachment, habit, and an instinctive drive toward community, rather than merely agreement and consent.

63. Gerald Doppelt, "Illiberal Cultures and Group Rights: A Critique of Multiculturalism in Kymlicka, Taylor, and Nussbaum," *Journal of Contemporary Legal Issues* 12 (2002): 672.

Be they explicitly liberal democrats, liberal communitarians, or proponents of multiculturalism, moderns tend to view human relations and human communities as in important ways disposable. Even contemporary communitarians and (what is much the same thing) multiculturalists accept the fundamentally liberal assertion that individual commitments are by nature artificial. Thus Charles Taylor, often seen as a leading figure in both communitarian and multiculturalist camps, argues that each of us needs to have some "background of things that matter" in order to define an identity for ourselves "that is not trivial." But this recognition that some things must matter to us if we are to form meaningful identities does not lead Taylor to recognize any particular thing or relationship as important, let alone natural. We may choose "history, or the demands of nature, or the needs of [our] fellow human beings, or the duties of citizenship, or the call of God, or something else." The important thing is to make a choice. The purpose of social life for Taylor is to maintain the grounds of such choice. And it does this by means of a social principle of fairness aimed directly at "equal chances for everyone to develop their own identity" through a variety of commitments that are not "in principle" tentative, though they may "break down."[64] Thus, for Taylor, our relations must be in principle important to us so that we may use them to form our own identities. But they are not in themselves of intrinsic importance to us, any more than any particular one is in itself natural to us. Perhaps most critically, for Taylor we moderns are "buffered selves," separated from the world around us by our various epistemological filters, and by an expressive interiority according to which we seek fulfillment in and through our own ideas of our selves, our goods, and the cosmos in which we reside.[65]

Liberal democrats and their communitarian critics share the conviction that society is rooted solely in convention, and that society is, in essence, a voluntary association through which we provide for the satisfaction of individual wants. Taylor's correction of some more simple-minded liberal assumptions regarding the nature of wants—his including identity and meaning through social participation as important wants—is highly salutary. Moreover, Taylor may be correct that the current, immanent frame or background of understanding continues to allow selves to genuinely pursue lives open to meanings that transcend individual human flourishing.[66] But, while Taylor may recognize the potential for human connectedness, it remains the case that his genealogy of "social imaginaries" or shared

---

64. Taylor, *Ethics of Authenticity*, 40–41, 50–52.
65. Taylor, *Secular Age*, 516.
66. Ibid., 544–46.

conceptions of reality points to a modern frame of buffered selves joined through political means for mutual, individual benefit.

Even multicultural, group rights to things like governmental support for the teaching of minority languages fall into the liberal democratic pattern and the individual-state-market grid. Demands for such rights rest on the assumption that the state has both the power and the legitimate authority to determine which languages people will speak in various venues and what forms of instruction will be allowed. Thus the state remains the center of rights recognition. Moreover, such rights are defended not because the groups so defended should be recognized for their own sakes, but rather because such groups are a necessary means for providing an equal, substantive opportunity to achieve personal autonomy to the individuals constituting those groups.[67] Thus, in keeping with Taylor's essentially liberal democratic espousal of "things that matter," multiculturalists seek to provide liberal democratic selves with greater opportunities for individual enrichment by showing "respect for the intrinsic value of the different cultural forms in and through which individuals actualize their humanity and express their unique personalities."[68] But the state must maintain its regulatory dominance over these potentially dangerous groups.[69]

Liberal democrats and communitarian multiculturalists view choice as the key to their primary goal of self-actualization or construction of one's own identity. This privileging of choice entails rejection of any set of standards or any order that might be seen as prescribing a given set of norms of behavior for all members of society. Such standards restrict the autonomy of the individual, limiting its sovereignty by pronouncing some choices wrong or bad. Made consciously, this rejection may have its benefits; it certainly rules out certain forms of theocratic or ideological tyranny and may militate against various forms of localized oppression. But one need not reject openness to recognition of the order of the universe, and the prescriptive implications of that order, in order to combat tyranny and

---

67. See Adeno Addis, "Individualism, Communitarianism, and the Rights of Ethnic Minorities," *Notre Dame Law Review* 67 (1992): 615, 631, arguing that group rights may be a temporary necessity to make up for past discrimination.

68. Steven C. Rockefeller, "Comment," in Charles Taylor, *Multiculturalism: Examining the Politics of Recognition,* ed. Amy Gutmann (Princeton: Princeton University Press, 1994), 87.

69. See Doppelt, "Illiberal Cultures," maintaining that minority cultures require group rights to further individual autonomy and ensure freedom to make life choices; Doppelt argues at 666 that meaningful choices and life options require "that individuals have access to a societal culture with which they identify as an expression of who they are."

oppression; that is, one need not insist upon a stringent distinction between *is* and *ought* such as to preclude foundational standards of human conduct. Indeed, one may argue that an essential goal of politics is to provide the forum within which people can discuss and come to an agreement concerning what role authorities of various kinds—including but not limited to strictly political authority—ought to play in encouraging people to conform their behavior to central norms. And the very multiplicity of authorities of a group-based social order, along with the respect for human dignity at the root of natural law theory, would seem to militate, more effectively than liberal democracy, against the concentration of power sufficient to bring oppression.

Indeed, one can argue that the current rejection of transcendent orders and standards in effect empowers the state to enforce its own conception of proper conduct (rooted in an understanding of toleration as the highest good, and requiring sometimes highly unnatural restraint from interference) even as it pushes more and more issues and powers into the hands of various market actors to control individual lives. Purely conventional relations, as we have seen, tend to reduce to market relations; the one remaining universal standard by which to evaluate our choices and relationships is a utilitarian calculus most readily understandable in terms of money. Thus, what Robert Nisbet calls the "cash nexus" has come to rule more and more of our lives.[70] Even rights, under these conditions, cease to protect us. More and more of our lives are taken up with tending to transactions with strangers against whose depredations we may assert our rights. And these rights, while formally enforceable, are beyond our capacity to defend in real life because few of us have either the time or the money to do so. Under such circumstances, those with the funds and the expertise to manipulate the legal system become increasingly powerful and immune to prosecution or restraint, even as the state takes on increased formal powers through its role as the protector of individuals. And all this time the transactions themselves become increasingly onerous and unfair as custom and social opprobrium lose their power to serve as checks on greed and abuses of unequal bargaining power. We become entrapped in the individual-state-market grid even as we lose our membership in the associations that once protected us from anonymous forces and allowed us to forge meaningful lives.

Our situation is all the more unfortunate because one of its primary sources, the liberal democratic view that objective standards make sub-

---

70. Robert Nisbet, *The Present Age: Progress and Anarchy in Modern America* (Indianapolis: Liberty Fund, 2003).

jective rights impossible, is false. Indeed, the very history from which liberal democrats have drawn this lesson shows quite the opposite to be the case. This is demonstrated in the very opening passage of Gratian's twelfth-century *Decretum*, which Tierney calls "the foundation of the whole subsequent structure of Western canon law": "The human race is ruled by two means, namely by natural law and usages. The law of nature is what is contained in the Law and the Gospel, by which each is ordered to do to another what he wants done to himself and is forbidden to do to another what he does not want done to himself."[71]

At the foundations of canon law, then, is a clear statement: natural law decrees that we must respect and show concern for all persons with whom we have dealings. And such concern and respect are the essential grounds of human rights. As Berman has shown, the development of canon law was premised on this respect for the individual person. Development of canon law—which protected individual persons through a system of rights—was part of a wider institutional development, by which liberty interests were fostered. Particularly important was what Berman has termed the Papal Revolution. Beginning in the eleventh century, the Catholic Church asserted its right, as an institution, to appoint its own bishops—a right that until then had been disputed and often violated by secular monarchs. By forging a consistent institutional integrity, and by using this base of authority to check (though certainly not control) the powers of monarchs and even, on occasion, to depose tyrants, the Catholic Church limited the power of secular government to control every aspect of the people's lives, and so made room for the flowering of civil society.

The Church was not the only source of law and rights during this era. A rich diversity of laws and legal jurisdictions during the Middle Ages furthered the person's individuality and rights. These jurisdictions established procedural rights and principles of equitable treatment. They also provided individual persons and groups with the means by which to protect their customs and self-rule against would-be oppressors. As Berman describes it,

> There were recurrent struggles between law and feudal class oppression, between law and the power of urban magnates, between law and ecclesiastical interests, between law and royal domination. Serfs who escaped to the cities claimed their liberty, under urban law, after a year and a day.

---

71. Gratian, *Concordance of Discordant Canons (Decretum)*, 1140, dist. 1, cited in Tierney, "Religion and Rights," 163.

Citizens rebelled against their urban rulers in the name of constitutional principles declared in the city charters. Barons demanded ancient rights and privileges from kings. Princes and popes fought one another, each claiming that the social-economic power of the other was being exercised in violation of divine and natural legal rights, against the spirit of the laws, and even against the letter.[72]

Medieval society itself abounded in creative tensions between and among individual persons and social groups. Even as the hierarchy of social and political orders was maintained and in many ways strengthened, individuals gained the capacity and right to appeal to a variety of courts and jurisdictions for the protection of their individual interests and rights. And people responded in part by forming a plethora of associations rooted in occupation, locality, family, and religion. These groups had their own rights and even their own legal systems through which they protected their members even as they pursued goals transcending those of their members.

This flowering of rights and associations was made possible by the growth of canon law and by the space, free from political control, provided by Church opposition to secular rulers. It was through the variety of corporate groups and legal jurisdictions that persons, individually and as members of a variety of groups, gained the power to escape arbitrary rule and to forge, with their fellows, procedures for fair adjudication.[73] Thus, where the Whig interpretation paints the rise of individual liberty as the story of reason's triumph, through the vehicle of the state, over the superstition of established religion, it would be closer to the truth to see the rise of ordered liberty as intimately connected with the increasing power of the Church to speak in its own voice, through its own bishops. One should not forget that the first section of the Magna Carta, that seminal document of liberties, declares that the rights of the Church shall not be violated by the king.

Questions of Size and Scope

We are not arguing that the Catholic Church somehow automatically brings with it the ordered liberty of societies and individual persons. The-

---

72. Berman, *Law and Revolution*, 43.
73. Ibid.

ologically, Christian contributions to conceptions of human rights have most to do with the doctrine of the person as made in the image and likeness of God—a doctrine that, in its details, is beyond the scope of this book. And the deplorable violence and oppression of the medieval era owed much to the selfish and corrupt conduct of religious as well as political and military figures. Our point, rather, is that the growth of human individuality, liberty, and rights has an essential grounding in the existence of a living, vibrant multiplicity of authorities. It is in and through the persistent exchange of ideas, experiences, and information possible only when each of us belongs to a variety of mutually enforcing and competing groups that we gain sufficient social grounding, self-confidence, and protection from arbitrary control to pursue full, meaningful lives and to protect meaningful human rights.

If we are to face successfully the current crisis of liberal democracy, if we are to maintain the integrity of rights such that each person's social nature is respected along with his or her need for a sphere of individual choice, we must rebuild healthy variety within healthy consensus. That is, if rights are to retain their power to protect individual persons without undermining even the most basic social order, there must be sufficient commonality of custom, habit, and belief such that a diversity of groups can cooperate as well as prevent one another from becoming dominant. The political nation-state cannot provide either the variety or the healthy consensus required for rights to flourish in their proper context. The nation-state is simply too large to form the kinds of personal attachments necessary to bind people to one another, or even to the state on any basis other than ideological zeal.

As Bertrand de Jouvenel pointed out, the modern democratic state in particular sees all "make-weights"—be they intermediary institutions, localized belief systems, or simple constitutional checks—as illegitimate barriers to completion of its task of effectuating the will of the majority.[74] Particularly given liberalism's call to liberate individuals from the confines of constitutive communities, the fostering of real, vital corporate associations is increasingly difficult in liberal democratic societies. As to individuals' attachment to the state, while some thinkers argue that we must foster increased loyalty to the "political community," this attachment further crowds out local attachments and, more damaging still, forges specifically political ties that subordinate other relations to political criteria. The result

---

74. Bertrand de Jouvenel, *On Power: Its Nature and the History of Its Growth*, trans. J. F. Huntington (Westport, CT: Greenwood Press, 1948).

is a thinning out of social relations and the elimination of any real variety of behavioral norms.

Neither does the multicultural model offer hope of a healthy combination of variety and consensus. Multiculturalists seek recognition of only very specific groups, defined by language, cultural practices, and other ties often summed up as ethnicity. The rights that multiculturalists seek to vindicate constitute claims by ethnic groups on the nation-state for public recognition of the validity of their cultural practices, maintaining languages in particular. This seems like a relatively innocuous demand, and one of potentially significant importance for human dignity, given the centrality of the nation-state in liberal democracies. But the multicultural program is fraught with danger in a time of increasing cultural pluralism. As religious and cultural differences within the same nation-state increase, differences over basic norms increase as well. When demands for public support for such differences is added to the mix, the obvious result is a splitting of people's loyalties and increasing cultural conflict, even unto violence.[75] Especially damaging is the narrowing of the range of possibilities for persons with which to identify and grow through interaction in groups small and local enough to foster lasting attachments not rooted in the pursuit of control over the state and its power to distribute goods and services. Continuing competition to control the state and its capacity to distribute rights and goods according to racial and other categories seems designed to increase conflict. And such conflict empowers the state, or the elites running it, to create, modify, or even destroy rights in the name of a more just order.[76]

If we are to live in a society that fully recognizes and protects the dignity of every person, we must reestablish a congruence between culture and government, such that there is a viable consensus regarding what is right and good to guide public policy. If people are to participate meaningfully in public and social life while having their rights protected, there must be meaningful agreement concerning the nature and importance of the primary groups within which such rights are exercised. If we cannot even agree on what a family is, how can we agree on what rights it should have? If we cannot agree on the nature of our common good, it seems non-

75. See Butler, "Affirmative Racial Gerrymandering," 600n10.

76. See generally Thomas Sowell, *Affirmative Action around the World: An Empirical Study* (New Haven: Yale University Press, 2004). Sowell examines the results of race-based governmental policies in five nations, finding that in every case those policies led to further social and economic stratification along with increased racial tension and state interference, including state-made classification systems.

sensical to argue that we can provide meaningful protection to everyone in the pursuit of their own goods.

This does not mean that each community must establish a nation-state sufficiently powerful to enforce a particular vision of the common good. That way lies tyranny. Rather, what is needed is that laws and rights grow from the particular culture of the specific people involved. And this means that the concentration of power and authority in the territorial nation-state accomplished over the last several hundred years must be redistributed. This is no call for a reversion to some utopian vision of the Middle Ages. Rather, it is a call for more imaginative thinking regarding the sharing of powers by political, economic, and social groups, along with a greater willingness to cede back to local associations the rights they once had, through which they empowered not only themselves, but also their members.

It is not necessary to eliminate nation-states—as if one could accomplish such a design. Rather, it is necessary for nations to begin recognizing not the mere right of ethnic groups to the use of their language in public, but rather the importance of self-governing groups such as towns, unions, professional associations, and other groups currently hampered by the drive for national and global uniformity. Some of these groups may cross ethnic lines, even as some ethnic lines, in fairness, ought to lead nations to voluntarily cede territory to new political entities such that self-governing peoples may replace ethnic conflict with the possibility of mutual forbearance.

Before serious thought can be given to such reshaping of political units to better serve the more primary associations of social life, however, we must rethink the nature of the good we seek. Defenders of liberal democracy claim that it by nature seeks maximal vindication of individual rights. And it is in this context that a rethinking of the nature, origins, and purpose of those rights is necessary. For rights are not merely judicially enforceable claims to various good things. They are, rather, a set of social realities, procedures by which we show respect for self-government by individuals and groups in their pursuit of a good life.

This volume consists of two parts. Essays in the first part retrace the origins and historical development of rights in the West, paying special attention to their political contexts and implications. They constitute an attempt to clarify the experience of rights within our tradition. Thus Brian Tierney examines the pivotal role of John Locke, seminal thinker of liberalism, at the center, rather than the beginning, of the development of rights in the West. In examining the concepts Locke inherited as well as those he bequeathed, Tierney shows that individual rights and atomistic individualism historically have not been one and the same, or even necessarily connected.

Gary Glenn's essay focuses on a central motif of liberal individualism—the notion of government as a social contract intended to protect individual rights and interests. By examining the idea of the social contract in Bellarmine's "premodern" and Burke's modern but nonindividualistic writings, Glenn shows the sense and extent to which respect for the person and for the necessary role of consent in public life transcend the false divide between medieval communalism and modern individualism.

George Carey's essay takes a document at the center of modern rights talk—the Declaration of Independence—and examines its roots in permissive natural law. Spelling out the common assumptions underlying this document, Carey shows the abiding relationship between natural law and natural rights in Western political thought. He also shows the extent to which American conceptions of rights in particular were grounded in a religious vision of the person and the purposes of public life.

Bruce Frohnen's essay traces the development of the practice of rights in the West, and especially in the Anglo-American context. Beginning before the Magna Carta, rights had a real, practical existence connecting persons and groups through an understanding of the importance of self-government and historically recognized custom as guards against tyranny and necessary aids to the search for a decent life. Increasing liberal hostility toward the rights of groups such as towns and corporations, he argues, has undermined not only groups, but also the rights of individual persons.

The second section of this volume addresses the need to rethink our understanding of the nature of existence if we are to understand rights and their proper place in our intrinsically social lives. Kenneth Schmitz directly addresses the ontological basis of rights by looking at the nature of the person and of the social relations that do so much to define each of us. In making claims of rights, Schmitz shows, each person acts on a series of social assumptions concerning the nature of himself and of social reality that require understanding, in particular, of the role that our relations with other people play in developing our rightful expectations and our social being.

In his essay examining a series of European legal thinkers, Paul Gottfried argues for the historical and cultural specificity of custom and the very idea of rights. The replacement of customary law by legal codes following the French Revolution and its Prussian successor, Gottfried shows, has broken down the historic identification of the customary with the rightful. This development, while in some cases salutary, nonetheless has dangerously empowered political elites centered in the nation-state and its transnational successors.

If one of the permanent truths toward which Gottfried points is the historical contingency of custom, another such truth, at the center of Kenneth Grasso's essay, is the socially embedded nature of the person. Grasso presents a critique of contemporary rights talk rooted in a social conception of the person and a corollary understanding of the limits of individualistic understandings of human rights.

Finally, Jonathan Chaplin draws the necessary conclusions from our social being in calling for an understanding of rights and the social order rooted in institutions. Because individual persons act through institutions, he argues, we must come to recognize, in our social and legal order, the importance of institutional self-government for a variety of groups throughout the social order.

Historical Roots of Modern Rights

Before Locke and After

Brian Tierney

In this paper I will explore some historical roots of our modern culture of rights by considering the work of John Locke, the teachings that he inherited, and his influence on modern rights theories. In addressing these issues I shall move from some very general comments to a discussion of some specific strands of thought concerning individualism, community, and natural law in Locke's work, with a final glance at the persistence of these themes in contemporary rights theories. I will argue basically that Locke's understanding of individualism and individual rights was rooted in a long-standing tradition of Western Christian thought, even though at present we often encounter these ideas in distorted or exaggerated forms.

On the most general level, the whole enterprise of seeking for historical roots requires some justification nowadays. Especially among medievalists, the current fashion is to emphasize the alterity, the "otherness," of the past—and the medieval world was indeed very different from ours. But medieval people were not just quaint aliens who believed in magic and witchcraft and improbable miracles. Their achievements were great; their thought is interesting; they helped to make the modern world what it is. And it has always seemed to me that one proper task of a historian—one reason for studying the past, even the medieval past—is to make our present-day world, the world we have to live in, more intelligible. Evidently we cannot achieve this end simply by imposing present-day ideas on the works of past thinkers. Instead, we need to understand the authors' writings "in their own terms" by considering the historical contexts within which they wrote and the particular circumstances that influenced their thought. But an important part of the relevant context in any age is the world of ideas—often taken-for-granted ideas—inherited from the past. It is from that perspective that I want to discuss the work of Locke, and then the modern world of rights.

This task is complicated by the fact that there does not exist at present any consensus about the philosophical or religious grounding of the rights that are asserted. Politicians typically pay lip service to human rights, but intellectuals are sometimes more skeptical. All the mainstream Christian churches now endorse the idea of human rights, and Pope John Paul II warmly embraced the principles of the United Nations' Universal Declaration on Human Rights when he addressed the UN in 1979. Yet nowadays some conservative Catholics are among the most severe critics of modern "rights talk." One of them, for instance, has observed that "Christianity actually has a deep resistance to the concept of human rights," and he expressed some uneasiness about the current *Catechism of the Catholic Church* because it refers to the "inalienable rights of the human person."[1]

It is not only the present status of human rights that evokes controversy; there is also disagreement about the early history of the idea. In a book written a few years ago called *The Idea of Natural Rights,* I discussed the contributions of a series of thinkers from the twelfth century to the seventeenth and the historical contexts within which they worked. And I thought that, in doing this, I had indeed explored the historical roots of modern rights. But my book had an evident limitation. It ended with the work of Grotius at the beginning of the seventeenth century, and so it failed to address a substantial body of current scholarship that asserts that a distinctive concept of individual natural rights did not emerge until later, in the age of Hobbes and Locke. These thinkers, it is argued, made a decisive break with the past by introducing a novel concept of natural rights that was inherently incompatible with the established tradition of natural law. This view is accepted almost as an article of faith by the followers of Leo Strauss, but it is not limited to them. The French author Michel Villey, who wrote very extensively on the early history of natural rights, also held that the modern notion of subjective natural rights was inconsistent with

1. Robert P. Kraynak, *Christian Faith and Modern Democracy: God and Politics in a Fallen World* (Notre Dame, IN: University of Notre Dame Press, 2001), 153, 182.

the classical idea of an objective natural right, understood as meaning "what is right" or "what is just."[2]

I am inclined to agree that the work of Hobbes does represent an aberration from earlier ideas about natural law and natural rights, though some scholars have seen even his work as derived from late medieval Scholasticism. But in any case his ideas have little to do with modern ways of thinking about human rights. Hobbes's characteristic teaching was that individuals have rights, but no duty to respect the rights of others; modern codes of human rights are concerned to enumerate rights that others are bound to respect. The situation is different with Locke. His rights did involve duties to others, and Locke is commonly cited as a major source of modern liberal ideas, including ideas about rights. But if Locke influenced modern thought only by making a break with the ideas of his predecessors, then an investigation of pre-Lockean thought would be only an antiquarian game, without any relevance for our understanding of modern concepts. Another possibility is that Locke's teachings were well grounded in earlier juridical and philosophical thought. The issue evidently requires some reconsideration.

Individualism before Locke

The assertion of an inherent incompatibility between Lockean natural rights and traditional natural law is sometimes expressed as a contrast between an individualistic and a corporative concept of society. Bryan Hehir, for instance, has maintained that a natural law ethic treats individuals as inherently sociable by nature and leads to an organic model of society, while a natural rights ethic is grounded on a conception of persons as autonomous individuals, so that there are profound differences between the two systems of thought.[3]

I will return to the relationship between natural law and natural rights in the work of Locke and his predecessors, but I want first to consider the issue of individuality and specifically the view that, in the seventeenth century, a new individualism replaced the corporative ethos of earlier Western society and introduced into political thought a novel idea of indi-

---

2. Michel Villey, *La formation de la pensée juridique moderne,* 4th ed. (Paris: Editions Montchrestien, 1975), 227.

3. J. Bryan Hehir, "Religious Activism for Human Rights: A Christian Case Study," in *Religious Human Rights in Global Perspective,* ed. John Witte Jr. and Johann D. van der Vyver (The Hague: Martinus Nijhoff, 1996), 1:100.

vidual natural rights. This argument, especially in its more extreme forms, fails to treat adequately either Lockean individualism or earlier corporatist and communitarian ideals. Nevertheless it is pervasive in the modern literature among both earlier and more recent thinkers. George Sabine, in his fine old book on political theory, noted that, in the seventeenth century, a new priority of the individual marked the principal difference between medieval and modern thought. Similarly, A. P. d'Entrèves asserted that "the new value was that of the individual." Leo Strauss maintained that Locke's political thought was "revolutionary" because "the individual, the ego, had become the center and origin of the moral world." C. B. MacPherson emphasized "a new belief in the value and rights of the individual" that reflected the realities of seventeenth-century economic life. Jack Donnelly observed, more simply, that the rise of a market economy in the seventeenth century "created separate and distinct individuals." Modern communitarians criticize the Lockean idea of rights because, they argue, it was based on a new doctrine of atomistic individualism. Charles Taylor contended that, for Locke, "people start out as political atoms."[4]

In spite of this consensus I have always been somewhat skeptical of the idea that we must wait until the seventeenth century before we encounter an onset of individualism. In my reading of medieval sources for more than half a century, the idea never occurred to me spontaneously that the people I was reading or reading about were not real live individuals, aware of themselves as individuals. Other medieval scholars have apparently had the same experience. One popular book on twelfth-century culture was called precisely *The Discovery of the Individual.* Then Alan MacFarlane found origins of individualism in the lives of thirteenth-century English villagers. A more common view holds that individualism really emerged in the fourteenth century, in the wake of William Ockham's nominalism. Others find the origin of individualism in the fifteenth century, in the world of Renaissance humanism. Or perhaps it was in the sixteenth century, with Protestant ideas on private judgment. One might also mention the Spanish neo-Scholastics as a likely source. I like especially a passage of Francisco Suarez, who argued that, even if the human race had

---

4. George Sabine, *A History of Political Theory* (London: George G. Harrap, 1937), 433; A. P. d'Entrèves, *Natural Law: An Introduction to Legal Philosophy* (London: Hutcheson's University Library, 1951), 54; Leo Strauss, *Natural Right and History* (Chicago: University of Chicago Press, 1953), 248; C. B. MacPherson, *The Political Theory of Possessive Individualism* (Oxford: Oxford University Press, 1964), 1; Jack Donnelly, *Universal Human Rights in Theory and Practice* (Ithaca, NY: Cornell University Press, 1989), 193; Charles Taylor, *Sources of the Self: The Making of Modern Identity* (Cambridge: Harvard University Press, 1989), 64.

remained in a state of innocence, it would still have increased and multi-plied. His reason was that "a multiplication of persons confers beauty and dignity on the whole race through the diversity of many individual per-fections."[5] One could go on and on. The truth is that depending on whom we choose to read we can find the individual discovered or invented in any century we care to look at, from the twelfth century onward.

We need to remember, though, that these individuals always lived in communities. Indeed, the twelfth century, which has been called an age of individualism, also saw the emergence of many new centers of corporate life—guilds, colleges, monastic houses, confraternities, communes. How-ever, the corporate *mentalité* that informed such institutions has sometimes been exaggerated, especially by an earlier generation of scholars influ-enced by Otto von Gierke. One of them wrote that a medieval city was not an association of individuals but a collective entity, *un être collectif;* another compared a medieval commune to a collection of social insects, like a swarm of ants or bees.[6] But in fact, whenever enough documentation sur-vives to give us an insight into the inner workings of a medieval commu-nity, we find individuals with their own characteristics interacting with one another, sometimes disputing with one another. Individuals within a community might be bound together by strong affective bonds of loyalty, but the idea of a medieval commune as an *être collectif* is a modern fantasy.

Medieval people did not see an antithesis between community loyalties and individual rights; they thought that the two things reinforced one another.[7] When a new commune was formed by conjuration—a group of individuals covenanting together—it would typically first of all seek a recognition of various rights and liberties for its members. The reality was reflected in medieval jurisprudence, especially in canon law. Medieval jurists all adhered to a doctrine of natural law with various shades of meaning and emphasis, but this did not preclude a concern for individual rights in their works. The jurists did not philosophize about the one and the many; instead they developed a complex structure of corporation law

5. Colin Morris, *The Discovery of the Individual, 1050–1200* (London: SPCK, 1972); Alan MacFarlane, *The Origins of English Individualism* (Cambridge: Cambridge Uni-versity Press, 1978); Francisco Suarez, *De opere sex dierum*, in *R. P. Francisci Suarez . . . opera omnia*, ed. A. D. M. André and C. Berton (Paris: Vivès, 1856), 3:381.

6. Georges de Lagarde, *La structure sociale et politique de l'Europe au XIVe siècle*, in *L'or-ganisation corporative du moyen âge à la fin de l'ancien régime* (Louvain: Bibliothèque de l'Université de Louvain, 1939), 109.

7. Jacques Maritain made a similar point in discussing modern society: "[T]here is nothing more illusory than to pose the problem of the person and the common good in terms of opposition." *The Person and the Commmon Good*, trans. J. J. Fitzgerald (New York: Scribner's Sons, 1947), 65.

that allowed for individual rights within corporate associations. In the field of political theory, Ptolemy of Lucca wrote, around 1300, that the end of government was to "preserve each one in his right."[8]

In the twelfth and thirteenth centuries we are in a world far removed from that of John Locke, but we can perhaps already discern some roots of the tradition that he would inherit. He too thought that the political community was a corporate association and that individuals had rights within it. And, as James Tully and others have pointed out, he did not really present individual persons as antisocial creatures, isolated atoms of humanity.[9] Locke saw no incompatibility in affirming a concept of human sociability while also upholding a doctrine of natural rights. Accordingly, he observed that "God . . . designed man for a sociable creature," and wrote of man's "love and want of society."[10] In Locke's work it was not the existence of human society as such that called for an explanation, but the coming into existence of a specifically political community.

Lockean Problems

Locke overtly presented his theory of natural rights as complementary to the established doctrine of natural law that he could find in many seventeenth-century sources and especially in the work of Richard Hooker. It is often observed that Locke quoted Hooker merely to give an air of respectability to his own more radical views. And this may be true in some instances; but it should not blind us to the fact that Hooker sometimes provided genuine support for views that Locke wanted to sustain. Many Locke scholars, probably most of them, realize this and acknowledge that Locke's work carried on an earlier tradition of natural law thinking. But this perception does not meet the objections of critics who assert that, although Locke did indeed write about a law of nature, he went on to propound views on the state as an artificial construct of reason and will, and on individual natural rights, that really were fundamentally incom-

8. Ptolemy of Lucca, *De regimine principum*, in *S. Thomae Aquinatis opera omnia*, ed. R. Busa (Stuttgart: Fromman-Holzboog, 1980), 8:558.

9. James Tully, *A Discourse on Property: John Locke and His Adversaries* (Cambridge: Cambridge University Press, 1980), 11, 24, 49. For further references on this, see A. John Simmons, *The Lockean Theory of Rights* (Princeton: Princeton University Press, 1982), 111n127.

10. *An Essay concerning Human Understanding*, ed. P. Nidditch (Oxford: Clarendon Press, 1975), 402 (3.1.1); Locke, *Two Treatises of Government*, ed. Peter Laslett (Cambridge: Cambridge University Press, 1970), 352.

patible with earlier concepts of natural law. Proponents of this view, however, often show little understanding of the earlier tradition that Locke is supposed to have abandoned. In this situation, we can probably best carry the argument further, not by general references to a preceding natural law tradition, but by specific inquiries into the historical background of some of Locke's characteristic teachings. The three topics to be discussed here are the idea of individual consent to government, the idea of self-ownership or self-mastery, and the existence of natural rights within a system of natural law.[11] Each of these themes involves, in one way or another, the ideas of individual rights and natural law, and each of them has been regarded by some scholars as radically innovatory; all three are of central importance in Locke's political thought.

Individual Consent to Government

The initial topic may seem to be a non-issue because, as is widely known, the idea of popular consent to government is often encountered in earlier sources. But the critics point out that, in these earlier theories, consent was always the consent of a corporate community, while for Locke individuals were the source of political authority. Tully, for instance, has written that "Locke's premise of political individualism is one of the major innovations in modern political thought."[12]

This argument runs into an obvious objection. In Locke's teaching, the consent that instituted a government was precisely the corporate consent of a community. Locke argued that a political society came into existence when a group of people "incorporated" and formed themselves into "*one Body Politick.*" A collection of separate individuals could act together only with the agreement of each single person, which, Locke observed, was "next impossible ever to be had." But once they were incorporated, the members of the community could act by the consent of a majority to institute a government for themselves.[13]

---

11. In discussing these themes I am in part summarizing the results of a group of my recent and forthcoming articles. See "Permissive Natural Law and Property: Gratian to Kant," *Journal of the History of Ideas* 63 (2001): 381–99; "Natural Law and Rights: Old Problems and New Approaches," *Review of Politics* 64 (2002): 389–420; "Corporatism, Individualism, and Consent" (forthcoming); and "Dominion of Self and Natural Rights" (forthcoming).

12. James Tully, *An Approach to Political Philosophy: Locke in Contexts* (Cambridge: Cambridge University Press, 1993).

13. Locke, *Two Treatises*, 2.348–50. Locke used the word *incorporate* over and over again in discussing the origin of government.

To be meaningful at all, then, the argument that Locke introduced a novel doctrine of individual consent must refer to the initial consent to establish a political community; and this is indeed one of the points where Locke is said to have made a break with past teachings. Charles Taylor, for instance, has observed that, in earlier thought, it was understood that a community could institute a government, but the existence of the community was just taken for granted; the important change in the seventeenth century was that the existence of the community itself had to be explained by assuming the prior consent of individuals. Michael Zuckert also has held that, in pre-Lockean thought, "the collectivity, or the corporation was the home and source of political power . . . and not the individual as in Locke." Zuckert also has maintained that Locke rejected the central doctrine of Aristotelian and Thomist political philosophy—the naturalness of political life—and envisaged instead a "state of nature" where a political community had to be created by human artifice. But, the argument continues, earlier thinkers who had accepted the Thomist view could not have imagined such a condition of humanity in which people lived under natural law but without any political institutions because, as Zuckert puts it, "natural law mandated and provided for political life."[14] For medievals, then, political society was natural; for Locke it was a work of human artifice; there is apparently a gulf between the two positions.

But this whole argument is based on a misunderstanding of medieval thought about natural law and human nature. According to the natural law that medieval jurists and philosophers knew, humans were by nature free and equal. For many of them, as for Locke, it was the fact of subordination under a government that called for an explanation. The Aristotelian teaching that the polis was natural to man in the sense that humans could flourish best in a political society was widely accepted—Locke himself thought that life in a political community was best for humans—but it was not taken to mean that such societies just came to exist naturally without any human initiative.

Giles of Rome made the point clearly in a very widely read work written toward the end of the thirteenth century. Although political society was natural to man in one sense, Giles pointed out, it was not natural in the same way that it was natural for a stone to fall or fire to heat. Natural law did not drive men willy-nilly into politically ordered communities;

14. Taylor, *Sources of the Self*, 193; Michael P. Zuckert, *Natural Rights and the New Republicanism* (Princeton: Princeton University Press, 1994), 226, 229, 230. Others who have contrasted Locke's individualism with an earlier tradition of corporate consent include Cary Nederman, Francis Oakley, Patrick Riley, and Paul Sigmund. On their views, see my forthcoming "Corporatism, Individualism, and Consent."

many people, Giles noted, still did not live in that way. The fact that the polis was natural in Aristotle's sense did not exclude the necessity for a political society to be actually brought into existence through "the work and industry of men" and "by human artifice" (*ex opere et industria hominum . . . ex arte humana*).[15]

There are various examples in the centuries before Locke of writers who envisaged a beginning of political society through individuals' consenting together to enter into compacts with one another. Already in the twelfth century the canonist Rufinus envisaged a state of affairs after the Fall of Adam when humans had lived without any ordered government and with only the law of nature to guide them. He depicted the human condition then as brutish and savage, rather in the manner of Hobbes. But, Rufinus allowed, men retained enough sense of justice to come together and enter into compacts and covenants with one another and so establish a body of law by which they could live.[16] There is perhaps a reminiscence of Cicero's *De inventione* here, but with a significant change. In Cicero's argument the scattered individuals were brought together by the skill of a great orator; in Rufinus's account they came together voluntarily to enter into compacts with one another.

In the next century Duns Scotus took up a similar theme. He imagined a group of strangers coming together to build a city. There would be no patriarchal or political authority among them, but they would feel the need of some governance. And so, Duns wrote, they could consent together that each individual would submit himself to the whole community or to a ruler whom they would choose.[17] Francisco de Vitoria also envisaged individuals uniting to form a political community, and he observed that they would all at first be equal since each had a natural right of self-defense.[18] Vitoria also noted, like Locke in a later age, that a unanimous consensus was not necessary to establish a government; a majority vote of the people concerned would suffice. Suarez provided the most detailed account before Locke of individuals consenting together to institute a political society. Among a group of scattered persons, he maintained, there would be no inherent ruling authority, but when the individuals came together to form

15. Aegidius Romanus, *De regimine principum libri III* (Rome: Antonium Bladum, 1556), 240, 320.

16. Rufinus, *Summa Decretorum*, ed. H. Singer (Paderborn, Germany: Ferdinand Schöningh, 1902), 4.

17. Duns Scotus, *Quaestiones in quartum librum sententiarum in Joannis Duns Scotus . . . opera omnia* (Paris: Vivès, 1891), 18:266 (4.15.2).

18. Francisco de Vitoria, *De potestate civile*, in *Obras de Francisco de Vitoria*, ed. Teofilo Urdanoz (Madrid: Biblioteca de Autores Cristianos, 1960), 159.

a political body, then the community could establish for itself any form of government it chose. The political community itself, Suarez emphasized, could be brought into existence only by "the special will and common consent" of the individuals who composed it.[19] If Locke had chosen to look for some earlier texts to substantiate his argument about individual consent, he would have found no shortage of authorities.

Self-ownership and Self-mastery

Locke declared, famously, that "every Man has a *Property* in his own *Person*. This no Body has any Right to but himself." But Locke also asserted that humans belong ultimately to God, that "they are his Property, whose Workmanship they are."[20] The two ideas are not really contradictory. In discussing the origin of property in general, Locke noted that it was held under the supreme dominion of God, and John Simmons has rightly argued that Locke conceived of ownership of self in the same way, as a sort of trust from God.[21]

Both ideas, self-ownership and divine ownership, were important to Locke's argument. Self-ownership expressed an idea of human autonomy. Because a man belonged to himself, he was not subject to anyone else except with his own consent; he was naturally free, endowed with "a Liberty of acting according to his own Will." And because he owned himself and his actions, he could licitly acquire property by his own labor. But because a man belonged also to God, he was not free to destroy or injure himself or another person.[22]

Locke's idea of self-ownership is another aspect of his work that has sometimes been seen as innovatory. C. B. MacPherson found in it a new kind of possessive individualism, where "the relation of ownership . . . was read back into the nature of the individual."[23] Zuckert, emphasizing a supposed contradiction between divine ownership and self-ownership, argues that Locke's doctrine "points toward his break with the entire premodern tradition."[24] But in fact the complex of ideas regarding self-ownership and

19. Francisco Suarez, *Tractatus de lege et deo legislatore*, in *Opera omnia*, ed. A. D. M. André and C. Berton (Paris: Vivès, 1856), 5:181 (3.2.4), 5:183 (3.3.6).

20. Locke, *Two Treatises*, 2.305 (emphasis in original), 2.289 (sec. 6).

21. Simmons, *Lockean Theory of Rights*, 102. See *Two Treatises*, 1.186: "[I]n respect of God . . . who is sole Lord and Proprietor of the whole World, Man's Propriety in the Creatures is nothing but that *Liberty to use them*, which God has permitted" (emphasis in original). Aquinas had taught the same doctrine centuries earlier.

22. Locke, *Two Treatises*, 2.327, 2.306, 2.289.

23. MacPherson, *Possessive Individualism*, 1.

24. Zuckert, *Natural Rights*, 276.

divine ownership that we find in Locke has a long prehistory in previous thought going back at least to the thirteenth century.

An initial difficulty in tracing this earlier history arises from the fact that the Latin word *dominium,* commonly used in pre-Lockean discourse, could mean either ownership or mastery, understood as control or rulership. But Locke used the English word *dominion* in both senses, and he too wrote of self-mastery as well as of self-ownership. Locke wrote, for instance, that man was "*Master* of his own *Life*" or "*Master* of himself and *Proprietor of his own Person,*"[25] here implying both relations, of mastery and of ownership. In tracing remoter anticipations of Locke's doctrine we need to consider both ideas.

I will begin with Aquinas since he is so often regarded as a prototypical medieval thinker. Aquinas expressed his own doctrine of autonomy in his teaching that humans are by nature free and equal, not subordinated to one another as a means to an end: "Nature made us all equal in liberty. . . . For by our nature no one is related to another as to an end."[26] Aquinas also expounded on "human dignity, by which a man is naturally free and exists for himself." He made various references to man's dominion of his acts (*dominium suorum actuum*) or dominion of self (*dominium sui*), and in these contexts he was concerned to express the idea of human freedom understood both as free will, the ability to make choices between different courses of action, and freedom from unjust subjection to another. According to Aquinas, humans differ from all other creatures precisely because "they have dominion of their actions through free choice."[27] In other discussions Aquinas also taught that humans' self-dominion made possible their ownership of external things. The various threads of argument were brought together in a passage from the *De perfectione,* where Aquinas was discussing renunciation of property and self-abnegation:

"Nothing is more pleasing to man than the liberty of his own will, for through this man is owner [*dominus*] of other things. . . . through this also he masters [*dominatur*] his own actions. . . . So in forgoing the judgment of his own will, through which he is master [*dominus*] of himself, he is found to deny himself."[28]

---

25. Locke, *Two Treatises,* 2.385, 336 (emphases in original).
26. St. Thomas Aquinas, *In quattuor libros Sententiarum commentaria,* in *Opera omnia* (Paris: Vivès, 1871), 1:255 (2.44.1.3). See also 1:613 (4.38.1.4): "There are some things in which a man is so free that he can act even against the command of the pope."
27. Aquinas, *Summa theologiae,* in *Opera omnia,* 2:610 (2.2ae.54.2), 355 (1.2ae.1.2).
28. Aquinas, *De perfectione spiritualis vitae,* in *Opera omnia,* 3:560. The idea that self-dominion made possible the ownership of external things was a commonplace of late medieval thought. There are occasional references to labor as a source of property right, but Locke's "mixing" metaphor is original with him.

In the texts of Aquinas, *dominium* is usually best translated as "mastery," though there is occasionally some ambiguity. Other thirteenth-century authors, including Peter John Olivi and Henry of Ghent, treated self-dominion more overtly as self-ownership. Olivi, by chance, used a phrase almost identical with one of Locke's. Locke noted that a man was "*Lord* of his own *Person* and *Possessions*." Olivi asserted that "each one is lord of himself and of his own" (dominus sui et suorum). Olivi also added a qualification like Locke's; a man was only lord of himself in things that were not contrary to God.[29]

Henry of Ghent addressed the issue of self-ownership by asking whether a criminal justly condemned to death had a right to escape if he could do so in order to preserve his life. Henry argued that two persons could have power over the same thing in different ways; one might have property, the other use. In this case the judge had a right to use the body of the criminal by imprisoning and even executing him, but only the criminal had property in himself "under God": "Only the soul under God has power as regards property in the substance of the body."[30] The conclusion of the argument was that the criminal's property right in himself prevailed; he could and should escape if an opportunity offered.

Among the later writers who addressed this theme I will mention especially Vitoria. His work is interesting because he first used the idea of self-ownership as a theological concept and then deployed it in a political context to defend the rights of American Indians. While discussing problems concerning property rights in his commentary on the *Summa theologiae* of Aquinas, Vitoria encountered an argument of Richard FitzRalph's. According to FitzRalph, since all *dominium* came from God, a person who excluded himself from divine grace by falling into sin could not be a true owner of anything. Vitoria replied by appealing to the doctrine of self-ownership. If FitzRalph were right, he argued, then a sinner would not be the true owner of his body or his acts and so would sin again in performing any bodily action—which Vitoria evidently regarded as absurd. Vitoria went on to argue here that man was the owner (*dominus proprietarius*) of his spiritual goods and of his "natural goods," such as his life and limbs. As owner of his own body, Vitoria argued, man could use it as he pleased; otherwise he would be a slave. Here again the natural freedom of choice was associated with freedom from servitude. Then Vitoria raised a problem that would recur in Locke's work: how could a man be owner of himself when

29. Peter John Olivi, *Quodlibet* 1 Q.17, ed. R. Spicciani, in *Studi Francescani* 73 (1976): 289–325. See 319, 321.

30. Henry of Ghent, *Quodlibet* 9 Q.3, in *Henrici de Gandavo opera omnia*, ed. R. Macken (Leuven, Belgium: Leuven University Press, 1983), 13:309.

he belonged to God, who was "lord of life and death"? Vitoria replied that "although God is the prime owner, still he grants dominion to man . . . not for every kind of use, but for licit ones." Self-ownership did not permit a man to kill or injure himself or another person.[31]

When Vitoria turned in a later work to a defense of Indian rights, he argued that God had granted dominion over worldly things to the whole human race; but he had to respond to an argument asserting that the Indians were incapable of ownership because they lived in a state of sin. Vitoria replied by reformulating the argument he had used against FitzRalph. If sin took away all rightful ownership, then a sinner would lose his natural ownership of his own body and his own acts. But, Vitoria argued, this was evidently not the case. A sinner still had the right to defend his own person.

Another argument that Vitoria discussed asserted that, according to Aristotle, all barbarians are natural slaves; hence the Indians were slaves and, as slaves, could not own anything. Here again Vitoria introduced the concept of self-ownership. Even if the Indians were inferior in intellect (which Vitoria did not concede) and so could be called natural slaves in Aristotle's sense, as better fitted to serve than to rule, still this did not mean that they naturally belonged to others and had no ownership of themselves or of their property. That would be a condition of penal servitude. No one was such a slave by nature, Vitoria insisted.[32]

Suarez also referred to ownership or mastery of self in various contexts scattered throughout his works, and he too used the concept to assert man's natural freedom. Suarez maintained that, as a rational creature, man was *dominus* of his acts; accordingly he was "naturally free and not a slave."[33] In arguing against the supposed tyranny of King James I of England, Suarez maintained that human freedom was grounded on the natural dignity of man and that this natural freedom included a power of ruling oneself but excluded involuntary subjection to another. Hence legitimate government had to be based on consent, on "human institution and election."[34] Locke would argue in the same way when he wrote against the supposed tyranny of James II.

Subsequently the idea of self-ownership was taken up by Grotius and then by the English Levellers. Among them, Richard Overton argued,

31. Francisco de Vitoria, *De justitia,* ed. V. Beltran de Heredia (Madrid: Associación de Autores Cristianos, 1934). FitzRalph used the word *dominium* to mean both "rulership" and "ownership," but in the contexts discussed above Vitoria was discussing specifically property right.

32. Francisco de Vitoria, *De Indis recenter inventis relectio prima,* in *Obras,* 654, 665.

33. Francisco Suarez, *De legibus,* in *Opera omnia,* 183 (3.3.6).

34. Francisco Suarez, *Defensio fidei catholicae,* in *Opera omnia,* 24:210 (3.2.11).

most strikingly, "To every individuall in nature is given an individual property by nature, not to be usurped by any: for everyone as he is himself, so he has a self-propriety."[35] When Locke took up this same theme, he was continuing in his own way a long-standing tradition of thought.

Natural Rights and Natural Law

After individual consent and self-ownership, a final theme we have to consider is one I mentioned earlier, a supposed opposition between traditional natural law and natural rights. Ernest Fortin, for instance, has maintained that the move from natural law thinking to an assertion of natural rights in the seventeenth century was not only *a* paradigm shift, but *"the* paradigm shift" in our understanding of justice and morality. On this view natural law is seen as a "higher law" that dictates the way we should live with its commands and prohibitions, while natural rights express a principle of human autonomy, of individual self-assertion, and the two doctrines are held to conflict with one another. Jack Donnelly, for instance, contended that liberties and entitlements distinguish rights from law so fundamentally that "law and rights point in different directions." Walter Berns stated the argument in an extreme form when he declared, "To espouse the one teaching [natural law] is to make it impossible reasonably to espouse the other [natural rights]."[36] Other scholars have argued that the only rights that can exist within a framework of natural law are rights to obey the mandates of the law; but, as Zuckert has observed, this implies nothing about "a realm of sovereignty or of free choice." Law directs our actions; rights leave us free to choose. A system of thought based on natural law must, then, be antithetical to one based on natural rights. And yet Locke certainly asserted a doctrine of natural law while also maintaining that humans are endowed with natural rights.[37] It seems, then, that we

35. Richard Overton, *An Arrow against All Tyrants* (London: Martin Claw-Clergy, 1646), 3.

36. Ernest Fortin, *Collected Essays*, ed. J. Brian Benestead (Lanham, MD: Rowman and Littlefield, 1996), 3:20; Jack Donnelly, "Natural Law and Right in Aquinas' Political Thought," *Western Political Quarterly* 33 (1980): 520; Walter Berns, *In Defense of Liberal Democracy* (Chicago: Gateway Editions, 1984), 8. In fact not all modern rights are based on human autonomy. Some are grounded on need or various entitlements. But "choice rights" represent the principal area where a conflict is said to exist between traditional natural law and modern natural rights.

37. Michael P. Zuckert, *Launching Political Liberalism: On Lockean Political Philosophy* (Lawrence: University Press of Kansas, 2002), 185; Locke, *Two Treatises*, 2.289: "The *State of Nature* has a Law of Nature to govern it . . ."

must either regard Locke's whole structure of thought as incoherent or else embrace the Straussian doctrine and assume that Locke did not really believe in the doctrine of natural law that he overtly presented.

But here again we are dealing with a misunderstanding of the earlier tradition of natural law. Pre-Lockean theories of natural law included an idea of natural rights. We have already seen that medieval and early modern thinkers before Locke were much concerned with human freedom understood both as free will and as freedom from subjection to others. Locke's way of expressing this was to state that we are free to exercise our rights "within the bounds of the law of nature" or "within the permission of the law of nature." But, in writing like this, Locke was again adhering to an old tradition of thought, one in which natural law was seen not as opposed to human freedom but as defining it. The ideas of natural law and natural rights had coexisted harmoniously enough for centuries before Locke. From the twelfth century onward, it was commonly held that natural law not only commanded and forbade, but also left to humans a wide range of discretionary behavior where they were free to choose their own courses of action and had a right to act as they chose. This tradition of thought flourished from the twelfth century to the eighteenth, when it was still vigorously asserted, especially among the professors of natural law in German universities. In the generation after Locke, Christian Wolff noted that the "law of nature is called permissive . . . when it gives us a right to act."[38]

Here again I can point to only a few steps in the earlier development of the doctrine. The idea of a permissive natural law first emerged in the writings of twelfth-century canonists who commented on Gratian's *Decretum*, their great collection of canonical texts. The issue arose when the Decretists considered the origin of individual property. According to Gratian, by natural law all things were common. How then could one justify the private property that actually existed? One solution argued that the law involved here was merely permissive. Natural law did not actually command that all property always be held in common, but only indicated that this was a legitimate state of affairs. It left humans free either to choose community of property or to assert an individual right of ownership, as they saw fit.[39]

Subsequent generations of jurists and philosophers used the idea of permissive law to carve out, so to speak, a sphere of human freedom and

---

38. Locke, *Two Treatises*, 2.287, 2.370; Christian Wolff, *Institutiones juris naturae et gentium*, in Christian Wolff, *Gesammelte Werke*, 2nd ed., vol. 26, ed. M. Thommam (Hildesheim: Georg Olms, 1969), 24.

39. For the relevant canonistic texts see my book *The Idea of Natural Rights: Studies on Natural Rights, Natural Law, and Church Law, 1150–1625* (1997; reprint, Grand Rapids, MI: Eerdmans, 2001), 67, 142–43.

autonomy within the realm of natural law itself. In one early development, the fourteenth-century canonist Johannes Andreae considered the nature of permission in civil law, canon law, and natural law. In the course of his discussion he distinguished three different kinds of permissive law. Such law could merely leave certain types of behavior unpunished, or it could forbid others from impeding a permitted behavior, or it could actually lend support to the permitted act. Duns Scotus approached the idea differently when he considered divine law. He maintained that in principle we are obliged to God in everything we do; but, he added, God does not ask so much of us; he demands only that we do not violate the precepts of the Ten Commandments. Duns's conclusion was that, where God does not specifically impose an obligation on us in the Decalogue, he leaves us to the liberty of our own wills.[40]

In the sixteenth century Vitoria made an explicit connection between permissive law and individual rights. Vitoria was trying here to extract a doctrine of natural rights from Aquinas's teaching on law, and he quoted Aquinas's statement that "law is the ground of right." Vitoria took this to mean that a right is what the law permits; he continued: "And so we use the word when we speak for we say, 'I have not a right [*ius*] to do this, that is it is not permitted to me or again, 'I have a right,' that is, it is permitted."[41]

Suarez also explored the relation between rights and permissive law when he faced an objection to the whole concept of permissive law that would also be raised by later critics. The nature of law is to impose obligation, but permission is opposed to obligation. Suarez replied that even permissive law did create obligation—not on the one who chose to act or not to act in accordance with the permission, but on others. Specifically, it imposed an obligation on judges not to punish for the permitted act. Suarez noted here that positive civil law sometimes had to permit behavior that was intrinsically evil—he mentioned fornication and adultery. But such permission meant only that the behavior was not prohibited by law. On the other hand, law permitting acts that were blameless in themselves conferred "a positive faculty or license or right."[42]

Suarez argued in a similar fashion when he considered the realm of natural law and the old problem of private property. Like the canonists, he maintained that a permissive natural law justified the acquisition of individual property, but he added an intricate argument to prove that the law

40. Johannes Andreae, *In titulum de regulis iuris commentaria* (Venice: Franciscanus Franciscanium, 1581), 64–65. For further discussion see my "Permissive Natural Law and Property"; Duns Scotus, *Quaestiones*, 19:161 (26.1).

41. Vitoria, *De justitia*, 64.

42. Suarez, *De legibus*, 57 (1.14.5), 62 (1.15.11).

also gave rise to a natural right. In another discussion he explained that many things could be done rightfully in accordance with natural law that were not commanded or forbidden but that were natural rights; and, he added, reason shows us what is permitted as well as what is commanded.[43]

Suarez emphasized humans' freedom to make their own maps of life in another context when he considered Aquinas's argument that the goal of life on this earth is felicity and that this goal is ineluctable. According to Aquinas, we cannot not want to be happy. Suarez did not dispute this, but he argued that the doctrine applied only to the one final goal and that there were many other particular goals where humans were free to choose.[44]

The tradition of permissive natural law that had developed by the seventeenth century did not assert only a right to obey the mandates of the law. Nor did it maintain, as one modern critic has argued, that we must "ask permission" of the law before acting. It was rather that natural law left large areas of human conduct undetermined by its commands and prohibitions; it recognized a realm of human autonomy where persons had a natural right to act as they chose. That is what Locke too meant when he affirmed a doctrine of natural law and of natural rights "within the permission of the law of nature."

Rights after Locke

The historical contingency that helped to shape Locke's teaching on rights was the constitutional crisis of the 1680s in England. Reflecting on an old tradition of thought in these new circumstances, Locke made his own distinctive contribution to the developing doctrine of rights, especially in his treatment of religious toleration, with its affirmation that "liberty of conscience is every man's natural right." But the development of a modern theory of human rights was far from complete in Locke's day. When we consider any living tradition, we deal with growth and change, but change in which each generation builds on the work of its predecessors. Modern human rights, though, are so different in their scope and content from anything that was envisaged in Locke's day that we still need to consider whether anything of the earlier tradition really survived among future generations.

43. Ibid., 141 (2.14.17), 163 (2.18.3).
44. Aquinas, *In quattuor libros Sententiarum commentaria,* in *Opera omnia,* 1.199 (2.25.1.2); Suarez, *De necessitate et contingentia effectum,* in *Opera omnia,* vol. 25, ed. A. D. M. André and C. Berton (Paris: Vivès, 1866), 713.

Locke's views were not widely accepted at first by the English Whigs for whom he wrote; they preferred to oppose Stuart absolutism by appealing to a supposed ancient constitution. But the Lockean idea of natural rights proved admirably suited for export, especially to the American colonies and to France. In those lands new circumstances arose in which natural rights proved relevant in the face of looming crises so that, by the end of the eighteenth century, each country had produced a document of major historical importance affirming the existence of such rights, the Declaration of Independence in America and the Declaration of the Rights of Man and the Citizen in France.

As regards America, during the past half century a complex dispute grew up concerning the extent of Locke's influence on colonial revolutionary thought. The relevance of Lockean ideas to the Declaration of Independence, with its assertion of God-given natural rights, seems self-evident. But various critics, emphasizing different sources, asserted the primary importance of other ideas in American thought, first the "country-party" ideology of English opposition propagandists, then the ideals of classical republicanism. Still other scholars continued to assert a primary role for Locke. As the discussion progressed, however, it became clear that these strands of thought are not mutually exclusive. The republican freedom to participate in government does not necessarily exclude a Lockean freedom from unwarranted government interference in one's individual affairs. And Zuckert showed how elements of Lockean thought existed within the country ideology of Trenchard and Gordon.[45] The tangled debate seems finally to have reached a consensus on this point at least, that Locke's thought was very important for the generation of the American Founding Fathers, whatever weight we attribute to other influences. And it was largely through their embedding in American constitutional documents that Lockean ideas on natural rights persisted into the contemporary world.

Even when this is understood, though, there remain problems concerning the nature of Locke's influence. Some followers of Leo Strauss maintain that Locke's teachings on natural rights were essentially the same as those of Hobbes and that, accordingly, Locke transmitted to the Founding Fathers an implicit doctrine of atheism, hedonism, and rationalism that was really incompatible with Christianity and with natural law understood as a higher law that provides norms of human behavior, even though Locke himself overtly affirmed his adherence to such traditional

45. Zuckert, *Natural Rights*, 297–305.

beliefs. Hence, in the American founding, elements of Locke's "radical and shocking intrepidity" came to be associated with conventional appeals to natural law, biblical revelation, and classical republicanism.[46] And this, it is argued, set up an enduring tension in American political thought. This whole argument, however, rests on Strauss's assertion that Locke's overt theistic teaching was deployed only to mask an esoteric skeptical doctrine, a view that has persuaded few Locke scholars. And in any case it was the overt Locke and his teaching about a divinely ordained natural law and natural rights that the American Founders knew and valued.

Knud Haakonssen contends in a different way that the eighteenth-century teachings stimulated by Locke's work still reflected a premodern way of thinking, essentially different from a modern conception of rights. Haakonssen argues that a "subjective theory of rights proper" would present rights as "the primary and fundamental feature of humanity." He associates the emergence of such rights with a new concept of individual autonomy understood as a human capacity for self-legislation rather than as a mere ability to obey the mandates of a supposed natural law. In Haakonssen's view, the emergence of such modern rights indeed "amounted to the philosophical death . . . of natural law thinking proper."[47] On this argument a considerable gap exists between modern ways of thinking about rights and the earlier ideas that we have discussed. But, as noted above, not all modern rights claims are grounded on assertions of human autonomy; some are derived simply from human need. Also, Haakonssen's argument is based in part on the view—a mistaken view, I have argued—that, within a system of natural law, a right is merely a power to fulfill the duties that the law imposes. Moreover, a capacity for self-legislation does not necessarily lead to a primacy of rights; rather, it results in a complex of rights and duties much as traditional natural law thinking does. Finally, there seems to be a logical incoherence in the argument. If rights depend on a capacity for self-legislation, then this, not the rights themselves, should be regarded as the "primary and fundamental feature of humanity" in the moral sphere. As Tibor Machan regularly observes, rights theories are always dependent on some more fundamental moral point of view.

If we accept that Locke's declared religious views provided a grounding for his own moral convictions, we are still left with a disagreement as

---

46. Thomas Pangle, *The Spirit of Modern Republicanism* (Chicago: University of Chicago Press, 1988), 276.

47. Knud Haakonssen, *Natural Law and Moral Philosophy: From Grotius to the Scottish Enlightenment* (New York: Cambridge University Press, 1995), 311, 314.

to what those convictions actually were and how they relate to his more rationalist arguments. Some scholars see Locke as a Socinian (or Unitarian), as some of Locke's contemporaries did; others regard him as a reasonably orthodox if latitudinarian Anglican. In either case, the fact that Locke introduced theological arguments into his political writings along with rationalist ones has given rise to a continuing debate about the contemporary relevance of Locke's theories. Among modern scholars, John Simmons has insisted most strongly on the continuing relevance of Locke's work; he maintains that Locke's theory of rights can provide a viable foundation not only for *his* political philosophy but for *ours*.[48] Simmons argues that Locke's political philosophy is logically detachable from his theological premises, so that it leaves the way open for a development of secular moral theories. John Dunn presents a different point of view. He maintains that Locke's rights theory was necessarily dependent on his theological commitments but holds that nowadays, paradoxically, we continue to find Locke's political theory attractive while firmly discarding the religious premises that make it intelligible.[49] Dunn's argument seems to me of dubious validity, while that of Simmons expresses a truth, though perhaps not the whole truth. Locke did provide both religious and secular arguments for his teachings, but the fact that the arguments were associated in his own mind does not prove that they were necessarily interdependent. The possibility of separating them had been apparent ever since Grotius framed his "impious hypothesis" ("even if there were no God . . ."); and Grotius in turn was echoing a fairly common tradition of late medieval philosophy.

In eighteenth-century America, to be sure, the question of "detachability" hardly arose. Instead, religious and secular arguments seemed to complement one another; New England preachers were quite happy to weave Lockean themes into their Calvinist sermons. But events took a different turn in France. There, the *philosophes* often admired Locke, but they developed their own theories of natural rights in a spirit of bitter animosity to established Christianity and especially to the Catholic Church, with the result that for a century an assertion of individual natural rights was widely seen as incompatible with Catholic religious doctrine. The idea still persists in some quarters. Pope Leo XIII reintroduced the language of natural rights into Catholic thought in his encyclical *Rerum novarum*, but a

---

48. Simmons, *Lockean Theory of Rights*, 199.
49. John Dunn, *The Political Thought of John Locke* (Cambridge: Cambridge University Press, 1969), 266–67.

modern commentator on the text has observed that this language was "neither native nor congenial to the older Catholic tradition."[50]

This remark reflects a misunderstanding of an earlier tradition of Catholic thought that, from the twelfth and thirteenth centuries onward, had contributed to the development of a doctrine of natural rights. But the fact that, for much of the nineteenth century, an assertion of the "rights of man" was seen as implying an attitude hostile to religion does indeed indicate that a doctrine of natural rights was logically detachable from Locke's religious premises. However, this should not be taken to mean simply that Locke's way of arguing made it possible for secular theories of rights to replace religiously grounded ones. There are indeed many secular theories of rights in the modern literature, based on a variety of philosophical premises—Kantian, Aristotelian, and consequentialist. But religiously grounded rights theories also continue to flourish. Indeed, some of the most successful rights movements of modern times have been inspired at least in part by religious convictions. One thinks of Dr. Martin Luther King Jr. in America and Desmond Tutu in South Africa. Dr. King appealed to St. Paul and Augustine and Thomas Aquinas in his *Letter from Birmingham Jail,* and Archbishop Tutu turned back to the scriptural language that described man as made in the image of God in asserting the dignity of all human persons. In a different religious sphere the Roman Catholic Church, turning its back on some recent history, has emerged in the last half century as a major champion of human rights. Locke's doctrine of rights can retain its relevance for the modern world, not only because it is separable from his own theological premises, but because it opens the way for further developments of both secular and religious rights theories.

Before we consider how far the three specific themes in Locke's work that we discussed earlier have persisted in modern political discourse, we need to glance at the historical context from which contemporary rights theories have emerged. The story from Locke's day to ours is not one of uninterrupted progress. Theories of natural rights reached an apogee in the eighteenth century. But in the nineteenth century they encountered increasing opposition, and not only from conservative religious sources. New movements of thought—Marxism, utilitarianism, anthropological relativism—all helped to erode belief in any natural rights common to all people. Then, in the years after World War II, there came a sudden, new flourishing of concern for universal rights, now called "human rights." The historical contingency that led to the change is well understood. The

50. Fortin, *Collected Essays,* 3:23.

new enthusiasm for human rights grew out of a horrified reaction to the atrocities of the Nazis during the war. As Michael Ignatieff succinctly observed, "Without the Holocaust, then, no Declaration," referring to the UN's Universal Declaration on Human Rights of 1948. Ignatieff saw the Declaration itself as "a studied attempt to reinvent the European natural law tradition," and he quoted Isaiah Berlin as saying that, "because these rules of natural law were flouted we have been forced to become conscious of them."[51] But the point is that within that old tradition of natural law there was embedded a doctrine of natural rights, and it was that aspect of the tradition that was revived. Moral outrage does not have to be expressed in a language of rights. But in this case a centuries-old tradition of natural rights already existed. It was "historically available," as Ignatieff again remarked, ready at hand to be taken up and applied to the circumstances of a new age. That is why an awareness of an old tradition can sometimes help us to understand modern movements of thought.

We can finally ask how far the three particular strands of thought that we discussed—individual consent, self-ownership, and permissive natural law—have survived among the multifarious modern theories of rights. As to the first, modern political scientists no longer base their theories on a Lockean idea of individual consent to government in a state of nature. But the underlying idea of humans' deliberating together in a prepolitical society about the institution of a government has been reinvented—one might say repristinated—in John Rawls's idea of an "original condition" and applied in a novel way in his very influential theory of justice.[52]

Our second theme, the idea of self-dominion, is surprisingly prevalent in the modern literature, and it is currently used to mean both self-ownership and self-mastery. Some writers, following C. B. MacPherson, attack the idea as a form of the possessive individualism that has led to all the (alleged) abuses of modern capitalism. Libertarians commonly take self-dominion as the foundation of their doctrine, with frequent references to Locke and even an occasional mention of Aquinas. Some left-wing authors have even used the idea of self-ownership as the starting point for socialist or egalitarian theories of society.[53]

51. Michael Ignatieff, *Human Rights as Politics and Idolatry* (Princeton: Princeton University Press, 2001), 80–81, 66.
52. John Rawls, *A Theory of Justice,* rev. ed. (Cambridge: Harvard University Press, Belknap Press, 1999).
53. For an example of each of these approaches see the following: Attracta Ingram, *A Political Theory of Rights* (Oxford: Clarendon Press, 1994); David Boaz, *Libertarianism: A Primer* (New York: Free Press, 1997); and Philippe van Parijs, *Real Freedom for All* (Oxford: Clarendon Press, 1995). Boaz refers to Aquinas at p. 95. See also Douglass Rasmussen,

Our third theme, the idea of rights within a framework of permissive natural law, invites comparison with Haakonssen's view that modern rights are based on a concept of human autonomy opposed to earlier natural law theories. But the issue is complicated. Medieval and early modern thinkers had their own ideas about autonomy, based on free will and self-dominion and a natural freedom from servitude, but there is no one generally accepted modern theory of autonomy to compare them with. Susan Brisson, for instance, has discussed six different types of autonomy that can be found in the current literature. But whatever idea of autonomy is adopted and although the language of natural law is not fashionable nowadays, it is still generally agreed that rights refer to a permitted range of actions and are limited by law—either by civil law or by some kind of moral law implied by considerations inherent in the concept of the right itself. Robert Nozick presented a libertarian view of society, but still he treated rights as constraints on behavior because they limit the ways we can act toward other right-bearers. "My property rights in my knife allow me to leave it where I will," he noted, "but not in your chest." And Nozick added here that we are free to choose only among "acceptable options."[54] Earlier thinkers, Vattel, for instance, expressed the thought by writing of a right to act within the realm of what is morally permissible; others, in still more old-fashioned language, wrote of rights "within the permission of the law of nature."

Looking at the whole modern picture, one can only conclude that, although much has changed, something still survives from an older tradition in the modern "welter" of rights and rights theories. There remains one last problem. As Mary Ann Glendon has pointed out, nowadays a language of rights has become so widely diffused, and often abused, that it threatens to infiltrate the whole of our moral discourse and to impoverish it.[55] It is the abuse of rights language, I suppose, that has led some conservative Christians to reject our whole culture of rights with phrases like "corrosive selfishness" and "narcissistic atomism."[56] But some people have always been selfish and narcissistic; the existence of such people is not just a product of a modern culture of rights; one could find plenty of

---

"Why Individual Rights?" in *Individual Rights Reconsidered,* ed. Tibor Machan (Stanford, CA: Hoover Institution, 2001), 127.

54. Susan Brisson, "The Autonomy Defense of Free Speech," *Ethics* 108 (1998): 312–39; Robert Nozick, *Anarchy, State and Utopia* (New York: Basic Books, 1974), 171.

55. On the modern "welter" of rights see Loren E. Lomasky, *Persons, Rights, and the Moral Community* (Oxford: Oxford University Press, 1987), 4; Mary Ann Glendon, *Rights Talk: The Impoverishment of Political Discourse* (New York: Free Press, 1991).

56. Kraynak, *Christian Faith and Modern Democracy,* 167; Fortin, *Collected Essays,* 3:23.

examples in the Old Testament. So we ought to give due weight to the proper use as well as to the abuses of modern rights language. Glendon provides good guidance here. She effectively skewered the abuses of "rights talk" in an early book, but she does not regard such abuses as inherent in the idea of human rights itself. In a later work she argues that they are not built into the founding program of the whole modern rights movement, the UN Universal Declaration on Human Rights, a document that Glendon, along with the late Pope John Paul II, has warmly praised. The Declaration, she points out, does not assert a selfish and atomistic individualism. It is grounded on the "inherent dignity" of the human person; it affirms that the family is "the natural and fundamental group unit of society"; it declares that "everyone has duties to the community."[57] Perhaps it is inevitable that abuses will arise, but they do not have to be embraced, they can always be resisted. The principle we should apply here, I think, is the old teaching that *abusus non tollit usum* (abuse does not take away rightful use).

The notion of natural rights or human rights had a long history in Christian thought before it assumed its more secular modern forms. The idea has always expressed an ideal never fully realized in practice, but it has provided a strong weapon against various forms of oppression in the past. Given the less amiable proclivities of human nature, we should probably do well to preserve the ideal for future generations. They too may find it useful to have such a notion "historically available" in the contingencies of their times.

57. Mary Ann Glendon, "The Rule of Law in the Universal Declaration of Human Rights," *Northwestern University Journal of International Human Rights* 2 (2004): 67–81.

Natural Rights and Social Contract in Burke and Bellarmine

Gary D. Glenn

The existence of natural rights and social contract language in pre-Hobbesian thought seems both little known and well known: little known to those of us who study the history of political philosophy, but well known to medievalists in the disciplines of philosophy and history,[1] as well as to theologians. While older histories of "political thought" and "political theory" were "at pains to stress the importance of the legacy which the medieval theorists of popular sovereignty, contract, and consent passed down . . . to the constitutionalists and consent theorists of the early modern era,"[2] more recent histories and studies tend to downplay or

---

1. Notably Francis Oakley, *The Medieval Experience: Foundations of Western Cultural Singularity* (New York: Scribner's Sons, 1974); Brian Tierney, *The Idea of Natural Rights: Studies on Natural Rights, Natural Law, and Church Law, 1150–1625* (1997; reprint, Grand Rapids, MI: Eerdmans, 2001); and Arthur P. Monahan, *From Personal Duties towards Personal Rights: Late Medieval and Early Modern Political Thought 1300–1600* (Montreal: McGill-Queen's University Press, 1993).

2. This observation (confirmed by my own study) is made by Francis Oakley, "Legitimation by Consent: The Question of the Medieval Roots," *VIATOR: Medieval and Renaissance Studies* 14 (1983): 304. As examples of the older histories, Oakley cites virtually all of them: Otto von Gierke, *Development of Political Theory* (New York: W. W. Norton, 1939); J. N. Figgis, *Political Thought from Gerson to Grotius, 1614–1625* (Cambridge: Cambridge University Press, 1916); Charles McIlwain, *Constitutionalism: Ancient and Modern* (Ithaca, NY: Cornell University Press, 1958); R. W. Carlyle and A. J. Carlyle, *A History of Medieval Political Theory in the West* (Edinburgh: Blackwood, 1915);

ignore the pre-Hobbesian medieval antecedents of these ideas.[3] The consequence is exemplified by the following statement from a preeminent student of the history of the idea of social contract: "The seventeenth and eighteenth centuries are commonly, and accurately, represented as the age of social contract theory."[4]

This change may be sufficiently explained by the fact that the older histories of "political theory" and "political thought" included political speculation and teachings drawn from political theologians. Leo Strauss, more emphatically than any other recent student of the history of political philosophy, articulates this change by explicitly distinguishing "political philosophy" from "political theory," "political thought," and "political theology."[5] These distinctions make the different grounds of what claims to be "political" knowledge more distinct and precise. But they also have the consequence of drawing our attention away from relevant writings that are beyond the boundaries of political philosophy as Plato and Aristotle as well as Machiavelli, Hobbes, and the rest of self-consciously "modern" philosophers understand it.

This study supposes that this contemporary tendency to downplay or omit pre-Hobbesian natural rights and social contract from the history of political philosophy might matter to how we understand modernity and what there is and is not room for within modernity's way of political thinking and living. And it seeks clarity about that question by investigating an old assertion about Edmund Burke by the historian of political philosophy Charles E. Vaughan and the criticism of that assertion by the student of Scholastic philosophy M. F. X. Millar, SJ.[6] Vaughan asserts that Burke

---

Harold Laski, "Political Theory in the Later Middle Ages," in *The Cambridge Medieval History*, vol. 8 (Cambridge: Cambridge University Press, 1911–1936); G. W. Gough, *The Social Contract: A Critical Study of Its Development* (New York: Oxford University Press, 1936); and George Sabine, *A History of Political Theory* (New York: Henry Holt, 1950).

3. Notably Leo Strauss and Joseph Cropsey, eds., *History of Political Philosophy*, 3rd ed. (1963; reprint, Chicago: University of Chicago Press, 1987); Strauss, *Natural Right and History* (1953; reprint, Chicago: University of Chicago Press, 1959); C. B. MacPherson, *The Political Theory of Possessive Individualism: Hobbes to Locke* (Oxford: Clarendon Press, 1962). Among contemporary students of the history of political philosophy, a major exception to this more recent tendency is Richard Tuck, *Natural Rights Theories: Their Origin and Development* (Cambridge: Cambridge University Press, 1979).

4. Patrick Riley, "How Coherent Is the Social Contract Tradition?" *Journal of the History of Ideas* 34, no. 4 (October–December 1973): 543.

5. See Strauss, "What Is Political Philosophy?" in *What Is Political Philosophy? And Other Studies* (Glencoe, IL: Free Press, 1959), 12–13.

6. Charles E. Vaughan, *Studies in the History of Political Philosophy Before and After Rousseau* (1925; reprint, New York: Russell and Russell, 1960), 2:53; M. F. X. Millar, SJ, "Scholasticism and American Political Philosophy," in *Present Day Thinkers and the New*

adopts "the language of contract" but gives it "a meaning which would have spread dismay among its authors." Burke transforms the "act of consent, which to Locke was all in all" into "a mere metaphor" which is "no true consent, no contract at all."[7] The reasons are that "the consent, so far from being actually given, is tacitly assumed . . . [and] so far from being matter of choice is imposed by the necessities of man's nature."[8]

Vaughan says that Burke's metaphorical social contract language is distinct from that of "the individualists" who were "its authors," not only as to its meaning but also "as to its scope and nature." Notice that, for Vaughan, the individualists are "*the* authors," for there was one, and only one, social contract theory, namely, that which was "devised to save the existence of indefeasible rights . . . by express stipulation in the contract from which every state took its origin." Vaughan grants that there are variations within that tradition, yet there remains a core "throughout," namely, the "unquestionable assumption" of indefeasible rights. Without that, the idea of social contract "would never in the face of all history and all probability . . . have seen the light" of day.[9]

To Vaughan's objection one might respond that Hobbes also teaches that the sovereign's power is based on contract and that subjects have natural rights. And, while one might say that the sovereign's power is limited to securing the subjects' self-preservation, yet that turns out not to be very limited. It would be strange to describe the sovereign's plenitude of legal power, combined with the subjects' lack of a legal right either to disobey or revolt, as "limited ends." Accordingly, Vaughan reads Hobbes out of the real social contract tradition.[10]

However, Vaughan argues that Burke's metaphorical use of social contract language so departs both from the meaning of "its authors" and from its development as to be outside that tradition. Locke, "the starkest and most consistent of the champions of that theory," is representative of their view that "the State is a partnership for merely material, and therefore limited, ends." In contrast, for Burke it is "a partnership for intellectual and moral ends . . . which, from the nature of the case, cannot possibly be lim-

---

Scholasticism: An International Symposium, ed. John S. Zybura (St. Louis: B. Herder, 1926), 327;

7. Riley, "How Coherent Is the Social Contract Tradition?" also regards Burke's contract language as "metaphorical" (543).

8. Vaughan, *Studies,* 2:53.

9. Ibid., 2:53, 60–61.

10. "[T]he first writer [Hobbes] to formulate it [social contract] in any detail . . . perverted it to ends the direct contrary of those for which it was manifestly devised. . . . he . . . forced a democratic theory into the service of autocracy." Ibid., 1:12.

ited."[11] Vaughan's claim then is that Burke enlists a language born of an effort to limit government, in the cause of unlimited government.

Vaughan is perplexed as to why, from Burke's own point of view, he "again and again . . . casts in his lot unequivocally with the theory of social contract." For social contract "squares" neither with his "doctrine of expediency" nor with "the incompatible theory of rights." He suggests that Burke "accepts" social contract "carelessly" perhaps because of "the hold which the doctrine of an original contract had laid upon men of his own generation."[12]

Millar's Objection

In contrast to Vaughan, Millar maintains that there is not one social contract theory, but two. He points out that Burke's statement on "the social compact" is so far from being "a mere metaphor" that it is the "older and sounder" tradition. Furthermore, Millar thinks that Vaughan's error of omission is not unique and that it exemplifies that "the historians and political scientists persistently ignore or evade" the fact that there are not one, but two traditions of social contract, equality, and government by consent of the governed.[13] Millar claims that the "older and sounder" tradition is found before Burke, in Robert Bellarmine's *De Laicis*, chapters 5 and 6. He suggests that Vaughan's puzzlement about Burke's use of contract language would be clarified by attention to these chapters.

If Millar would turn out to be onto something, it would seem to clarify Vaughan's puzzlement in the following way: Burke would be seen as transporting into modernity ideas of social contract and rights hitherto presented under cover of, or at least in company with, political theology. It would then be fair to ask whether there is room in modernity for such ideas as something other than metaphor. To investigate Millar's claim, those of us who study history of political philosophy, and who seek to understand precisely how modernity both departs from and inherits elements of premodern thought, cannot take for granted that these ideas are simply modern, as Vaughan and self-consciously modern students of social contract and consent now tend to do.

At stake in this investigation of whether this is only one tradition or two are the following questions: How does the substance of consent and social

11. Ibid., 1:11, 2:53, 54.
12. Ibid., 2:60, 61.
13. Millar, "Scholasticism and American Political Philosophy," 327n39, 327–28.

contract presented in a theological context differ from that of "the individualists," especially the commonly recognized consent and contract theories
of Hobbes, Locke, Paine, and Rousseau? Alternatively, if all genuine consent and contract are necessarily "individualist" and antitheological, can
there be a place within either philosophical or political modernity for those
whose understanding of contract and rights is situated in a theological context?[14] And have we political scientists all but forgotten the latter tradition
because, like Vaughan regarding Burke, we find it simply unintelligible
because it is so radically incompatible with philosophical modernity?

Studying Bellarmine across the Medieval/Modern Divide

Bellarmine's *De Laicis: or, The Treatise on Civil Government*[15] is explicitly an
explanation and defense of "the Church." Its external structure is political

14. Strauss argues that philosophical modernity is antitheological in its foundations.
"The founder of modern political philosophy is Machiavelli . . . [who was the first to
effect] an amazing contraction of the horizon. . . . the narrowing of the horizon . . . was
caused, or at least facilitated, by anti-theological ire." "What Is Political Philosophy?"
40, 43–44. Recent studies by modern political philosophers that point to this antitheological foundation are Vicki Sullivan, *Machiavelli's Three Romes: Religion, Human Liberty,
and Politics Reformed* (DeKalb, IL: Northern Illinois University Press, 1996); Paul D.
Cooke, *Hobbes and Christianity: Reassessing the Bible in Leviathan* (Lanham, MD: Rowman and Littlefield, 1996); and Steven B. Smith, *Spinoza, Liberalism, and the Question of
Jewish Identity* (New Haven: Yale University Press, 1997). One relevance of this line for
the present study is summarized by Allan Bloom: "When bishops, a generation after
Hobbes's death, almost naturally spoke the language of the state of nature, contract
and rights, it was clear that he had defeated the ecclesiastical authorities, who were no
longer able to understand themselves as they once had." *The Closing of the American
Mind* (New York: Simon and Schuster, 1987), 141–42. Bloom appears unaware that the
language of natural rights and of contract were part of pre-Hobbesian Christian political thought. However, Bloom may be correct about the state of nature. Certainly Bellarmine rejects the idea.
15. The incomplete *De Laicis: or, The Treatise on Civil Government*, trans. Kathleen E.
Murphy (New York: Fordham University Press, 1928), introduction by M. F. X. Millar,
SJ, is the only published English translation of Robert Bellarmine's *De Laicis*. This edition will be cited parenthetically in the text and notes as *DL*. What appears to be Murphy's translation, but completed by the addition of chaps. 16 and 19–22, trans. James
Goodwin, SJ, is available online at http://www.catholicism.org/pages/Laity.htm. *De
Laicis* is apparently Bellarmine's only work translated into English. Its full title is *De
Laicis sive Saecularibus*, which means "Concerning the Laity or Those in the World."
Saecularibus needs a bit of explaining. In classical Latin, it means "of, or belonging to,
a saeculum," and *saeculum* means "an age, a people, a generation," with the connota-
tion that it endures over some period of time. In Church Latin, it means "in the world"
as distinguished from "in the Church." *De Laicis* is the last part of Bellarmine's broader
work, *De Controversiis*. Parts 1 and 2 deal with "two branches of the Church," namely,
"the clergy and monks," respectively, and *De Laicis* deals with "the third" branch (9).

theology in the sense that it is addressed to those who believe in biblical revelation, both Old and New Testaments, and in "the Church" that developed from them. Thus what for Bellarmine counts as a basis for political *knowledge*—scripture and the writings of "the Fathers" (*DL*, 11–12)—does not count as knowledge for those who follow self-consciously modern thought. For that modernity (and perhaps modernity as such) rejects as knowledge both revelation and the theology developed out of it, and limits what it accepts as knowledge to what can be known to unassisted human reason. In this respect, at least, Machiavelli's "effectual truth" and the epistemology of Descartes's *Meditations* and Locke's *Essay concerning Human Understanding* take the place of revelation and theology.[16]

Modernity's transformation in what constitutes both knowledge and the grounds for knowledge would seem to make suspect the meaning of any premodern language and ideas that continue to be used in modernity. In particular, it should make believers cautious about the view represented by Millar that there is an unbroken, "sound tradition" of political ideas "which connects Plato and Aristotle, St. Augustine and St. Thomas, with our own [American] Constitution."[17]

The same caution would apply to the older histories of "political thought" and "political theory" cited by Francis Oakley in "Legitimation by Consent." These tend to present the development of these ideas as simply ongoing recombinations of ingredients, variations without fundamental transformations of meaning. The emphasis of these histories, in contrast to MacPherson's and Strauss's, is on continuities and the medieval "roots" of ideas like "consent of the governed."[18] That is, these

---

In this context, it seems most accurate to understand *saecularibus* as meaning that the laity is both "in the church" and "in the world," in contrast to the clergy and monks, who are "in the church" but not "in the world."

16. "From the earliest beginnings of liberal thought . . . there was a conscious, if covert, effort to weaken religious beliefs, partly by assigning—as a result of a great epistemological effort—religion to the realm of opinion as opposed to knowledge." Bloom, *Closing of the American Mind*, 28.

17. Millar, introduction to *Treatise on Civil Government*, 8. For present purposes, the relevant ideas, or at least language, contained in this tradition are that government by consent of the people (understood in a certain way) "is a necessary condition to the legitimacy of all secular power" and "the correct idea of the equality of men" (6).

18. This view is represented in the nineteenth century by Archbishop John Ireland. See "Patriotism," a speech given before the New York Commandery of the Loyal Legion of Civil War Veterans, April 4, 1894, in *The Church and Modern Society: Lectures and Addresses*, by John Ireland, 2 vols. (St. Paul, MN: Pioneer Press, 1905), 1:165. A recent interpretation and critique of Ireland's thought in this matter is my "Archbishop John Ireland and Orestes Brownson on Whether There Are Catholic Antecedents of the Declaration of Independence," *The Catholic Social Science Review* 12 (2006).

histories reveal little sense of "the roots" having been pulled out of the earth and replanted in soil that has been leached of all but residual theological nourishment, or of new seeds being sown and wholly new flora being grown on the new continent discovered by "that greater Columbus"[19] and those who came after him. But this is, I take it, what the self-consciously modern philosophers thought they were doing. Even Riley, who says that "the social contract tradition" is characterized by "an importance given to will which never appeared before in the history of political philosophy" and that Christianity "made individual choice and responsibility so important" and was "the main force in effecting the change from classical to modern political philosophy," does not seem to consider how that change affected the premodern Christian social contract teaching of the political theologians. Millar represents the twentieth-century Catholic variant of this view that tends to see modernity in general, and the "new nation" brought forth in 1776 in particular, in a way that emphasizes the continuity, rather than the radical transformation, of ideas.

There exists a nineteenth-century Catholic countertradition (if one informed and competent thinker constitutes a tradition) to Millar's view. Orestes Brownson argues that Hobbes, Locke, and Rousseau had given new content to the old Christian idea of "social contract." He regards this new content as having "abused the phrase borrowed from the theologians and made it cover a political doctrine which they would have been the last to accept." He says Hobbes originated this modern tradition and "imagined a state of nature antecedently to civil society in which men lived without government, law or manners, out of which they finally come by entering into a voluntary agreement [either] with some one of their number to be king and to govern them, or with one another to submit to the rule of the majority."[20] Brownson contends that Locke and Rousseau followed Hobbes, though Locke and Rousseau had more regard to the liberty of the people than to the power of government.

Brownson argues that the Declaration of Independence follows the modern view both that "civil society, the state, the government *originates* in this compact" and that government "derives its just powers from the consent of the governed." Contrary to the premodern Ciceronian/Catholic theological

---

19. Strauss so describes Machiavelli in *Natural Right and History,* 177. Strauss regards Machiavelli, along with Hobbes, as the founder of political modernity's new moral orientation, as Descartes' *Meditations* and Locke's *Essay concerning Human Understanding* were of modern philosophy's new view of what constitutes knowledge.

20. Orestes A. Brownson, *The American Republic* (New York: P. O'Shea, 1865; reprint, Wilmington, DE: ISI Press, 2002), 45. Citations are from the ISI Press edition.

tradition, this modern view regards neither society nor government as natural, but both rather as wholly artificial. They are both created by the consent of individuals, and so individuals may "uncreate them whenever they judge it advisable." Individuals are morally obliged neither to remain in it nor to obey the law made by consent of the majority. Society has no rights that individuals are morally obligated to respect "except such as it derives from individuals who all have equal rights."[21]

By asserting that the powers of the government are derived from the people rather than ordained by God, this modern social contract view "deprives the state of her sacredness . . . and hold on conscience." It consecrates not civil authority but "the right of insurrection [revolution]." This is why "the [modern democratic] age sympathizes, not with authority in its efforts to sustain itself and protect society, but with those who conspire against it—the insurgents, rebels, revolutionists seeking its destruction. The established government that seeks to enforce respect for its legitimate authority and compel obedience to the law, is held to be despotic, tyrannical, oppressive." As a result, the governments "now in the civilized world" are "the logical or necessary result of the attempt to erect the state on atheistical principles . . . for political atheism . . . can sustain itself only by force since it recognizes no right but might." No modern government "can sustain itself for a moment without an armed force sufficient to overawe or crush the party or parties in permanent conspiracies against it."[22]

That Locke Points Us to Bellarmine

Modern students of the history of political philosophy read Locke's *Two Treatises of Government*, the first of which is a critique of Robert Filmer's *Patriarcha*. But *Patriarcha* repeatedly attacks Bellarmine[23] and Francisco Suarez[24] by name, in addition to Calvin "and all those who place supreme power in the whole people."[25] Filmer objects to both these "Papist" and

---

21. Ibid., 33.

22. Ibid., 80–81.

23. Robert Filmer, *Patriarcha*, ed. Johann P. Somerville, in *Patriarcha and Other Writings* (Cambridge: Cambridge University Press, 2000), chap. 1, pp. 1, 2 (twice), 3 (three times); chap. 2, pp. 1 (twice), 4 (twice), 5, 9, 10; and chap. 3, p. 9. There is one additional reference simply to "The Cardinal" (chap. 2, p. 9). (There are sixteen mentions of Bellarmine in all.)

24. Ibid., chap. 2, pp. 2 (three times, including once "Suarez the Jesuit"), 3, 4 (five times), 5 (twice). (There are ten mentions of Suarez in all.)

25. Ibid., chap. 2, much of pp. 1–10.

"reformed" teachings because they profess that men are by nature free from subjection and are hence "at liberty to choose what form of government [they] please" and that "the people or multitude have power to punish" and even "depose their prince" if "he transgress the law of the kingdom."[26] Filmer, then, reminds us that natural freedom from subjection to another, natural liberty to choose the form of government, and some kind of right to overthrow the established government are taught by these pre-Hobbesian thinkers.

Though Filmer also attacks Calvin,[27] it seems the "Jesuits" or "Papists" are by far his bigger target. He cites Bellarmine and Suarez by name twenty-six times, Calvin only twice. He cites Aristotle by name twenty-three times,[28] about the same number of times approvingly (five) as critically (four), but eleven times by way of clarification. The effect of the clarifications is almost always to deny Aristotle's authority to the Jesuit advocates of "democratical" government. Thus, Filmer focuses his criticism on the *conjunction* of Aristotle with these Catholic democrats.

One can say then that Locke attacks Filmer for attacking natural freedom, government by consent of the governed, and social contract, which certainly is the language, and may be the ideas, that Locke would afterward make famous for modernity. Since Locke points us back to Bellarmine, attention to the latter's pre-Hobbesian[29] rights and consent teachings is not fabricating an historical connection that did not already exist.

Notwithstanding that Locke thus refers us to Bellarmine, at least two problems discourage a modern student of political philosophy from taking Bellarmine seriously. First, *De Laicis*, the political text quoted by Filmer, is structured by the Reformation/Counter-Reformation conflict in which modern scholars are no longer interested since that conflict was settled by what J. N. Figgis calls "a revolution" that "substituted the civil for the ecclesiastical authority" and thereby created "a gulf . . . between medieval and modern thought."[30]

---

26. Ibid., chap. 1, p. 1.

27. Ibid., chap. 1, p. 1; chap. 2, p. 9.

28. Ibid., chap. 1, p. 1; chap. 2, pp. 1 (thirteen times), 3 (four times), 4 (where he says he will "leave off Aristotle and return to Suarez" and after which Aristotle is only cited approvingly and in opposition to Suarez), 10, 17; chap. 3, pp. 8, 9.

29. Bellarmine was born in 1542 and died in 1621. *De Controversiis,* which includes *The Treatise on Civil Government,* appeared in four volumes between 1586 and 1594. See John Clement Rager, *The Political Philosophy of St. Robert Bellarmine* (Spokane, WA: Apostolate of Our Lady of Siluva, 1995), 13. Hobbes's political teaching is in *De Cive* (1642), *Elements of Law* (completed in 1640 and published in two parts in 1649 and 1650), and *Leviathan* (1651).

30. Figgis, *Political Thought,* 3, 4, 12. This "gulf" does not seem to lead Figgis to see it

Second, much of Bellarmine's argument in *De Laicis* appeals to theological evidence as well. He supports his arguments with citations to scripture, to the fathers such as Irenaeus, Abelard, and Tertullian, and to Reformation theologians Calvin and Luther. He cites as evidence the miracle of Constantine and his army's seeing the cross in the sky and Christ's subsequently appearing to Constantine and explaining what the sign meant. Modern students of political philosophy, insofar as they are decisively influenced by modernity's rejection of Revelation as knowledge, cannot take this seriously as evidence.

On the other hand, as we will see, Bellarmine also utilizes strictly philosophical and rational arguments and evidence. For example, he argues that "all the philosophers" agree with scripture and the Church fathers that it is an error that political rule is as such incompatible with how human beings should live.[31]

In making arguments and using evidence that appeal to reason alone, Bellarmine seems to follow both St. Thomas Aquinas's example and his explicit teaching that the truth arrived at by unaided reason and the truth arrived at from Revelation should not be contradictory. If they seem to contradict each other, then we have made a mistake, in understanding either what reason or what Revelation teaches. I will look carefully at whether Bellarmine follows Aquinas in this respect in chapters 5 and 6 of *De Laicis* to see whether we can take the political teaching of the work seriously as political philosophy rather than as theology. I turn now to those chapters in Burke to which Millar points us, and to their congruence with political philosophy on this side of the medieval/modern divide.

Burke and Chapter 5 of *De Laicis*

Bellarmine does not use "natural rights" language in either chapter 5 or chapter 6 of *De Laicis*. Nevertheless, I will argue that Burke follows Bellarmine's arguments from these chapters to attempt to transform modern natural rights language.

Chapter 5 consists of eight paragraphs. The first two initially look like a fundamentally Aristotelian defense (though Aristotle is not explicitly mentioned) of the necessity of political rule. "The nature of man is such that he is a social animal" because he cannot be self-sufficient alone. He "is born without clothing, without a home, without food, lacking all necessities,"

---

as having effected any fundamental alteration in medieval, as distinguished from modern, ideas of natural freedom and social contract.

31. Ibid., 12.

with only "his hands, and reason by which he can prepare all instruments" (*DL,* 20). And "even were each one sufficient to himself for the necessities of life, yet he would never, unaided, be able to protect himself from the attacks of wild beasts and robbers," which necessitates "men to assemble and to ward off attacks with their combined strength." In addition, the society thus necessitated by man's nature makes it possible "to exercise justice," which is "the virtue determining equity among many" (*DL,* 21).

The end of paragraph 2 takes a non-Aristotelian turn. The "instruments" and "the arts and sciences" that man is born capable of developing "were developed after a long time and by many men." This emphasis is not found in Aristotle, or at least Aristotle makes little of it,[32] but Burke's political teaching makes much of it.

Bellarmine cites Aristotle by name for the first time in paragraph 3 as declaring "that man is by nature a civil animal, more so than the bees . . . and any beast" because why else "has the gift of speech and of hearing, that is, of clearly perceiving words, been bestowed upon him?"

In paragraph 4, in addition to social life, man's nature further necessitates political rule. The first reason is that "it is impossible for a multitude to hold together for any length of time unless there be one who governs it, and who is responsible for the common welfare" (*DL,* 22). The second reason is a purely rational analogy to the soul understood in a Platonic / Aristotelian manner: "if there were not in each of us a soul to govern and unite the parts and powers and conflicting elements of which we are made, immediately all would disintegrate." To show that these strictly rational arguments for the necessity of political rule agree with Revelation, Bellarmine cites Proverbs 2: "Where there is no government, the people shall fall" (*DL,* 22–23).

Since we cannot fulfill our nature's needs on our own because it takes longer than the life span of any single man and individuals cannot develop them on their own, we need "a teacher" (*DL,* 20) who lives longer than any single man. Not merely society, but *civil* society appears to be that teacher.

Burke builds on this idea of civil society as a necessary teacher to create an alternative to Hobbes, Locke, and Rousseau's natural rights. The "real rights of men," he points out in *Reflections on the Revolution in France,* are

---

32. At least this turn is not found in the *Nichomachean Ethics* or the *Politics.* Thomas Lindsay of Seton Hall University, with whom I consulted about this matter, noted that neither of us can say with certainty that it might not be in the *Eudemian Ethics,* the *Magna Moralia,* or the *Economicus,* since we have not studied them. In addition, the *Economicus* is now thought spurious, and we do not know whether Bellarmine might have had it and thought it was Aristotle's.

those of "the civil social man."[33] He grants that there are "natural rights, which may and do exist in total independence of" government. However, these are the rights of "uncovenanted man"[34] and as such "are absolutely repugnant" to "civil society." This is because "in order to secure the advantages of civil society" one must "divest himself of the first fundamental right of uncovenanted man, that is to judge for himself, and to assert his own cause" and largely "abandon the right of self-defense, the first law of nature." Since "men cannot enjoy the rights of an uncivil and a civil state together," to "secure some liberty" in civil society, natural men must "surrender in trust . . . the whole of it" (*RRF*, 52). As a consequence, what natural liberty can be kept in civil society is a practical matter of "convention" or agreement rather than a matter of abstractly logical inferences, or deductions, from pre-political natural rights. "The moment you abate any thing from the full [that is, pre-political natural] rights of men, each to govern himself, and suffer any artificial positive limitation upon those rights, from that moment the whole organization of government becomes a consideration of convenience" (*RRF*, 53).[35]

As Burke spells out what those rights are, the relevance emerges of Bellarmine's emphasis on the length of time required to develop the instruments of self-sufficiency, and the need for teaching them to each new generation. For "the real rights of men . . . are their advantages" developed by earlier generations and handed down (and in that sense "taught") to later generations: that men have a right to live by civil law, a right to "justice as between their fellows," "a right to the fruits of their industry," "a right to the acquisitions of their parents," a right "to the nourishment and improvement of their offspring," a right "to instruction in life," and "a right to a fair portion of all which society, with all its combinations of skill and force, can do in his favour" (*RRF*, 55, 51).

These rights are "the real rights of men," not in the sense that they were original and pre-political, but in the sense that they have been gleaned out of those pre-political rights by the "long experience" (*RRF*, 51) of civil society. Each generation has learned what natural liberty it is wise to give up to secure what can be kept, under ever-changing circumstances, and each generation has handed down that learning to later generations. In particular,

33. Edmund Burke, *Reflections on the Revolution in France*, ed. J. G. A. Pocock (Indianapolis: Hackett, 1987), 51–52. Hereafter this work will be cited parenthetically in the text and notes as *RRF*.

34. The phrase *state of nature* does not occur in *Reflections on the Revolution in France*.

35. Vaughan's reaction to these passages on rights is "shock. . . . they have the effect of pulling the reader up short, of making him ask how in the world they ever got there." *Studies*, 2.54.

"the science of government . . . requires . . . more experience than any person can gain in his whole life" (*RRF*, 53). In light of this, and in contrast to the direct appeal to pre-political natural rights of Hobbes, Locke, Rousseau, or Paine, "we [Englishmen] claim and assert our liberties as an entailed inheritance derived to us from our forefathers, and to be transmitted to our posterity . . . without any reference whatever to any other more general or prior right" (*RRF*, 29). This way of society's discovering from experience and handing down to later generations what civil liberty can be, Burke calls "prescription."[36]

As Bellarmine does not use natural rights language, neither does he speak of "prescription." However, Burke's prescription seems indistinguishable from what Bellarmine calls "the law of nations." That law permits "the consent of the people to decide whether kings, or consuls, or other magistrates are to be established in authority over them"; and also whether "there be legitimate cause, to change a kingdom into an aristocracy, or an aristocracy into a democracy, and vice versa." Consent of the people, so understood, "derive[s] from the law of nations, not from the natural law," yet the law of nations is "a sort of conclusion drawn from the natural law by human reason." It is derived, somehow, but apparently not in any direct, necessary, merely deductive, or inevitable way. "[H]uman wisdom and choice" (*DL*, 27) are justly involved in its derivation, along with the legitimate differences of opinion that accompany such a manner of thinking. Accordingly, both the regime question and revolution may lawfully be decided differently by different peoples under different circumstances.

The resemblance to Burke's prescription is striking. However, Burke asserts that prescription not only is "a part of the law of nature" but is "a great fundamental part" of it (*RRF*, 133). Hence, one must ask if this does not contradict Bellarmine's insistence that the law of nations is distinct from natural law. Perhaps technically it does, but it is not clear how substantive the contradiction might be. Bellarmine and Burke agree that the right of a particular people to consent to who should rule them is derived in some way from what they both call "the law of nature." And they agree that the manner in which the answer is derived gives some scope to what Bellarmine calls "human wisdom and choice." So, it may be that the difference between Bellarmine's "law of nations" and Burke's "prescription" might only be the difference between the greater precision of the political philosopher, in view of his audience, versus the political rhetoric of the philosopher/statesman, in view of his.[37]

36. In contrast, for the French revolutionaries "there is no prescription against nature" (*RRF*, 196).

37. For those who take notice of this sort of thing, and even regard it as evidence, the

Burke's prescription is a claim to what one has, and is entitled to have, based on longtime possession. However, it is not merely tradition. Its being part of the law of nature provides a defense against the criticism that Burke's appeal to prescription is a version of historical or cultural relativism and therefore fails for the same reasons that these relativisms fail. This criticism owes its plausibility to the sharp contrast Burke repeatedly draws between the "rights of men" (taught by the French revolutionaries) and his assertion that Englishmen claim and assert their liberties on the basis of prescription "without any reference whatever to any more general or prior right." It would be relativism either to deny that some transsocietal standards like "rights of men" exist at all or to assert that they exist but have no relation to the "rights of Englishmen." To avoid the relativism problem, Burke distinguishes the *basis for claiming* liberty in civil society from its ultimate and transcendent, but remote and "primitive,"[38] *source*. The basis for claiming rights is "prescription." But the "rights of men" that Burke defends are "the rights of men in civil society." Those rights are "not made in virtue of natural rights." All men, wherever and whenever they live, have transpolitical rights, but these rights are not the proper basis for claiming rights in civil society. Because Burke understands man as by nature political, the rights that may be properly claimed in civil society are political. While rights' origin may be pre-political and therefore transpolitical, their substance in civil society is given shape by prescription.

This distinction between the *basis for claiming* rights in civil society and their remote and primitive *source* also squares his claim that prescription is part of natural law with the seeming denial of "any more general or prior right." Burke grants, in passing, that "natural rights . . . may and do exist in total independence" of government (*RRF,* 52). But since these rights are "absolutely repugnant" to civil society's existence, they can neither continue unabated in it (*RRF,* 52) nor be appealed to directly as the basis of rights in civil society.[39] What *can* be appealed to directly in civil society is how our ancestors learned to modify and restrict natural rights in order to "secure some liberty" (*RRF,* 52). What those modifications and restrictions have to be cannot be taught by "abstract rule," but only by

---

only time the phrase *law of nations* occurs in *Reflections* is in the same paragraph that has the greatest density of the use of the word *prescription* (four times in this paragraph out of a total of eleven in the whole work). This paragraph is also the only one where *natural law* occurs and one of only two paragraphs in which *law of nature* is used (*RRF,* 133–34).

38. Edmund Burke, "Thoughts on French Affairs," in *Works of the Right Honourable Edmund Burke* (London: John C. Nimmo, 1887), 4:342.

39. Burke does not object if they are appealed to "in the schools," where the "subtilty" of "political metaphysics" is less politically dangerous (*RRF,* 51).

"long experience" (*RRF*, 53, 51). The intergenerational contract is constituted by the older generation's teaching what has been learned from that
experience and the younger generation's learning it. "Prescription" so
understood is the basis both for learning and for claiming what liberty is,
but it is not liberty's ultimate source.

Still, Burke grants implicitly that the pre-political and "full rights of
men" must remain the remote source and continue to somehow provide a
standard of right for every civil society. "What is the use of discussing a
man's abstract right to food or medicine? The question is upon the method
of procuring and administering them" (*RRF*, 53).

Burke explicates this thought with a remarkable metaphor. These "full"
and "primitive" rights, "like rays of light which pierce into a dense
medium, are by the laws of nature refracted from their straight line" (*RRF*,
54). This metaphor seems meant to show that something can be the indispensable source of life, like the sun, but still must remain remote from
human life in order not to destroy it. To that end, the "dense medium" of
the earth's atmosphere is necessary to moderate the sun's full intensity.
Similarly, the dense medium of civil society's "prescriptions" is necessary
to moderate the "abstract perfection" of the "full rights of men" so that the
attenuated rights become compatible with civil life.[40]

Burke might be thought to go beyond Bellarmine in making prescription
the only basis for publicly claiming and asserting civil liberties. Certainly
Bellarmine does not make such an argument explicitly, nor is it an evident
inference from anything he explicitly says. Yet this may be the difference
only between the philosopher/theologian, who is laying out the theory
and just needs to be concerned to state cogently the abstract teaching or
"principles," and the philosophical statesman, who is putting the theory
in practice and also has to be concerned about how to make the principles
improve rather than harm the civil order.

Having established in chapter 5 both man's natural sociality and polit-
icality by rational arguments that do not require (though they evidently
agree with) Revelation, Bellarmine appears to digress in the last three
paragraphs. He turns to attack a view "that there was formerly a time
when men wandered about in the manner of beasts" and that eventually
"through the eloquence of some wise orator, they were induced to assemble and to live together" (*DL*, 22).[41] This view, which neither he nor Burke

40. The theological equivalent might be that the basis and source of these primitive
rights is divine but that the full amplitude of the divine is incompatible with human
life. Moses, even as deliverance and the law were at hand, was told, "Thou canst not
see my face: for there shall no man see me, and live." Exodus 33:20.

41. The source here is Cicero's *De inventione*, trans. H. M. Hubbell, 1.1–2.3 (Cam-

calls a "state of nature," Bellarmine attributes to "Cicero and other pagans"[42] who lack the "Revelation of God" that "the first men immediately built cities."[43] He gives no merely rational evidence that men immediately built cities, just as he gives no merely rational arguments that men were created. As political philosophy, therefore, this argument has (for moderns) no weight.

This attack upon "Cicero and other pagans" who lack Revelation is curious. For it is not necessary in defending his merely rational argument that human nature requires society and political rule. He has already made that Aristotelian argument, and he could have proceeded to support it by Aristotle's alternative anthropological account from book 1 of the *Politics*. Men are born with needs, but they are born into households, which combine into villages, which combine into cities seeking fulfillment of those needs. So why does Bellarmine go out of his way to quarrel with Cicero about the merely historical question of whether "the first men" lived in society? It does not particularly matter to Bellarmine's argument *how* the first men lived. What matters is *what* human nature requires.

One explanation for this seeming digression might be that, while attacking Cicero's argument is not important to establish Bellarmine's political teaching, attacking it *is* important to defend the scriptural account of man's origins. The Ciceronian "state of affairs" could not "have existed at any time. For Adam was a very wise man, and without doubt did not allow men to wander about like beasts, and Cain, his son, even built a material city; before Cain and Adam, man did not exist" (*DL*, 23).

A second explanation might be that Cicero's account still persists. "[W]hoever undertakes the praise of eloquence usually makes this statement even now" (*DL*, 22). The teaching of pagan rhetoricians remains a

---

bridge: Harvard University Press, 1960), 5–9; the context is Cicero's account of the origin of "eloquence": "For there was a time when men wandered at large in the fields like animals and lived on wild fare; they did nothing by the guidance of reason, but relied chiefly on physical strength; there was as yet no ordered system of religious worship nor of social duties; no one had seen legitimate marriage nor had anyone looked upon children whom he knew to be his own; nor had they learned the advantages of an equitable code of law. And so through their ignorance and error blind and unreasoning passion satisfied itself by misuse of bodily strength, which is a very dangerous servant." At that point a "great and wise" man "assembled and gathered" men "scattered in the fields and hidden in sylvan retreats" to transform them, by "reason and eloquence" and "in accordance with a plan," from "wild savages" into "kind and gentle folk."

42. Obviously Bellarmine consulted a different text of Cicero than Brownson did.

43. "[T]he first man to found a city and start a political kingdom before the Flood was Cain, as Augustine shows from Gen[esis] IV, the first to do this after the Flood was Nimrod" (*DL*, 11). Bellarmine cites Augustine, *The City of God,* bk. 4 and chap. 1.

challenge, not only to Revelation's teaching about human origins, but to the primacy of Revelation-based theology over the teachings of those who understand human things from the standpoint of rhetoric.[44]

A third consideration might be that, since Bellarmine's political teaching relies approvingly on pagan political philosophers like Aristotle, it might be useful to distance himself, where it does not matter substantively, from "other pagans" who are philosophers. Even theologians might make such unobtrusive use of the art of rhetoric.

I conclude that the apparent digression[45] to attack Cicero's teaching about "the first men" and the importance of eloquence is not necessary to Bellarmine's political teaching, but rather to other matters of importance to a Christian theologian. It does not matter to his political argument whether "the first men immediately built cities." What matters is that we must "make and prepare many things, which we cannot do without the help of others" (*DL,* 22). If one asserts that the first men lived as Cicero says they did, all that needs saying in reply is that (1) that was contrary to their nature's needs and (2) besides Aristotle shows they did not live that way anyway.

Burke and Chapter 6 of *De Laicis*

Chapter 6 begins by affirming the goodness and lawfulness of political power according to both Revelation and "natural law." The theological argument is that "political power is of God."[46] The merely rational arguments are that it is "a primary instinct of nature" that the human race should not perish,[47] that political rule is necessary to that end, and hence that such rule is a "necessity from the nature of man." From these merely rational premises, which had been defended in chapter 5, he infers that political power *as such* "does not depend upon the consent of men" (*DL,*

44. One is reminded of the parallel Socratic defense of the superiority of philosophy over rhetoric in Plato's *Gorgias.* The rhetoricians seem to have been a problem from more than one point of view.

45. The "digression" consists of three of the chapter's eight paragraphs.

46. Bellarmine cites Augustine, *The City of God,* bks. 4 and 5; and Proverbs, chaps. 7, 1, and 6, and Daniel, chaps. 2 and 4.

47. This "primary instinct" for the preservation of the species as such is of course at odds with the assertion of the Hobbesian and Lockean "individualist's" social contract teaching that the strongest desire of our nature is for individual self-preservation. "Consent of the people" will presumably have quite different political meanings depending on whether it is undergirded by this assumption or by Bellarmine's opposite assumption.

24). That men must be ruled politically is a "necessity" of both divine and natural law and hence is not, as a matter of right, subject to consent. However, what the regime should be and who should rule are, as a matter of right, up to the wisdom and consent of the people.

Recall that Vaughan objected that Burke's contract was neither "true consent" nor "contract" because Burke regarded it as a "necessity" of man's nature. "Necessity," Burke contends, is part "of that moral and physical disposition of things, to which man must be obedient by consent or force." We have the capacity to disobey that "disposition," but doing so means violating that "inviolable oath which holds all physical and all moral natures each in their appointed place." This "law" preserves a "world of reason, and order, and peace, and virtue and fruitful penitence" against the alternative world of "madness, discord, vice, confusion and unavailing sorrow" (*RRF,* 85).

This most extensive and important statement of Burke's idea of contract is supported partly by philosophical and partly by theological arguments. The philosophical part echoes Bellarmine's merely rational argument. Since the ends of civil society "cannot be obtained in many generations," the contract is "a partnership not only between those who are living, but between those who are living, those who are dead and those who are to be born." The theological part is: "Each contract of each particular state is but a clause in the great primeval contract of eternal society, linking the lower with the higher natures, connecting the visible and invisible world, according to a fixed compact sanctioned by the inviolable oath which holds all physical and all moral natures, each in their appointed place."[48] This imagery alludes to the medieval "great chain of being," which was at least partly based on Revelation. As to what "inviolable oath" refers to, I would be grateful to be instructed.

Vaughan's objection that Burke's idea of contract is "no true consent" would seem to imply that, from the "individualist's" view of contract, either there are no such "necessities" or there are no such adverse consequences as Burke sees from failing to consent to them. Insofar as Hobbes, Locke, Rousseau, or Paine would admit "necessities" of human nature, these would refer either to other living human beings or to material nature. Other men are a threat to my self-preservation, and material nature threatens us with famine and poverty. Creating, entering, remaining in, or leaving civil

---

48. To repeat, Bellarmine does not speak in either chap. 5 or chap. 6 of this interconnection of generations as a "contract." Neither does he use the word *contract* to describe the relation of the people and the regime or rulers to which they consent.

society is a choice, not a necessity. Thus, nothing in their thought sees any-thing resembling a duty of the present generation to the past.

This is rather explicitly the view of America's most famous individual-ists, Thomas Jefferson and Thomas Paine. As Jefferson put it, "The earth belongs to the living, not to the dead. . . . We may consider each generation as a distinct nation, with a right, by the will of its majority, to bind them-selves, but none to bind the succeeding generation, more than the inhabi-tants of another country." And in Paine's words, "Every age and generation must be as free to act for itself, in all cases as the ages and gen-erations which preceded it. . . . I am contending for the rights of the living, and against their being willed away, and controlled and contracted for, by the manuscript assumed authority of the dead."[49] Evidently each genera-tion is *de novo* and free to do as it pleases with the experience, discoveries, and political and social order handed down to it.

Unless one assumes, as Vaughan seems to do, that society itself is formed by consent; that is, unless one assumes the reality of the state of nature, Burke's idea of contract is a plausible alternative to the individu-alists. Bellarmine helps us see that it is more than a mere metaphor. This disagreement about whether the society, as well as the regime, results from consent, has surprisingly far-reaching consequences. For Burke it means that society is an intergenerational contract with the real rights of men being the advantages inherited from the work of past generations. In return for these free gifts of the past to the present, a gratitude is due that takes the form of a moral duty that restrains what any given generation is morally permitted to consent to. Each generation is the custodian, not the owner, of society and its inherited benefits. In contrast, for Vaughan, Jef-ferson, and Paine, the contract is not intergenerational. What the present generation gets from the past is primarily the moral and legal right to reject whatever it has inherited. It has no duties, either of gratitude for unearned and undeserved benefits received or of repayment by passing them on to the future.

While the first two paragraphs of chapter 6 teach that political rule does not depend upon the consent of men, beginning with paragraph 3 neces-sity abates and a consent appears that someone not in thrall to Vaughan's individualists might recognize as at least plausible. It now turns out that only political power in general does not depend upon consent. However, both the form of rule and who rules, do. Divine law gives political rule to

---

49. Thomas Jefferson to John Wayles Eppes, June 24, 1813, in *Thomas Jefferson: Writ-ings* (New York: Viking, 1984), 1280–81; Thomas Paine, *The Rights of Man*, in *Two Clas-sics of the French Revolution* (New York: Doubleday, 1989), 277–78.

no particular man. So "in the absence of positive law, there is no good reason why, in a multitude of equals, one rather than another should dominate. Therefore, power belongs to the collected body," which is free to delegate it either to one or to several rulers. And not only does it depend on consent whether the form of rule is monarchy, aristocracy, or democracy, but this consent has teeth: Bellarmine maintains that "if there be legitimate cause, the people can change a kingdom into an aristocracy, or an aristocracy into a democracy, and vice versa" (*DL*, 24). This justice of changing regimes, and *a fortiori* changing individual rulers, justifies revolution in the strict Aristotelian sense of *metabole*.

Vaughan is correct that for Locke, but not for Burke, consent is all in all. One reason is that Lockean consent has to create, not merely civil society and government, but society itself. Before Locke's social contract there was only the state of nature. In contrast, the contract that Burke affirms is not an original contract that creates society.[50] With Bellarmine,[51] Burke affirms that consent, somehow understood, authorizes both the regime and the ruler. However, it is consent without an original contract, consent grounded in the naturalness of both society and civil society. It is consent that applies only to the *development* of civil society and government and not to the *origins* of society as such.

Conclusion

Judging from Bellarmine alone, it is apparent that there exists a pre-Hobbesian political teaching that lawful government is, by consent of the governed, understood as including a title by the law of nations (itself an inference from natural law) to change regimes and rulers for cause. And that teaching is, in a manner, carried into modernity by Burke. But the manner in which he does so is important. Bellarmine restrains himself from using words that might encourage individual or collective willfulness regarding regime change, such as *rights* and *indefeasible rights* or *inalienable rights* and *right of revolution* might do. As a premodern Christian moralist, he seems inclined to the classical and biblical view that human willfulness, especially political willfulness, needs taming more than fostering and that it is the duty of political teachers to emphasize the former

---

50. Burke once speaks of "the original contract between king and people" (*RRF*, 54). However, this is obviously not what Vaughan means by the "original contract" that forms society.

51. And with a broader pre-Hobbesian tradition that is not included in this study.

rather than the latter. Bellarmine attempts to do this by teaching what is right or just for the people to do, rather than what are the rights that they can claim. Burke practices a similar restraint by not speaking in *Reflections on the Revolution in France* of a "right of revolution," while admitting that revolution is sometimes necessary. He defends the Revolution of 1688 as "an act of necessity in the strictest moral sense in which necessity can be taken" (*RRF,* 16). But while necessity justifies and makes it "right," Burke does not admit a right to choose revolution.[52] To make a revolution is "a necessity that is not chosen but chooses" (*RRF,* 85). "But with or without right [justification] a revolution will always be the last resort of the thinking and the good" (*RRF,* 27).

I believe it has been substantiated that Millar was onto something in asserting that Bellarmine's thought casts helpful light on Burke's understanding of consent of the governed and contract. In particular, reading Burke in light of Bellarmine shows that Burke has an intelligible social contract teaching, though it is in sharp contrast to Hobbes or Locke, to say nothing of Rousseau. Burke does not simply restate Bellarmine. He appears to adapt Bellarmine's thought in order to moderate the consequences of modern individualist thought. To the extent that this interpretation is correct, we cannot simply quote Bellarmine justifying government by consent or justifying the people's changing of regimes as if it means the same thing, for instance, as Locke or the Declaration of Independence. Bellarmine's teaching may be an antecedent, but we cannot assume it is also a root (as Millar and the histories and studies cited above in notes 2 and 4 do).

Burke's adaptation of Bellarmine's consent teaching is of the same sort, that is, as his modification of what Burke would call "rights." While Bellarmine speaks of earlier generations' learning and handing down to future generations, he calls neither the advantages to the present generations "rights" nor the relation of generations a "contract." Instead he puts in Aristotelian terms the need for self-sufficiency, obtainable in society especially over a long period of time.

Burke would later translate these thoughts into a kind of rights language in an apparent attempt to provide a more moderate alternative to

52. Locke also does not speak of a "right of revolution." Indeed, the word *revolution* does not occur in *Two Treatises of Government.* But he speaks of a "right of" something or other 106 times and a "right to" something or other 125 times. This possessive, even egoistic, language is on this side of the medieval/modern divide, while Burke's use of right as justification, and even duty, is on the other side. Instead of "necessity" as a justification and standard, Locke says only "the people shall be judge." He chooses to answer the question "who decides" rather than "what is the standard." *Two Treatises of Government* (London: Dent and Sons, 1924), 228.

modern, individualist "rights of men" language. One might argue that what Burke adds to Bellarmine by doing so is only a drawing out of what is already implicit. That argument would be as follows. Each generation of a particular civil society receives benefits and advantages from previous generations. By accepting these benefits, however implicitly, the latest generation incurs moral duties to preserve, add to, and teach them to still later generations. It would be the vice of ingratitude to simply reject these duties, as individualist contract theory seems to do.

In contrast, gratitude seems to have no place in Locke's political teaching. Neither *grateful* nor *gratefulness* occurs at all in *Two Treatises*. The word *gratitude* occurs six times, always having to do with the gratitude of children to parents. All but one of these instances occur in *Second Treatise*, chapter 6. *Gratitude* never occurs in a political context. The relevance of this observation is that Locke insists on the radical difference between paternal (or parental) power, on the one hand, and political power, on the other. One seems entitled to conclude that gratitude has nothing to do with Lockean politics.

On the other hand, what Burke does here may be more than drawing out what Bellarmine left implicit. Burke's contract, at least in some formulations, has a tendency to be or become legal obligations rather than either moral obligations or mere chords of memory.[53] A legal duty to obey the will of past generations is different from a moral duty to preserve that is derived from gratitude.[54] At any rate, Paine understands Burke in the former manner, and it brings forth Paine's most passionate protests against later generations' being "forever bound" by the consent of earlier generations.

53. "The mystic chords of memory" is Lincoln's language from his *First Inaugural Address*, March 4, 1861. It expresses a sort of Burkean (certainly not Lockean) thought to the effect that, if North and South can allow themselves to be bound together by these memories (which are "the better angels of our nature"), we can remain one nation. The rhetoric appeals not to abstract and individualistic Lockean equality and natural rights, but to the emotionally binding sentiments of a remembered shared past.

54. This is a point insisted upon by Locke even regarding parents. "It is one thing to owe [parents] honour, respect, gratitude and assistance; another to require absolute obedience and submission." *Two Treatises*, 139.

Natural Law, Natural Rights, and the Declaration of Independence

George W. Carey

In 1945 the noted constitutional historian Charles Warren pointed out, "It is a singular fact that the greatest event in American history—the Declaration of Independence—has been the subject of more incorrect popular belief, more bad memory on the part of the participants, and more false history than any other occurrence in our national life." Warren was preoccupied with the early partisan efforts to claim exclusive credit for the Declaration, but key elements of his indictment clearly apply to the current popular understanding of its theoretical dimensions, particularly its "all men are created equal" clause and its assertions regarding "unalienable Rights." So much would seem apparent from the uses to which the Declaration is put in contemporary America: from the sublime, as being a statement of the nation's goals and aspirations, to the ridiculous, as mandating the "right" of same-sex marriage.[1]

---

1. Charles Warren, "Fourth of July Myths," *William and Mary Quarterly* 2 (July 1945): 237. Such views regarding the legitimacy of gay marriage have been frequently expressed by its proponents. A more subtle argument to this effect based on the Declaration of Independence is offered by the historian Joseph J. Ellis: "Abraham Lincoln once observed that America was founded on a proposition, and that Thomas Jefferson wrote it. He was referring, of course, to the section of the Declaration of Independence that begins, 'We hold these truths to be self-evident . . .' The reality, though, is that we are founded on a debate over what Jefferson's proposition means. And the current struggle over gay marriage is but the most recent chapter in that longstanding Amer-

While significant differences abound today concerning the theoretical underpinnings of the Declaration and its purpose—differences too numerous and complex to pursue here—this was not the case during the revolutionary period. Indeed, there was a substantial consensus in this period concerning its status and meaning. One of the purposes of this undertaking is to set forth and examine the assumptions and ways of thinking that produced this consensus. A second and closely related objective is to consider the ramifications of this consensus for understanding the place of the Declaration, natural law, and natural rights within the American political tradition.

The Declaration: Consensual Foundations

The Declaration of Independence was, to begin with, almost universally viewed by the colonists as a proclamation and justification of independence. As Philip Detweiler emphasizes, controversies over the meaning of its phrasing on "self-evident" truths were not to be found in the revolutionary period or the decades immediately following. Moreover, Detweiler notes, "the self-evident truths [of the Declaration] were seldom employed by those who formulated wartime propaganda." Rather, for most Americans of this period, "[a]ttention centered upon the conclusion—the announcement of independence."[2] On the basis of his researches, Detweiler concludes that Carl Becker was quite correct in maintaining that "during the revolution, as a matter of course, men were chiefly interested in the fact that the colonists had taken the decisive step, at this time, of separating from Great Britain."[3]

Jefferson's well-known views regarding the meaning of the Declaration, penned in 1825, a year before his death, point to another of its features about which there was consensus. As he put it, "with respect to our rights, and the acts of the British government contravening those rights, there

---

ican argument." Ellis concludes that while "debate over gay rights has just begun," the spirit of the Declaration accords "great advantage to the side in favor of expanding the scope of individual rights" and that "everyone who has bet against the expansive legacy has eventually lost." "A New Topic for an Old Argument," *New York Times*, February 29, 2004, A22.

2. Philip F. Detweiler, "The Changing Reputation of the Declaration of Independence: The First Fifty Years," *William and Mary Quarterly* 19, 3rd ser. (October 1962): 558.

3. Carl Lotus Becker, *The Declaration of Independence: A Study in the History of a Political Idea* (New York: A. A. Knopf, 1942), quoted in Detweiler, "Changing Reputation," 558.

was but one opinion on this side of the water. All American whigs thought alike on these subjects." And, he maintained, "an appeal to the tribunal of the world was deemed proper for our justification," after the colonists were "forced . . . to resort to arms for redress. . . . This was the object of the Declaration of Independence." He was quick to add that discovering "new principles," presenting "new arguments, never before thought of," and saying "things which had never been said before" were not among its purposes. Rather, he continued, its objective was "to place before mankind the common sense of the subject, in terms so plain and firm as to command their assent, and to justify ourselves in the independent stand we were compelled to take," but not, he emphasized again, to set forth an "originality of principle or sentiment." It was to be "an expression of the American mind," formulated "to give to that expression the proper tone and spirit called for by the occasion."[4]

Jefferson concluded his remarks by elaborating on the foundations and character of this "expression," pointing out that "its authority rests . . . on the harmonizing sentiments of the day, whether expressed in conversation, in letters, printed essays, or in the elementary books of public right, as Aristotle, Cicero, Locke, Sidney, &c."[5] As such it could be seen as a statement of the public mind, perhaps reflecting, as few public documents before or since, a deep and genuine consensus. Yet, it must be asked, what was the precise nature of this consensus? What were the common understandings upon which the Declaration rested? Answering these questions requires an exploration of the theoretical framework of the Declaration, perhaps the most important dimension for a coherent understanding of its meaning.

At one level the answers to these concerns are easy to come by because, as Jefferson's comments clearly suggest, the Declaration's justification for separation is cast in terms of a widely accepted social contract theory, outwardly similar to that employed by John Locke in his *Second Treatise.* Such a view gains support from the research of Philip Hamburger, who remarks that while it is debatable "whether Locke, Sidney" or "other European writers" had the greatest influence on American thinking, it is nevertheless the case that the colonists "extracted highly generalized notions" about natural rights, the state of nature, and the origins of government from these sources. While, Hamburger observes, educated Americans were probably "knowledgeable about the ideas espoused by particular

4. *Thomas Jefferson: Writings,* ed. Merrill D. Peterson (New York: Viking Press, 1984), 1501.
    5. Ibid.

European theorists," far more Americans "only became familiar with—or only retained—a relatively simple approach abstracted from the details of the foreign treatises."[6]

In its most rudimentary form the social contract theory postulated individuals living without government in a state of nature, enjoying equal liberty and natural rights (discrete portions of the natural, equal liberty), the exercise of which conformed with natural law (usually God given and/or derived from reason). Because not all individuals obeyed the natural law and also because there was no acknowledged common superior to settle disputes that arose between individuals, people formed governments through contract by unanimous consent. As will be apparent in the discussion below, not all contract theories were exactly alike: differences existed over the context and source of natural law, as well as over the character of rights. Nevertheless, this theory provided the rough framework within which issues such as the limits of obedience to government, the obligations of the citizens to authority, the legitimate powers of government, and *inter alia*, the need for virtue and restraint were discussed before and during the founding period.

An examination of the selections in *American Political Writings during the Founding Era, 1760–1805*[7] certainly lends support to Hamburger's thesis concerning the prevalence of this social contract mode of thinking. Of the thirty-four selections, largely essays and sermons, that preceded the Declaration, thirteen embraced the compact mode of thought to one degree or another in addressing the need for government, natural rights, the nature of liberty, the limits of government, and related concerns. Virtually every essay dealing with the origins of government and its general character, the impending break with Great Britain, or the need for virtue and civil order employed this framework. What is more, most of the essays that embraced the social contract approach also reflected and integrated Christian teachings, largely by reference to "natural law" or the "law of nature." As Simeon Howard, for instance, put this matter in a 1773 Boston sermon, "In a state of nature, or where men are under no civil government, God has given to every one liberty to pursue his own happiness in whatever way, and by whatever means he pleases, without asking the consent or consulting the

6. Philip A. Hamburger, "Natural Rights, Natural Law, and American Constitutions," *Yale Law Journal* 102 (January 1993): 914, 915.

7. *American Political Writings during the Founding Era, 1760–1805,* ed. Charles S. Hyneman and Donald S. Lutz, 2 vols. (Indianapolis: Liberty Press, 1983). These two volumes are generally considered to be the most comprehensive and representative collection of the political writings of the founding period.

inclination of any other man, *provided he keeps within the bounds of the law of nature."* And Silas Downer, writing as "A Son of Liberty" in 1768, antici- pated to some degree an argument presented in the Declaration by assert- ing that government "was instituted to secure to individuals that natural liberty"—that is, "that liberty which the GOD of nature hath given us"— which Great Britain had, without "right," "deprived them of."[8] In sum, from the thrust of the political writings prior to the Declaration and the lan- guage of the Declaration itself, whose opening passages were cast in the mold of social contract theory, one can readily appreciate what Jefferson meant when he wrote that it was but "an expression of the American mind."

Nor can there be much doubt about the "harmonizing sentiments" to which Jefferson referred. Widespread agreement prevailed concerning the most significant and more specific elements of the contract or compact the- ory.[9] Locke's depiction of conditions in the state of nature, for instance, was widely accepted, and, accordingly, virtually all commentators of this era held that in this state men were endowed with "natural liberty." According to Ronald Peters, who has closely studied the complexities of the compact theory underlying the Massachusetts Constitution of 1780, natural liberty was understood to be "a power of self-determination in respect to all things, being bounded only by the laws of nature and God." Peters notes that the "corollary" to "natural liberty," namely, "the concept of natural equality" or "an equality of liberty," was also universally sub- scribed to.[10] Hamburger, surveying a wider range of sermons and essays,

---

8. Simeon Howard, "A Sermon Preached to the Ancient and Honorable Artillery Company in Boston," in *American Political Writings,* 1:187 (emphasis added); Silas Downer, "A Discourse at the Dedication of the Tree of Liberty," in *American Political Writings,* 1:99, 100.

9. While a few of the sermons and essays set forth in some detail the contractual ori- gins of society and government and the nature and substance of natural liberty and rights, they still do not offer a comprehensive picture of the theoretical framework that prevailed during the revolutionary era. The election day sermon of Samuel West ("On the Right to Rebel against Governors") on the eve of the Revolution is perhaps the fullest. Here he sets out to understand "the nature and design of civil government" with the end of examining the limits of civil disobedience. West's treatment, however, does not delve into certain complexities and refinements that are necessary for under- standing fully the Declaration's assertion of "unalienable rights." *American Political Writings,* 1:410–54.

10. Ronald Peters, *The Massachusetts Constitution of 1780: A Social Compact* (Amherst: University of Massachusetts Press, 1978), 24. There are very substantial reasons why Peters's analysis of the Massachusetts Constitution of 1780 is highly relevant for an understanding of the Declaration. An important one is that the Massachusetts experi- ence from even before the Declaration to the adoption of the 1780 Constitution bore

sees essentially the same understanding prevailing. He finds that natural liberty was understood to be "the undifferentiated freedom individuals had in the state of nature or the absence of government." He, too, points out that an equality of liberty was assumed and that natural liberty was clearly understood to be bounded by "natural law." As remarked above, this understanding formed the basis for explaining the emergence of civil government: to wit, civil government emerged from the fact that some individuals did not obey the law of nature in the exercise of their liberty; that is, they transgressed the bounds of natural law. There being no common authority to rectify these transgressions, each individual was judge of his own cause, which, in turn, meant that there could be no equity or justice or even personal security. To remedy this state of affairs, individuals contracted to form a civil government, but in so doing they parted with portions of their natural liberty in order to "preserve the residue."[11]

Given the prevalence of the social contract framework during and before the revolutionary period, it would have been noteworthy, even startling, had a different framework been used in the Declaration to justify or explain separation. Yet this was only a framework, a skeleton, so to speak, of a more complex theory whose terms and components—their meanings, substance, and relationship—had already been elaborated upon in much narrower circles, particularly among the educated elite familiar with modern European political theory.

Natural Law

In many ways the most important element of contract theory is natural law, largely because it prescribed the boundaries or limits of natural liberty. According to Peters, "the law of nature was seen" by the Congregationalists who predominated in New England "to be part of the law of

---

some resemblance to a "state of nature" since it lacked a formal government. On this point see the introduction to *The Popular Sources of Political Authority,* ed. Oscar Handlin and Mary Handlin (Cambridge: Harvard University Press, 1966). The very state that had taken the lead in the movement toward separation found itself in a condition where the principles of the Declaration could readily be applied in practice. (In this regard, it should be remarked as well that Massachusetts was the first state to found a new government on the consent of the governed.) Beyond this, the application of the contractual approach to the practical task of framing a government compelled an elaboration and refinement of this approach. This, in turn, offers a better understanding of what Americans at the time of the Declaration understood to be their rights and liberties.

11. Hamburger, "Natural Rights," 908, 931.

God." The law of God, in turn, would be affirmed in two ways: first, as revealed in the Bible; and second, through the moral sense implanted in men by God. The two were not seen as exclusive of one another: man's implanted moral sense, for instance, would reaffirm the revealed morality of the scriptures. Peters points out that there were specifics that were seen to comprise natural law, "specific tenets" that constituted the "natural rights of men." These rights, he notes, "were perceived in terms of freedom to act," and no individual could be legitimately prevented from exercising a natural right. And "[e]ven were [an individual] to be prevented from taking an action to which he had a natural right, his right to take that action remains inviolate. By providing this normative standard, natural rights establish the basis upon which rested the moral law of the state of nature." In determining what constitutes a natural right, "reason" also came into play: man had a right to do that which was necessary to deal with the con- ditions of the state of nature—for example, to support and protect his exis- tence. To this effect Peters quotes from Samuel West's 1776 sermon: "[W]hatever right reason requires as necessary to be done is as much the will and law of God as though it were enjoined us by an immediate reve- lation from heaven, or commanded in the sacred scriptures."[12]

The emphasis on the divine origins of the natural law that Peters finds in Massachusetts is undoubtedly attributable to the state's strong Congre- gationalist roots. As might be expected, Hamburger's survey, broader in scope, reveals both similarities and differences concerning the sources of natural law. The similarity consists in the underlying assumptions relating to the state of nature, namely, that individuals possess an equality of lib- erty and that individuals have a right to preserve themselves and their lib- erty. The differences involve the means for deriving the natural law. As Hamburger points out, the underlying assumptions provided the foun- dations for individuals to "reason" about what is needed to "preserve" liberty. Or, if not "reason," some derived the natural law from prudential judgments about what conditions would serve this end. Moreover, Ham- burger notes, some reasoned that natural law could be extended to embrace certain duties or even a comprehensive moral code. For example, because government is necessary to preserve liberty, individuals could be said to have duties that insure that government perform its functions sat- isfactorily. Or, even more expansively, some held that "man's social char- acter" provided not only "an additional ground" why "individuals should not violate the equal rights of others," but also the basis for "a more com-

12. Peters, *Massachusetts Constitution*, 75.

plete set of moral rules." On Hamburger's showing, "A natural right was simply a portion of . . . undifferentiated natural liberty." For Americans of the founding era, he finds, natural rights were generally cast in terms of "life, liberty and property, or life, liberty and the pursuit of happiness," the latter formulation, of course, that used by Jefferson in the Declaration. Natural rights, he also remarks, could take more specific form—for example, "the free exercise of religion," "freedom of conscience," or "freedom of speech and press."[13]

It is important to note that despite their differences over the derivation of natural law, Americans of the founding era still had ample grounds for meaningful dialogue given their shared understanding of the conditions in the state of nature to which this natural law, however derived, would apply. First, as already indicated, they assumed that individuals in the state of nature enjoyed equal liberty and that they were entitled to do that which was necessary to support their existence. And second, they all acknowledged that natural law set the limits to the exercise of natural liberty. For the most part, moreover, there existed widespread agreement about what these limits on natural liberty should be. Hamburger, on this point, approvingly cites Thomas Rutherford to the effect that, though there were philosophical disagreements surrounding the sources of natural law, "the disagreements did not greatly affect what eighteenth-century men understood to be the theory's moral and political conclusions." Rutherford, for his part, argues that while moralists see different sources of and reasons for obedience to the natural law ("instinctive affections, or an innate moral sense," "certain abstract relations or fitness of things," the realization of happiness, or a combination of these), "they are agreed about the law, to which we are obliged," and "they concur in establishing the same rules of duty."[14] To this it should be added that there was a recognition in the sermons and essays of the period that different communities might come to different judgments regarding the extent to which natural liberty should be limited or regulated. "In every state," Howard observed, "the members will, probably, give up so much of their natural liberty, as they think will be most for the good of the whole. But different states will judge differently upon this point, some will give up more, some less, though with the same view, the publick good."[15]

13. Hamburger, "Natural Rights," 924, 925, 919.

14. Thomas Rutherford, *Institutes of Natural Law,* 2nd American ed. (Clark, NJ: Lawbook Exchange, 2004), quoted ibid., 925.

15. Howard, "A Sermon Preached," 188.

Natural Rights

Howard's observation leads to another major element of contract theory, namely, the status of rights in the context of civil society. Peters makes much of the fact that rights were thought of as either alienable or unalienable. Peters notes in particular the reasoning of Theophilus Parsons embodied in the "Essex Result," according to which alienable rights are those of which individuals "may choose to divest themselves . . . on the condition that they receive an equivalent in return."[16] As Peters points out, given this understanding, life, liberty, and property, three of the most commonly asserted rights, have to be considered "alienable" rights. That is, as he puts it, "[m]en do as a matter of fact give up their right to live, and their liberties, and under the Constitution men could be compelled to give up their power of controlling their lives, liberties, and property."[17] Such, indeed, would be the case under the Massachusetts Constitution that Parsons and others would eventually endorse. Of course, in "surrendering" these rights, individuals receive equivalents in return—for example, security, advancement of the common good—that make the surrender more than acceptable from the individual's perspective, as well as from that of natural law.

Peters, relying again on the "Essex Result" and the analysis of Parsons, turns to examining the character of unalienable rights. Not unexpectedly, he finds that one of their characteristics is that there can be no equivalent for their surrender. As he puts it, "Where no equivalent can possibly be received for a particular right, the individual presumably is not free to give up the right, and it is therefore an unalienable right." Delving into this matter more closely, he observes that what is really at stake when individuals enter civil society is not the surrender of the rights themselves, but the relinquishing of control over their exercise. Thus, the question becomes, as Peters phrases it, "When would the power to control a natural right be of such importance so as to be unalienable?" The answer he provides, derived from a close analysis of Parsons's position, is that the importance of unalienable rights stems from their "inherent" nature, that is, from their being "essential to the very existence *as a human being* of him who possesses [them]." Rights of this character are "literally impossible for that individual to forfeit" control over; they are unalienable because they "cannot be physically alienated." Thus, Peters concludes, there are "two senses in which a right may be unalienable: when it is impossible for

16. Peters, *Massachusetts Constitution*, 78.
17. Ibid.

an individual to give it up and/or when it is impossible to receive an equivalent."[18]

Peters remarks that the "right of conscience" can be considered the "prototypical unalienable right" because on all counts it qualifies for this status: individuals simply could not part with the responsibility of making moral choices, nor could they receive any possible equivalent. This right was also regarded as highly crucial because it was so closely attached to religion, as being indispensably necessary for individuals to make those moral choices upon which they would ultimately be judged by God. This required and presupposed, as Peters points out, that "individuals would have the freedom to make decisions in matters of conscience."[19] Thus the understanding of one Samuel Stillman regarding "THE SACRED RIGHTS OF CONSCIENCE" apparently reflected a commonly held view, at least among the Congregationalists, regarding their status, namely, that they "can neither be parted with nor controled, by any human authority."[20]

The right of conscience, as students of the era well know, was intimately involved in the growing controversy over the propriety of a state-established religion or, at another level, nondenominational state support for religion, and insight into the matter of what was considered to constitute unjust interference by "human authority" or government can be gained by examining this controversy. Article 2 of the Massachusetts Constitution declares that "all men" have a "right as well as a duty . . . to worship the SUPREME BEING." It affirms that no punishment or harm will befall any individual "for worshipping God in the manner and season most agreeable to the dictates of his own conscience; or for his religious profession or sentiments." In the very last portion of the article, however, there is a caveat: the individual is free to practice or exercise his religion "provided he doth not disturb the public peace, or obstruct others in their religious worship."[21] Yet, as Peters points out, no one seemed to take exception to this particular provision; even the unalienable status of the right of conscience would not protect practices that might be detrimental to the community or an abridgment of equal rights.

Intense controversy did arise, however, over provision for the public support of the ministry in Article 3—support justified on the premise that "the good order and preservation of civil government, essentially depend

18. Ibid., 76, 77 (emphasis in original), 80.

19. Ibid., 81.

20. Samuel Stillman, "The Duty of Magistrates in Patriot Preachers of the American Revolution," quoted in Peters, 80 (emphasis in original).

21. Massachusetts Constitution of 1780, pt. 1, art. 2, reprinted in Peters, *Massachusetts Constitution*, 196 (emphasis in original).

upon piety, religion and morality."[22] The arguments offered against this provision varied. One variant, most forcefully presented by an author writing as Philanthropos, a widely used colonial pseudonym, raised concern about the limits, if any, of state power with regard to matters of conscience: if the majority can compel support for ministers because doing so is beneficial for society, then what is to prevent the majority from, say, incorporating its notions of Christian doctrine into the constitutional fabric on the grounds that this would redound to the common good? Not unrelated to this argument was another that questioned whether the scope of governmental authority could legitimately extend to matters of conscience. Peters finds the gist of this argument in Philanthropos's reasoning to the effect that "the *power* of the legislature depends upon the right of the people. If the latter have not the *right*, the former cannot have the *power*." The town of Westford forcefully expressed this view in holding that "no Man Ought or of Right can be compelled to attend any religious Worship or maintain any ministry contrary to or against his own free will and consent."[23] The issue, as Peters makes clear, did not relate to altering the minds or the inner thoughts of individuals. Rather, it revolved around whether the positive powers accorded government in Article 3 (for example, that of supporting the ministry) were among those that individuals could legitimately be commanded to comply with. The opponents of state-supported religion regarded the unalienable right of conscience to place such powers outside the realm of public control.

The answer provided by Parsons to this line of thought is of interest because it places the status of the right of conscience—as well as other unalienable rights—into a wider context. While Parsons does agree that efforts to change or compel beliefs would constitute a violation of the right of conscience, he sees "the great errour" in the argument of those opposing Article 3 as "not distinguishing between liberty of conscience in religious opinions and worship, and the right of appropriating money by the state." Noting that "no power is claimed" in Article 3 to direct or control "the faith" of individuals, he goes on to remark: "The authority derived from the constitution extends no further than to submit to the understandings of the people the evidence of truths deemed of public utility, leaving the weight of the evidence, and the tendence of those truths, to the conscience of every man."[24]

22. Massachusetts Constitution of 1780, pt. 1, art. 3, reprinted in Peters, *Massachusetts Constitution*, 196.

23. Peters, *Massachusetts Constitution*, 82–83 (emphasis in original), 85.

24. Theophilius Parsons, *Defence of the Third Article of the Massachusetts Declaration of Rights* (Worcester, MA, 1820), quoted ibid., 87.

Parsons's defense of Article 3, which presumably reflected the views of a majority in Massachusetts, certainly bears out Peters's assessment that "the unalienable rights of man do not set great limits on the power of civil society." As Peters points out, the right of conscience, perhaps the most basic of all rights, did not "preclude political coercion in favor of religion."[25] Certainly one of the reasons for this can be found in the firm and widely shared conviction, consistent with natural law, that the very survival of the civil order depends on cultivation of "piety, religion and morality." In sum, to the extent that the right of conscience can be considered the prototype, it was understood that unalienable rights could be narrowed or confined in the civil society by considerations of social needs and the common good.

While Peters places stress on the distinction between alienable and unalienable rights, Hamburger is careful to distinguish between natural and acquired rights. During the founding period, he notes, while Americans only "occasionally" drew distinctions between the two types of rights, the grounds for the distinction were clear and widely shared. Natural rights were those that could be derived from the natural liberty individuals enjoyed in the state of nature, whereas acquired rights, such as habeas corpus and trial by jury, "did not exist in the state of nature." The acquired rights were also "civil rights," protected by constitutions and laws, "rights that could exist only under civil government."[26]

Hamburger's major contribution is providing a better understanding of how those of the founding period and beyond looked at the relationship between natural rights and natural law. As previously noted, natural rights, which can be looked upon as portions of natural liberty, were bounded or confined by natural law. As Hamburger explains, this was well understood at the time of founding, so that normally any assertion of a natural right implicitly carried with it the realization that it was limited by natural law. In other words, for Americans of the founding period, "natural rights did not suggest the existence of expansive rights without substantial restrictions." This realization helps to explain the attitudes of late-eighteenth-century Americans toward natural rights—attitudes that seem "unsystematic, contradictory, and even paradoxical" to modern scholars.[27] Focusing on the freedoms of speech and press, Hamburger notes the difficulties modern students have in reconciling the language of the First Amendment, where these freedoms are couched in absolutist

25. Peters, *Massachusetts Constitution,* 89.
26. Hamburger, "Natural Rights," 921–22.
27. Ibid., 956, 910.

terms, with the ready willingness of the founding generations to accept limitations on them.[28] The answer, of course, is that these eighteenth-century Americans understood that natural rights, including freedom of speech and press, carried with them the limitations of natural law. In Hamburger's words, "Americans [of this period] frequently said or assumed that certain types of speech or press—including blasphemous, obscene, fraudulent, or defamatory words—lacked or should lack constitutional protection."[29]

Individuals upon entering civil society surrendered their natural rights, save for those "as were reserved by a constitution, or, much less securely, were left unimpeded by their other civil laws." What secured the benefits in civil society of those natural rights that were surrendered was the understanding that civil laws should reflect natural law. Thus, to quote Hamburger once again, "If physical natural liberty was subject to natural law already in the state of nature, and if civil laws reflected natural law, then the imposition of civil laws did not reduce natural liberty."[30]

This is not to say that there were no complications involved in determining the fidelity of civil law to natural law. Understandably, given the general character of natural law, there could be differences of opinion about how it applied to specific situations or conditions. This fact, significantly, led to the recognition that there could be substantial differences in the civil codes of nations without any of these codes necessarily transgressing the natural law. Furthermore, civil laws, which applied to specific circumstances or conditions in the context of the civil society, necessarily had to be more specific and detailed than natural laws.[31]

With Peters, Hamburger affirms that Americans simply assumed that constitutions would be structured upon "the natural law principles of

---

28. Hamburger points to Alexander Meiklejohn, who found a "paradox" or "apparent self-contradiction" in the fact that the First Amendment "'does not forbid the abridging of speech' and yet, 'at the same time, it does forbid the abridging of free speech'" (Hamburger, "Natural Rights," 912; quoting from Meiklejohn's *Political Freedom: The Constitutional Powers of the People* [New York: Harper, 1960], 21). Citing Leonard Levy's *Emergence of a Free Press* (New York: Oxford University Press, 1985), Hamburger remarks upon Levy's concern to resolve the seemingly schizophrenic positions of the founding generation regarding freedom of the press by maintaining "that they understood freedom of the press to be defined by the traditional common restraints upon the press, including seditious prosecutions." But, as Hamburger points out, Levy's explanation is at best partial and does not deal with the question of "how eighteenth-century Americans reconciled their highly restrictive laws with their claim that the freedom of speech and press was a natural right." "Natural Rights," 911.

29. Hamburger, "Natural Rights," 935.

30. Ibid., 930, 947–48.

31. Ibid., 942–44.

equal liberty and self-preservation." Yet, he maintains, they were aware of the fact that "the people might adopt a constitution that did not adequately preserve their natural liberty or that otherwise failed to conform to the implications of the natural law." Consequently, natural law provided the measure of constitutions, "means by which the people could measure the adequacy of their constitutions." And what if they judged their constitution inadequate, as failing to reflect natural law? Then, according to Hamburger, the people could remedy the situation by amendment or alteration of the constitution—presumably to the extent of adopting a new constitution—or, if that were impossible given the political landscape, "by revolution."[32]

The Declaration: Unalienable Rights and Equality

This survey of the contractual mode of thinking that prevailed at the time of the Declaration of Independence, though brief, is sufficient to indicate the broad areas of agreement and to identify certain difficulties surrounding the interpretation of key provisions of the Declaration. These difficulties as intimated at the outset arise with regard to two relatively specific but interrelated phrases in the second sentence of the text, beginning "We hold these truths," specifically the "all men are created equal" clause and the portion that places "Life, Liberty, and the pursuit of happiness" among "unalienable Rights." A convenient point of departure is to turn again to the meaning and status of "unalienable Rights."

As noted previously, Peters cannot see how the rights of "life, liberty, and property" could be considered unalienable largely because from his perspective they are and have traditionally been controlled or regulated as if they were alienable rights. Peters is obviously correct concerning their regulation and control. Americans took it for granted that society (that is, majorities) could regulate all manner of concerns relative to these rights, even to the extent of imposing capital punishment. The major safeguard against arbitrariness with regard to regulation was the "due process" established by the positive laws that conformed with natural law. But in recognizing this, Peters faces a difficulty in light of Article 1 in the "Declaration of Rights" of the Massachusetts Constitution, which holds: "All men are born free and equal, and have certain natural, essential, and unalienable rights; among which may be reckoned the right of enjoying

---

32. Ibid., 940.

and defending their lives and liberties, that of acquiring, possessing, and protecting property, in fine, that of seeking and obtaining their safety and happiness."[33] This article, as Peters sees it, cannot be interpreted to hold that "life, liberty, and property" per se are unalienable. Rather, from his perspective, what is unalienable is the "enjoying," "acquiring," and "protecting" associated with these rights.[34] Moreover, as previously pointed out, Peters demonstrates—using for this purpose the prototypical unalienable right of freedom of conscience—that, in reality, unalienable rights really did not impede popular control in any significant way, that they could not be given a meaning that would impede majorities from acting pursuant to the common good and welfare.

Peters's analysis may be understood as an effort to square unalienable rights with the principle of popular control of government, to avoid what would appear to be a contradiction in the theoretical design underlying the Massachusetts Constitution whereby unalienable rights could be interpreted to trump majority rule. Still, his analysis leaves us to wonder in what meaningful sense unalienable rights are unalienable; for instance, to recur to his notion of unalienable rights, majorities are and have traditionally been free to regulate and control the "enjoying," "acquiring," and the like associated with liberty and property. Put otherwise, the distinction he draws between "property" and "protecting property" in determining what is unalienable does not, in fact, hold up. Consider, for instance, Article 10 of the Massachusetts "Declaration of Rights": it provides, in effect, that property may be taken for public use with reasonable compensation.[35] Society's reach, thus, legitimately extends not only to control over the use of property (which as noted above is presumably alienable), but also to its possession, which renders it difficult to determine precisely what is unalienable. What emerges from Peters's account is that the theory underlying the Massachusetts Constitution seeks both popular self-government and the goals attributed to natural law, the major one being rule that advances the common good and welfare. This underlying theory, it should be noted, does not embrace the position commonly attributed, rightly or wrongly, to John Locke, which has gained considerable currency in modern times, to wit, there is "a body of innate, indefeasible, individual rights

33. Massachusetts Constitution of 1780, pt. 1, art. 1, reprinted in Peters, *Massachusetts Constitution*, 196.

34. Peters, *Massachusetts Constitution*, 78.

35. Massachusetts Constitution of 1780, pt. 1, art. 10, reprinted in Peters, *Massachusetts Constitution*, 198: "And whenever the public exigencies require, that the property of any individual should be appropriated to public uses, he shall receive a reasonable compensation therefor."

which limit the competence of the community and stand as bars to prevent interference with the liberty and property of private persons."[36]

Peters's analysis points in the direction of reducing unalienable rights to their essence by way of emphasizing that they really constituted no barrier or hindrance to society's pursuing the common good. In my view, however, Hamburger's analysis leads to the same conclusion in a simpler and more direct manner. Simply put, on his showing, all natural rights—alienable and unalienable—are bounded, regulated, or controlled by natural law; in other words, it was understood that these rights inherently embodied or contained within them the restrictions and caveats of natural law. Obscenity, slander, and defamation, for instance, were not part of the right of freedom of speech. Likewise, individual actions or behavior contrary to natural law were no part of liberty. Viewed in this manner, unalienable rights could be subject to regulation or control by society through positive law in accordance with natural law, that is, in order to preserve or advance the general welfare. And this is where, ultimately, Peters's analysis leads.

To return to the Declaration and its assertion of unalienable rights, the text seems clear enough: there are these unalienable rights, "Life, Liberty, and the pursuit of happiness," which "Governments are instituted" "to secure." From this it is but a short step to the proposition that "whenever any Form of Government becomes destructive of these ends, it is the right of the people to alter or abolish it, and to institute new Government, laying its foundations on such principles and ordering its powers in such form, as to them shall seem most likely to effect their Safety and Happiness."[37] In light of what Peters and Hamburger have written, these particular passages pose no basic problems.

There is, it should be noted at this point, another view concerning the status of the unalienable rights, one that directly bears upon Peters's analysis of unalienable rights; it is a view that is linked, as well, to an interpretation of the "all men are created equal" clause. In the decade leading up to the Declaration, an understanding took hold that Americans were a people separate from the English, that under the existing arrangement there were, in fact, "two peoples" joined only in their allegiance to the king. So much is reflected in that portion of the first sentence of the Declaration that reads "When . . . it becomes necessary for one people to dissolve the political bands which have connected them with another . . ." Logically following this is an

36. George H. Sabine, *A History of Political Thought,* 3rd rev. ed. (New York: Henry Holt, 1950), 529.

37. Declaration of Independence, para. 2 (U.S. 1776).

assertion that this "one people" is going "to assume among the powers of the earth, the separate and equal station to which the Laws of Nature and of Nature's God entitle them."[38] This language would suggest that what follows should be read in a "corporate" sense, that is, that with the "all men are created equal" clause, Americans are asserting an equality as a people with the British people. In this context, then, the "unalienable rights" are those that belong to the people in their corporate or collective capacity and, as such, these rights are unalienable in the sense set forth by Peters: they cannot be parted with, that is, transferred to another people. Nor can they be controlled or regulated by another people. In this account, it is critical to note that once government is established, these rights ("Life," "Liberty," "pursuit of happiness") lose their unalienable status; a majority or whatever sovereign power there be, in keeping with natural law, may regulate these rights to promote the well-being of society.

There is abundant evidence to support this corporate view. A common theme in the sermons and political essays leading up to the Revolution is that the colonists were not being treated as equals with their British counterparts. The belief prevailed among the colonists, as Stephen Hopkins put it in 1764, that they were "justly and fully entitled to equal liberty and freedom with their fellow subjects in Europe."[39] This point was put most forcefully by an anonymous pamphleteer, Britannus Americanus, who argued two years later that the "indefeasible rights" of the "people of *New* England" were the same as those of "*Old* England," "they being *fellow subjects,* and standing on *equal* footing."[40] British policy clearly did not reflect this equality, and this proved to be the major source of discontent that eventually led to separation.

Despite this, there are still grounds for interpreting this clause outside of the corporate context. For starters, if the equality of men was to be understood in the corporate context, the phraseology would seem to pose some difficulties. "All men" means *all men,* perhaps best understood as the entire universe of men undifferentiated with regard to national or social groupings or identification. If the corporate view was intended, then some other way of stating this might have been devised, a phraseology that would have reflected the equality between Americans, who identified themselves as "one people," and the British nation. Moreover, the assertion of the equality of all men—and equality between them, not a cor-

---

38. Declaration of Independence, para. 1 (U.S. 1776).
39. Stephen Hopkins, "The Rights of Colonies Examined," *American Political Writings,* 49.
40. Britannus Americanus, *American Political Writings,* 89 (emphasis in original).

porate equality—fits in with the widely accepted contractarian understanding that men enjoy equal liberty in the state of nature, that this equality is basic for understanding many of the injunctions of the natural law.
As Hamburger puts it, for instance, "none had a moral right to exercise his
liberty in a way that infringed on the equal freedom of another person."[41]
The upshot is that the reference to "all men" being "created equal" accords
with the predominant mode of thinking in a context quite apart from the
corporate or collective interpretation.

Having said this much, however, it is clear that even if the clause is given
the most expansive meaning, as applying to men in undifferentiated fashion, its purpose is clearly to advance the proposition that the Americans
were (as presumably are other peoples) as entitled as the British to unalienable rights. Consequently, the corporate view is, in effect, not very far from
the surface, even given this undifferentiated understanding. So much is
evident from the political landscape at the time the Declaration was written, as well as its express purpose and the internal logic of its argument.

In the last analysis—and what should not be lost sight of in discussing
the complexities surrounding rights—it makes little difference whether
the corporate or what has here been dubbed the undifferentiated interpretation is accepted. The two views present essentially the same understanding of rights, the origins of government, and the substance and role
of natural law. And, most importantly, the two interpretations are alike in
viewing the Declaration's purpose as that of establishing popular self-
government in which, in the end, majorities rule in conformance with natural law. It cannot be overlooked in this connection that many of the
specific grievances against the king that comprise the main body of the
Declaration involve measures that undermine colonial self-government.
In keeping with its purpose, the theory underlying the arguments of the
Declaration does not in any way enshrine individual rights in the sense
they are generally understood today. True enough, it may be justifiably
inferred that the drafters accepted the mandate of natural law for "due
process," which would serve to curb arbitrary and capricious government.
Again, it is of some significance to note that many of the specific grievances relate directly to breaches in due process as it had come to be understood over time in the common law. And these guarantees of due process
did involve individual *acquired* rights. Yet, it is clear that the drafters sub-
scribed to the proposition that these acquired rights could be changed or
amended by majorities if the common good warranted.

41. Hamburger, "Natural Rights," 927.

Finally, to the question that has recurred in one form or another over the course of American history, how inclusive was the "all men are created equal" clause intended to be? Here a few observations on this matter must suffice. In light of the subsequent controversies that have arisen over this clause, an important aspect of this question involves how the "one people," the "nation," or the political community was conceived by those who drafted the Declaration. Historically speaking, a people comes to define itself through a process or evolution with which the theory underlying the Declaration does not deal. The contractarian theory, this is to say, simply assumes that there is a people who want to be one politically. As such it really has no hooks to grapple with the questions surrounding key issues, for example, What are the limits to the community? Who stands outside its bounds and why? Moreover, contract theory is largely ahistorical, taking no cognizance of the complex processes by which communities come to identify themselves, much less the traditions, cultural norms, beliefs, and such that have, in fact, determined the hierarchy within the community or society that, in turn, is determinative of who is to rule.[42] To put this in more specific terms, it seems evident that the drafters of the Declaration thought that mature, white males—particularly those with a stake in the community—would comprise the lawmaking portion of a community. Such a view was, so to speak, a "given" of their time, a "given" that was probably shared by the largest excluded group, mature white women. But restricted suffrage did not mean that women and children were in any way to be denied the advantages of civil government, nor were they to be treated in a manner inconsistent with natural law.

Slavery did involve difficulties on this score. Slaves, unlike women and children, were not considered by many to be members of the community. Thus, they could be and were treated as a separate group, apart from the society and not entitled to equal liberty. In addition, there was the thorny problem posed by the very institution of slavery itself, namely, that its very existence served as a reason to exclude slaves from participation in the political process since they were under the control of their masters and in no position to render independent judgments. These considerations serve simply to highlight the fact that the social contract mode of thought itself

---

42. To this point Edmund Burke explains: "As in the abstract, it is perfectly clear, that, out of a state of civil society, majority and minority are relations which can have no existence; and that in civil society, its own specific conventions in each incorporation, determine what it is that constitutes the people, so as to make their act the signification of the general will." *Further Reflections on the Revolution in France,* ed. Daniel E. Ritchie (Indianapolis: Liberty Classics, 1992), 167.

has little to say about the criteria for inclusion into the community or full participation in the political processes. Being able to exercise independent judgment or having a stake in the society, for instance, are criteria for inclusion that are independent of the theory used to declare independence. What that theory does hold is that if majorities—no matter how small a portion of the population they may initially be—want to extend full membership and political rights to those initially excluded, they are free to do so. Beyond this, the institution of slavery within a self-defined community is also undermined by the tenets of natural law, external to the contract paradigm, that recognize and assert human dignity.

The American Political Tradition: Natural Law and Natural Rights

Certain conclusions, central to what we believe is a proper and fuller understanding of an important dimension of the American political tradition, follow from this analysis. One relates to the place of the Declaration of Independence within that tradition: is the Declaration, as many have contended, both the source and the foundation of the American political tradition in the sense of providing the theoretical framework for understanding its nature and contours, for discerning its aspirations and goals, and for evaluating the constitutional system and its achievements?[43] My

43. That the Declaration of Independence has long been regarded by many as the basic founding document of the American political tradition scarcely needs documentation. It is encountered in many forms. William J. Bennett, for example, by way of supporting the message of President George W. Bush's second inaugural address, notes that, with the opening words of the second paragraph ("We hold these truths to be self-evident . . .") "a new nation—our nation—was born. And before Thomas Jefferson put the final sentences in our Declaration of Independence, he labeled the 'truths' and 'ends' of government, not just means. . . . No nation in the history of the world has come as close as we have to abiding by these norms of government, enshrined in our conscience, identified as the idea around which the United States of America was founded." "A Call for Dignity," *Washington Times*, January 28, 2005, A18. The idea of the Declaration's giving birth to the nation is, of course, attributable to Abraham Lincoln's Gettysburg Address. Robert N. Bellah finds the Declaration to represent the "normative core" of "the American civil religion." He finds that the Gettysburg Address is a restatement and rededication to this civil religion. "The Revolution and the Civil Religion," in *Religion and the American Revolution*, ed. Jerald C. Brauer (Philadelphia: Fortress Press, 1776), 55. Most of the writings of Harry V. Jaffa affirm a very similar view of the Declaration while seeing Lincoln as a champion of its values. See his *Crisis of the House Divided: An Interpretation of the Issues in the Lincoln-Douglas Debates* (Garden City, NY: Doubleday, 1959) and *A New Birth of Freedom: Abraham Lincoln and the Coming of the Civil War* (Lanham, MD: Rowman and Littlefield, 2000).

analysis of the Declaration would hardly support according it such a central role simply because, taken as a whole, it can so easily be linked to the political thought and processes that prevailed throughout the colonial period and the core differences that led to separation from England. Understood in this light, the Declaration is part of a continuous American political tradition and is entirely compatible with the principles of deliberative self-government that emerged and flourished during the colonial period. This is to say, the Declaration does not prescribe ends or goals that government is obliged to realize; it does not assert rights that are inviolable, rights that cannot be modified or altered by deliberative majorities for society's well-being. Rather, consonant with the principles of the prevailing contractarian thought of the era, it asserts that when a government violates natural rights and contravenes or ignores natural law, "the People" have "the Right . . . to institute new Government . . . as to them shall seem most likely to effect their Safety and Happiness."

It also follows from this understanding that there is no inherent conflict between the ideals of the Declaration and those of the Constitution.[44] On the contrary, given the inadequacies of the Articles of Confederation, the Declaration even anticipates that the people will form a new government to meet their needs. As well, the institutions and processes established by the Constitution are designed to allow for the reflection and deliberation necessary for a people intent upon operating within the confines of natural law.

Finally, this approach to understanding the Declaration acknowledges and takes into account the significant role and function of natural law in the political thinking before and during the founding period, particularly the stress on the need for an effective government, operating under the rule of law and capable of modifying, limiting, or advancing natural rights in accord with the common good. Indeed, it should be noted, the political thought that predominated in this era, reflected in the Declaration, is

---

44. It is an article of faith among most Progressive historians that the "democratic" values enshrined in the Declaration were significantly altered or abandoned by those who wrote the Constitution. The thesis that the Constitution was a reaction to the egalitarian values of the Declaration was first advanced by James Allen Smith in *The Spirit of American Government* (New York: Macmillan, 1907). As Douglass Adair noted, this thesis was widely accepted by the 1950s, judging from his survey of American history texts. "The Tenth Federalist Revisited," in *Fame and the Founding Fathers*, ed. Trevor Colbourn (New York: W. W. Norton, 1974). As historian Richard F. Gibbs remarked, this thesis portrayed the Declaration "as the ultimate expression of Revolutionary ideals, to wit, egalitarianism, popular majority rule, and human rights," whereas the Constitution was "cast in the role of a counter-revolutionary reaction in support of monied privilege, minority rule, and property rights." "The Spirit of '89: Conservatism and Bicentenary," *University Bookman* 14 (Spring 1974): 54.

entirely conformable with the main tenets of traditional natural law theory rooted in Christian teachings. The natural law, as Heinrich Rommen concluded after an extensive survey of its development, recognizes the need for positive law given the fact that men are not angels and are predisposed to "disorder" rather than order. Rommen emphasizes as well the necessary interrelationship between natural law and positive law: "[N]atural law and positive law are, as the Christian Doctrine of natural law expresses it, directed immediately to each other. The natural law calls imperatively for the specification of positive enactments, even though it is at the same time the measure and guideline of the positive law." He informs us that the primary end of political institutions within the general framework of natural law "is to establish an order and unity of cooperation among free persons and free associations of persons in such a way that they, while they freely pursue their individual and group interests, are nevertheless so coordinated that they realize at the same time the common good under the rule of law." Ultimately, he holds, it is the natural law that provides the measure of the "legal positive order," that is, determines whether the order is "unjust" and stands in need of change.[45] In sum, to go no further, there is nothing in the political thought leading up to and embracing the Declaration that is incompatible with Christian natural law principles. Quite the contrary, these principles seem to have been essential elements in American political thought before and during the founding period.

Yet, today, the Declaration and its theoretical underpinning are viewed in almost an entirely different light, as authoritatively setting forth an American creed or civil theology at whose center reside egalitarian notions along with inviolable, individual rights. This understanding, of course, ignores the tradition leading up to the Declaration, since it regards the Declaration, as we remarked above, as our "founding" document that provides the guiding principles and basic values of the tradition. That the Declaration has assumed such a critical role in defining the American tradition is one matter. Still another, more central to our purpose, is the interpretation given to its key passages that has spurred a profusion of spurious rights claims on the part of individuals and groups, claims that acquire legitimacy because of the hallowed status of the Declaration. Put another way, the rights set forth in the Declaration and their derivatives are taken seriously in contemporary political discourse, but they now take on a new character, different from that which they possessed during the founding

---

45. Heinrich A. Rommen, *The Natural Law: A Study in Legal and Social History and Philosophy,* trans. Thomas R. Hanley (1947; reprint, Indianapolis: Liberty Fund, 1998), 221–22, 235, 236.

era. Modern rights claims, this is to say, are asserted without any regard for the dictates of natural law.

Brian Tierney, in the conclusion of his fine work dealing with the historical development of natural rights thought, observes that "nowadays" we find a "luxuriant array of rights inhering in various classes of humans—rights of ethnic minorities, rights of women, rights of children, rights of gays, lesbians, bisexuals, rights of the handicapped, rights of consumers, rights of smokers and nonsmokers, and so on almost endlessly." As he notes, however, rights inhere as well for "animals," "unborn generations," and even "trees." From Tierney's vantage point, this development "can erode any sense of community and the common good, values that the earlier rights theorists never lost sight of." Beyond this, as Mary Ann Glendon points out, the assertion of rights, which can be and is matched with the assertion of competing rights, leads to a sterile debate in the public arena.[46] The participants in the debates, moreover, usually possess a "rights mentality" that renders compromise or accommodation very difficult, if not impossible, since this would tend to bring into question the status of the "right" asserted by acknowledging the claims of a countervailing "right." In short, considerations of the common good and the well-being of society have not played a prominent part in contemporary debates involving rights claims and counterclaims.

John Courtney Murray also took note of this development and inquired whether in the mid-twentieth century the traditional natural law teachings were still "alive" and part of the American ethos.[47] He took the occasion to examine critically the main elements of Locke's thought, which he considered to be responsible for the seeming eclipse of natural law. In this endeavor, he made several points that differentiate between the understanding of natural law he derives from Locke's teachings and that of traditional Christian natural law. Certain of his conclusions seem highly pertinent for understanding why the modern perceptions of the Declaration and rights have assumed the form they have, whether or not we can rightly attribute these perceptions to Locke's teachings. This is to say, whether or not Murray's analysis of Locke's theory is correct, his conclusions point to widely held assumptions and perspectives that have served to give new meaning and form to natural rights.

---

46. Brian Tierney, *The Idea of Natural Rights: Studies on Natural Rights, Natural Law, and Church Law, 1150–1625* (Atlanta: Scholars Press, 1997), 346; Mary Ann Glendon, *Rights Talk: The Impoverishment of Political Discourse* (New York: Free Press, 1991).

47. John Courtney Murray, *We Hold These Truths* (Kansas City, MO: Sheed and Ward, 1960).

One of the most fundamental of Murray's points is that, whereas traditional natural law thinking regards man as a social being, part of a web of associations, institutions, and relationships, all necessary for his moral and intellectual development, "Locke's individualism completely deprives society of any organic character." Specifically, "[i]n Locke's theory," contrary to basic tenets of traditional natural law, "all forms of sociality are purely contractual, they have no deeper basis in the nature of man than a shallow 'reason' that judges them useful" with no recognition of the natural and formative role of social institutions, voluntary associations, and such that stand between the individual and his government. Consequently, from Murray's perspective, Locke's understanding of the common good is truncated, consisting "merely in the security of each individual in the possession of his property." Or, as Murray put it in another place, Locke's nominalism compelled him to conceive of the common good "as nothing in itself," not as "qualitatively distinct from individual goods, but simply a symbol for the quantitative sum of individual goods." Finally, Murray contended, due to Locke's "individualism," his law of nature "results in a complete evacuation of the notion of the 'rights' of man." His state of nature is "simply a pattern of power relationships" without any "*ordo juris*, and no rights in any recognizably moral sense," so that government, a "third power," becomes the arbiter of "right." Thus, "right" is ultimately what the majority, the "greater force," declares it to be.[48]

Murray's analysis raises critical questions for serious students of the American political tradition because, as we have noted throughout, there is an obvious connection between Locke's social contract theory and the key second paragraph of the Declaration of Independence. Thus, we must ask, in what ways did the founding generation buy into Locke's teachings?[49] To what extent, if at all, did they understand Locke's theory as Murray understood it?[50] Indeed, has Murray presented an accurate picture of

48. Ibid., 306, 305, 309, 307–8. Many Locke scholars are not as certain as Murray on this point. As Willmoore Kendall put it, there is a "riddle" in Locke's *Second Treatise*. Is Locke saying, "right is that which the majority wills," or "the majority always wills that which is right"? *John Locke and the Doctrine of Majority Rule* (Urbana: University of Illinois Press, 1941), 133.

49. While most students see the heavy hand of John Locke in the Declaration of Independence and the political thinking of the founding era, others do not. See, for instance, John Dunn, "The Politics of Locke in England and America in the Eighteenth Century," in *John Locke: Problems and Perspectives*, ed. J. W. Yolton (Cambridge: Cambridge University Press, 1969).

50. On this matter we should remember that Locke's theory fit in very well with the Christian covenantal tradition in which the traditional natural law played a crucial role. It could well be, perhaps probably is, that the founding generation did not understand

Locke's assumptions and guiding principles?[51] These questions, albeit in slightly different form, have been and are at the center of a continuing debate over the character of the American tradition. Yet, for our purposes, we should note one simple fact: those who drafted the Declaration did hold to the belief that natural rights had to be conformable with natural law. Whether they read Locke in this fashion or not is irrelevant for our purposes. At the same time, I repeat, whether Locke is the responsible party or not for separating natural rights from natural law, Murray's analysis is still highly useful for identifying the reasons why this separation has come about in modern times, as well as for appreciating the centrality of that separation for understanding and explaining the character of modern rights claims. Understandably, with the disappearance of natural law, the origins and foundations of natural rights have also been lost, resulting in a seemingly endless proliferation of claims to individual and group rights quite apart from concerns about the common good.

What is more, the notion of unalienable rights, either for individuals or for groups, that grows out of social contract thinking sans natural law, leads us away from the understanding of the relationship between representative institutions and natural rights that, as I noted above, is implicit in the Declaration. Rights, even those deemed unalienable, as we have seen, were considered in the founding period as amenable to legislative regulation, qualification, or modification consonant with natural law. But today, those who assert unalienable rights seek the recognition and realization of these rights on the most secure foundations and in their fullest, most undiluted form, that is, possessing a substance and status conformable with their unalienable character unaffected by natural law. In the American context this comes down to attaching them to the Constitution, the recognized fundamental law, principally through judicial sanction, thereby placing these rights beyond the reach of legislative majorities. This process conforms with the modern versions of social contract theory, namely, that rights inhere to individuals or groups and, as such, are beyond the legitimate reach of government and most certainly legislative or popular majorities.[52]

I conclude simply by noting that a reading of the Declaration of Independence apart from the natural law tradition is not only misleading, since

---

Locke to be saying what many modern theorists, such as Murray, attribute to him. Indeed, the proper interpretation of Locke remains an issue of contention today.

51. Brian Tierney, for example, while sharing Murray's views on natural law and natural rights, views Locke's teachings from a far more sympathetic perspective.

52. The most notable example of this is the Supreme Court's decision in *Roe v. Wade*, 410 U.S. 113 (1973), where the Court employed the "right of privacy" to legalize abortion.

it conveys a false picture of a more complex and sensible American political tradition, but dangerous as well. It fosters the belief that the realization and exercise of rights supersedes the common good and well-being of society. Suffice it to say, no decent and orderly society can long endure when such a belief prevails.

Individual and Group Rights

Self-Government and Claims of Right in Historical Practice

Bruce P. Frohnen

In this essay I relate the rise and fall of corporate rights, particularly within the Anglo-American tradition. My purpose is to show the manner and extent of the linkage between individual and group rights in its historical development in European and especially British public life, and to show the manner of the decline of group rights, especially those of municipalities and business corporations in the United States. Toward the end of this essay I will sketch an overall inference from this inquiry, namely, that as individual and group rights were linked in their development, so too have they been linked in their erosion. More specifically, insistence on seeing rights in purely individualistic terms has resulted not just in the erosion of group rights, but also in the erosion of individual rights—particularly those individual rights aimed at meaningful participation in social, political, and economic life.

Rights can be understood both as claims of right to specific goods and as realms of licit choice, autonomous behavior, or, as emphasized here, self-government. Indeed, the two senses and kinds of rights are connected. Those who would participate meaningfully in self-government are aided substantially by the possession of justiciable rights. For example, if one is blocked from voting, it is useful, to say the least, to have a claim of right that will be heard by an impartial tribunal. And such rights owe much in their character and development to more simple and deep-rooted notions of commutative justice, such as the ability to demand that a party to a contract keep his or her bargain. Unfortunately, too much emphasis on rights in merely this commutative sense undermines rights of self-government or reduces them to mere parts of an inchoate realm of individual choice in which rights of participation are severely endangered. If the numerous groups below the level of (that is, smaller, more local, and more intimate than) the state are denied their subsidiary rights of self-government, their members also lose important rights, as the state concentrates increasing and increasingly unchecked power in itself.

Group Rights and the Medieval Church

In seeking the wellsprings of rights, scholars in recent decades increasingly have looked to the middle ages. Historical studies have made clear that the medieval era was one of remarkable fertility in the development of both concepts and practices related to the rights of the person. This revisionist scholarship has had to contend with an entrenched set of assumptions according to which rights could not have had any meaningful place in the society of the middle ages because these were times of religiously based communalism. Rights, on this view, are the purview of scientifically minded individualists, and so could not have come about before the rise of individualism in the philosophy of the early modern era.[1]

The misconceptions at the root of this vision are threefold: first, that rights are by nature individualistic; second, that the Catholic Church— seen as the dominant force of this era—as an institution was hostile in both thought and practice toward individual rights; and, partly from the second, third, that the middle ages were inherently anti-individualistic. History shows a markedly different picture. Medieval Europe was home to integrated societies in which individual persons and groups were intimately connected, in which the medieval Church served as both a bulwark against secular claims to absolute power and as a source of legal thought and practice directly productive and protective of rights. The Church's thought and practice were rooted in the very integrated vision of person and community central to the era. And this was the context within which rights developed as practical means for the mediation of disputes regarding the governance and self-governance of persons and groups.

The medieval Church took the leading role in forming practices and theories of rights. The Church was able to take such a role because, by the end

1. The relevant literature is reviewed in the introduction to this volume.

of the eleventh century, it had won from secular rulers recognition of its own right to self-government, including important immunities from secular controls. Spurred by the success of its pope in the late eleventh century in solidifying his right to appoint his own bishops, the Church rationalized its internal structures in large measure by systematizing rules and edicts into a coherent canon law—which Harold J. Berman has referred to as "the first modern legal code."[2] The canon law was a comprehensive legal system that set out the rights of the Church as a self-governing corporate entity whose members also had rights, particularly on account of their specific place within the Church hierarchy and its various subgroups.

Canon law rights governed both individual persons and groups and controlled a wide variety of issues, including clerical exemptions from civil duties, taxes, prosecutions, and forced testimony; the ability of ecclesiastical organizations such as parishes, monasteries, and charities to form and disband, accept and reject members, and acquire and alienate property; and the ability of religious conformists to worship, evangelize, maintain religious symbols, participate in the sacraments, and educate their children.[3] Development of these rights both limited the reach of secular governments and came to permeate the laws of other jurisdictions, buttressing other corporate groups and coalescing into more general procedural rights.

Much of this argument has been made before and need not be rehearsed here. Rather, I wish to add to existing theoretical arguments and generalized historical narratives a concrete tracing of the development of legal rights in practice, both within the Church and within the wider societies of the middle and succeeding ages. Central to this retracing, however, is an understanding of corporate groups themselves, especially as such groups existed before the rise of liberal individualism.

A corporate group was a self-governing body of persons joined in pursuit of common ends. Each such group often cooperated and often competed with other groups—many of which incorporated many of the same individual persons. Thus it is only by understanding medieval society in its fundamental order, as a community of communities, with each negoti-

---

2. Harold J. Berman, *Law and Revolution: The Formation of the Western Legal Tradition* (Cambridge: Harvard University Press, 1983), 199.

3. John Witte Jr., "Law, Religion and Human Rights," *Columbia Human Rights Law Review* 28 (1996): 18. See also p. 17: "Many of the common formulations of rights and liberties in vogue today were first forged not by a John Locke or a James Madison, but by twelfth and thirteenth century canonists and theologians."

ating interests, goods, and rights claims with other groups, with the state, and with group members, that we can understand the origin and nature of rights.[4]

As its name suggests, the corporate group incorporated within itself various individual persons. These persons became in important ways constituents of the group, without losing their individual identity and status. The group was greater than the sum of its parts, having its own ends as well as its own history and character, without thereby erasing the ends of those making it up. Legal practice reflected this understanding. For example, current legal doctrine dictates viewing a corporate entity (almost exclusively a business enterprise) as separate from its more or less passive shareholders. In this way the state justifies granting corporations limited liability, thereby allowing shareholders to escape the obligations incurred by their corporation. In earlier eras, by contrast, members of a corporation (be it a town, guild, or other group) shouldered a kind of joint and several liability. Each member of the corporation was liable for its acts, including, for example, citizen liability for the taxes of one's town.[5] By the later fifteenth century, what would now be considered a charter of incorporation still did not bestow limited liability, even while it bestowed on the town the so-called five points of incorporation: the right to have perpetual succession; the right to a common seal; the right to sue and be sued; the right to own property; and the right to issue bylaws—that is, to have its own will, though one for which corporation members were personally responsible.[6]

The corporate group integrated what today would be called public and private means and goals. Corporate groups were not radically individualistic, as economic concerns are viewed today. The corporate group was no mere nexus of contracts.[7] Nor was it a "group person," as for legal historian Otto von Gierke.[8] Rather, the corporate group incorporated individual persons into a group—it caused people to join together for a common end. Moreover, such common ends were seen as producing public goods, not merely private profit. Even the most specifically economic of corporations retained their communitarian character. As late as the seventeenth century,

4. That this understanding of society remains powerful and even necessary is shown by essays in this volume penned by Jonathan Chaplin and Kenneth Grasso.

5. H. Ke Chin Wang, "The Corporate Entity Concept (Or Fiction Theory) in the Year Book Period," *Law Quarterly Review* 59 (1942): 498, 507–8.

6. Susan Reynolds, *An Introduction to the History of English Medieval Towns* (Oxford: Clarendon Press, 1977), 113.

7. See for example Stephen M. Bainbridge, "Competing Concepts of the Corporation (A.K.A. Criteria? Just Say NO)," *Berkeley Business Law Journal* 2 (2005): 77.

8. See Chaplin's excellent discussion in this volume.

after the initial movement toward limited liability had commenced, Berman notes

> the invention of the joint stock company as a means of bringing investors together to engage in a common cause, often of political as well as economic significance. Thus a 1692 act of Parliament granting a corporate charter to a Company of Merchants of London to carry on trade with Greenland recited the great importance of such trade, how it had fallen into the hands of other nations, and the need to regain it by the joint efforts of many persons. Similar recitals of a public purpose marked the corporate charters of other joint-stock companies. These were, to be sure, entrepreneurial activities intended to be profitable to the shareholders. At the same time, the enterprise depended on the close cooperation of many like-minded people, who were motivated partly by a desire to participate with others in a joint venture serving a public cause. . . . Nothing is more symbolic of the "spirit of capitalism" in England in the late seventeenth century than the creation of the joint-stock company called the Bank of England, which was founded by act of Parliament in 1694 principally in order to finance the government's war against France.

The bank was incorporated as "one body politick and corporate."[9]

Thus capitalist business corporations, supposedly the most atomistic of economic structures, were, at least in their beginnings, in significant ways communalist. We have, here, an important corrective to the view that history is the story of the individual's increasing liberation from medieval communal structures, be they political, legal, or economic institutions or the belief structures of religiously rooted traditions. We also have an important insight into the nature of the corporate group for most of its history. It was an integrative community aimed at some common good deemed consistent with the common good of society. Thus corporate groups were neither mere collections of individuals fitting into some category, nor management-run entities allowing passive investment through some form of market.

Though communal, the corporate group was not inchoate. It had a definite structure—that of "an organic union of a head and members."[10] As late as the seventeenth century, the Bank of England was chartered as "The

9. Harold J. Berman, *Law and Revolution II: The Impact of the Protestant Reformations on the Western Legal Tradition* (Cambridge: Harvard University Press, 2006), 26.

10. Brian Tierney, "Origins of Natural Rights Language: Texts and Contexts," in Tierney, *Rights, Laws and Infallibility in Medieval Thought* (London: Variorum, 1977), 171.

Governor and Company" of that bank.[11] To understand the nature and importance of this structure it is best to look to the model of corporate groups, the medieval Catholic Church.

The Church was the central corporate group of the middle ages. It was deemed to have rights to self-government through appointment of its own officers and in other areas—spelled out, for example, in the Magna Carta's opening section, which declared that the English Church "shall be free, and have her whole rights, and her liberties inviolable."[12] All Christians were incorporated into the one Body of Christ—the Church. But the Church had a head—the pope—and "was defined juristically as consisting at least in part of a network of corporate entities." These entities, including dioceses, cathedral chapters, monasteries, and religious orders, were defined as corporations, governed through members' consent and combining a web of individual rights with corporate existence.[13]

In the corporation of the Church, the pope had rights spelled out in the canon law on account of his position as head. These rights included the right of holding the property of the Holy See (though not necessarily in exclusive possession). The pope also had the right to intervene in any contentious local process. But the pope's rights were limited by the rights of others. Specifically, litigants had the right to receive justice from the pope—he could defer their suits, but not simply deny them any process. The pope also was limited by the corporate relationship, including by procedural protections afforded to those below him in the hierarchy. The pope could not intervene where cardinals or bishops were exercising their rights without satisfying strict procedural safeguards. And the pope could not remove a cardinal from office without the consent of the entire assembly.[14]

This last limitation points us toward the rights of the college of cardinals. That group had a corporate right to elect the pope through a set of procedural rules protecting the right of individual cardinals to participate in the vote. The cardinals also had substantial say in the governance of the Church. For example, the pope was required to get the consent of the cardinals for certain actions. In instances requiring consent, failure to procure it could lead to invalidation of the papal act.[15]

---

11. 5 and 6 William and Mary c. 20 (1694), discussed in Berman, *Law and Revolution II*, 342–43.

12. Reprinted in Bruce Frohnen, ed., *The American Republic: Primary Sources* (Indianapolis: Liberty Fund, 2002), 92.

13. Charles Reid, *Rights in Thirteenth-Century Canon Law: A Historical Investigation* (PhD diss., Cornell University, 1995), 6, 310–12.

14. Ibid., 322, 321, 366, 215–16, 356, 377.

15. Ibid., 395, 393–94.

There were numerous other rights accruing to individuals as members of corporate groups within the Church. The members of individual religious corporations possessed a series of identifiable rights. These rights depended, in nature and form, on each person's status within the salient group. For example, the bishop had a right to his *cathedraticum*, a fixed sum to be paid to him by the churches of his diocese.[16] The cathedral canon held some rights in common with the other members of the cathedral chapter, but also held individual, justiciable rights, such as that to his own *prebend*, or claim to receive revenue.[17] Bishops had a right to visit, inquire into, and impose punishment or correction either on monasteries as a whole or on their individual members.[18] And the link between individual and group is made even more clear by the fact that the mayor himself was limited in his rights by those of the group that acted for the borough—the borough council.

Boroughs, Corporations, and Charters in England

Canon law set forth the rights of the medieval Church, along with the rights of persons and subsidiary groups within it. But Church law had an impact throughout society; it was neither insular nor isolated. Like the Church, canon law interacted with persons and groups outside itself, influencing them in a variety of ways. There were many sources of law and judgment during the middle ages: canon law; merchant law; various local, customary laws; and geographical "royal" laws chief among them. Because jurisdictions overlapped, there was conflict and cross-fertilization of procedures and rules of decision. For example, ecclesiastical courts often would hear any case in which a specific sin was alleged. In response, secular rulers actively competed for litigants so as to retain and enhance their own power and influence.[19] This was true, for example, of the English royal or common law, which was rooted in the decisions of particular judges in particular cases and borrowed heavily from canon law precepts.[20]

Canon law, which Berman refers to as "the Constitutional Law of the Church,"[21] helped shape corporate groups within the Church, and found

---

16. Ibid., 165–66.

17. Brian Tierney, "Religion and Rights: A Medieval Perspective," *Journal of Law and Religion* 5 (1987): 171.

18. Reid, *Rights*, 197.

19. See Berman, *Law and Revolution II*, 221–24.

20. See generally William W. Bassett, "Canon Law and the Common Law," *Hastings Law Journal* 29 (1978): 1383.

21. Berman, *Law and Revolution II*, 215.

its analogy in English law and English corporate groups. Here I focus in particular on the English borough. The word *borough* denotes a population center that was rather vaguely defined but had certain characteristics enhancing its importance and its communal character. Boroughs, growing physically and legally from early royal military encampments, enjoyed greater self-government, rights, and freedoms than other localities in medieval England.[22]

By the thirteenth century, the English borough could be likened to a religious order—one of the important corporate groups within the Church. Like an order, a borough would have "a permanent purpose that keeps it together[,] just as a religious house is kept together by the purpose of glorifying God." A freeman of Norwich, for example, had the civil purpose of protecting the franchises and liberties of that borough. Moreover, boroughs developed corporate personality. Their lands and affairs belonged to the group, rather than simply to individuals. In addition, "the administrators for the time being [were] a legally organized body, a body which [perdured] while its members" came and went. And this body transacted "business as a body by means of meetings and votings and resolutions; the motive power [was] not . . . the will of a single man."[23]

England itself was conceived as a corporation with the king as head. The king/head had specific rights, but was limited in those rights by the corporate, law-bound nature of his relationship with his subjects. His rights also were limited by the doctrine of *ultra vires,* according to which actions taken outside customary limits and procedures were invalid.[24] As bishops were not mere creatures of the pope, so secular corporations in the medieval era were not mere creatures of the king. Charters, or "formal documents describing the rights and obligations on each side of a feudal relationship,"[25] were common means by which both kings and lesser lords granted privileges (generally for a price) to burgesses or local borough leaders.[26] Charters from the Crown played an important role in establishing corporations and their laws. During the medieval era, "[g]radually English law came to view charter grants as grants of corporate status."[27]

---

22. Frederick Pollock and Frederic William Maitland, *The History of English Law before the Time of Edward I* (Cambridge: Cambridge University Press, 1968), 634–38.

23. Ibid., 686.

24. Eric Enlow, "The Corporate Conception of the State and the Origins of Limited Constitutional Government," *Washington University Journal of Law and Policy* 6 (2001): 1, 7–8.

25. Joan C. Williams, "The Invention of the Municipal Corporation: A Case Study in Legal Change," *American University Law Review* 34 (1985): 369, 378.

26. Reynolds, *An Introduction,* 135. Burgesses were those wealthy enough to pay borough dues.

27. Williams, "Invention of the Municipal Corporation," 381.

By 1200, boroughs were receiving seals with their charters, which their heads used to commit the whole in conducting business.[28] Charters were not the sole source of borough rights. Medieval corporations could be formed by act of Parliament, prescription, or common law as well.[29] But charters provided a particularly clear and enforceable statement of corporate rights.

The English monarchs' reliance on sales of charters, increasing quickly in the reigns immediately following the conquest of 1066, produced demands for more liberties and for more secure and generalized rights. Such demands eventually culminated in the rebellion that produced the Magna Carta. That document declared the rights of individual barons to be free from unlawful imprisonment and a variety of royal taxes and other actions. It also declared the rights of the Church and of boroughs and the city of London to self-government. The document did not itself create such rights, but rather solidified and furthered an existing tradition or "precedent of municipal privilege."[30] As Frederick Pollock and Frederic William Maitland point out, the Magna Carta was a grant of "certain liberties" by King John to the men of England "as he had granted them to the men of Cornwall and the men of London," that is, as a corporate charter for a borough.[31]

As corporations, boroughs held important rights of self-government. They officially could not pass new legislation unless that right was specifically granted by the king. But even the right to legislate did evolve. Among the earliest local laws was a building code for the city of London, which was justified as an exercise of the city's recognized right to declare and follow local custom.[32] Boroughs also held numerous economic rights rooted in local control. They maintained borough monopolies on various goods, as well as freedom from certain taxes and feudal incidences.[33] These rights spurred development of further corporate groups and rights rooted in the medieval guilds, which were separate from the boroughs and maintained their own courts.[34] Individuals also gained rights from borough membership—including freedom from personal service to the nobility.

Perhaps the most sought-after right was that of a borough to appoint its own officials and thereby control its own internal affairs. Boroughs more

28. Pollock and Maitland, *History of English Law,* 683.
29. Joseph S. Davis, *Essays in the Earlier History of American Corporations* (Cambridge: Harvard University Press, 1917), 2–3.
30. J. C. Holt, *Magna Carta* (Cambridge: Cambridge University Press, 1992), 55.
31. Pollock and Maitland, *History of English Law,* 674.
32. Ibid., 660–61.
33. Holt, *Magna Carta,* 57–59.
34. Pollock and Maitland, *History of English Law,* 674, 664–65, 660–61, 667.

or less achieved a more general right to self-government by obtaining rights to appointment of more or fewer local officials. Grants of the "farm of the borough" made citizens corporately responsible for the annual royal dues, and transferred to them the right to appoint the reeve—the official who accounted to the Crown for payment of those dues.[35] Over the medieval era, boroughs sought with varying success to purchase rights to appoint their own local judges, mayors, bailiffs or tax collectors, and coroners to oversee the bailiffs.[36] With these rights, a majority of the burgesses could act for the whole, with each individual member exercising rights of control through the group.

The most important local official of boroughs was the mayor. Reeves and bailiffs might be appointed by the burgesses, but still had financial and administrative responsibilities to the king. Mayors, on the other hand, were purely urban officials. They both symbolized the borough's unity and served as its head. As the head of the corporate group of the borough, the mayor was the nexus of individual and group rights. Individual burgesses had the right to choose their mayor. The mayor as an individual had the right to exercise the powers of his office. And the borough as a corporate body had the right to act through the mayor, to be free from interference from lords and even from the king in areas protected by the charter and to control the burgesses' common destiny in terms of legal proceedings, economic activity, and everyday, customary relations. Thus, in the borough we see the inherent linkage between the rights of individuals and the rights of groups. The groups' right to self-government was bound up with the rights of the mayoral office—exercised by an individual on behalf of the group—and protected the rights of other individual persons to engage in political and economic self-government and to be free from a number of outside controls.

Boroughs and the Right to Due Process

There are deep connections between corporate rights developed in borough charters and the rights of individuals, including such putatively natural rights as that to due process of law. The Magna Carta gave rights to trial according to "the law of the land"—a phrase that referred to local customary procedures and eventually was redubbed "due process." Local

---

35. Reynolds, *An Introduction,* 102–3.
36. Pollock and Maitland, *History of English Law,* 656–57.

burgesses had the right to appeal to the king their claims that local laws and procedures were unfair.[37] Moreover, the enforceable, legal status of charters brought the king under the law and established norms according to which every person had a right to the enforcement of his or her rights—to a process by which they might enforce rights gained through charter or usage.

The English ability to keep their monarch within the confines of corporate office enabled them to prevent establishment of the personal absolutism of other monarchs, such as France's Louis XIV. As Alexis de Tocqueville observed, French kings took it upon themselves to curtail, sell, resell, and finally abolish towns' charter rights in pursuit of personal power and money.[38] The English king's power in this area was limited in that rights granted in perpetuity could be revoked only for cause or lack of exercise.[39] The key device for establishing this principle was the common-law writ of *quo warranto*.

Quo warranto was used to inquire into the authority by which a public office was held or a franchise claimed. It had been used early on by the king as a tool of arbitrary revocation. However, it soon became an instrument of due process. Its development in important ways was the development of the rights of both groups and individual persons. By establishing due process as a norm in charter proceedings, *quo warranto* reinforced the developing right to proceedings according to usage or the law of the land.

Perhaps the most significant development of *quo warranto* took place during the reign of Edward I (1272–1307). Edward carried out a general inquiry into local franchises and governmental conduct. He ordered claimants to appear before itinerant judges riding in circuit "and if it was found that they actually held any franchise, a writ of *Quo Warranto* would be served on them, requiring them to show by what warrant they claimed to have the liberty of wreck, or gallows, or view of frankpledge, or return of writs, or whatever it might be."[40] If the party answered the writ successfully the franchise was maintained. If not, the putative franchise was confiscated by the Crown.

---

37. Ibid., 661.

38. Alexis de Tocqueville, *The Old Regime and the French Revolution* (Garden City, NY: Doubleday Anchor, 1955), 42. This is not to say that all grants of charter rights in England were permanent; many required repeated confirmation, sometimes involving difficult bargaining with the king.

39. Pollock and Maitland, *History of English Law*, 667–68. Of course, kings frequently sought to act unilaterally on this, as in most areas.

40. Helen M. Cam, *Liberties and Communities in Medieval England* (New York: Barnes and Noble, 1963), 173.

Edward rarely abolished anyone's franchise. The usual result of an adverse ruling for a claim in *quo warranto* was the imposition of a substantial fine, followed by the granting of a royal charter. Besides revenue, then, what did Edward seek? Not franchises' revocation, but rather their precise definition, along with recognition of the king's power to revoke them for misuse: "If the abbot of St. Albans had the right to appoint his own coroner for the liberty of St. Albans, he took on himself the responsibility for seeing that the coroner's rolls were duly kept, and that the coroner was available when required; when these conditions were not fulfilled the king took back the privilege and appointed a coroner himself."[41]

Edward's aggressive program was aimed at increasing royal control over local administration. But, whether intentionally or not, it also helped establish due process rights in the guarantee of "each man's own liberty, warranted by a charter, upheld in the courts." This due process went so far as to show that the king, as a person, was not above the law. For example, when one Earl Warenne was called to defend his Stamford charter in Lincolnshire, he claimed that Edward himself had granted it. Edward's attorneys asserted the defense that, prior to becoming king, Edward had usurped the liberties in question and, therefore, had had no power to grant them.[42] Thus Edward won his case—Stamford lost its preexisting charter. But the king in effect admitted that he was limited in his power by preexisting rules, procedures, and substantive law. Further, the charters themselves, and thus the king's powers, by the sixteenth century at the latest were deemed incapable of either changing the common law or altering the rights and duties of private persons as fixed by that law.[43]

Charters, then, were not seen as aberrations from common law, trumping its general provisions only in specific, narrowly defined cases. Rather, charters reinforced and expanded rights and procedures within the common law. They were particularly powerful and valued instruments. For example, when James II misused the *quo warranto* proceeding as a means to gain control over the boroughs and pack Parliament, resistance was so fierce that he restored the confiscated charters—before eventually fleeing during the Glorious Revolution of 1688.[44] But municipal rights were not

41. Pollock and Maitland, *History of English Law,* 180, 207. Pollock and Maitland continue: "All through the reign the juries of the countryside were being invited to tell the king's justices in eyre what they knew of persons who had had liberties granted to them and had used them otherwise than the grant prescribed."

42. Ibid., 183, 176.

43. W. S. Holdsworth, "English Corporation Law in the Sixteenth and Seventeenth Centuries," *Yale Law Journal* 31 (1922): 382, 392.

44. James II's conduct had the unfortunate effect of bringing *quo warranto* proceedings into ill repute.

limited to the specific provisions of charters. Indeed, during the earlier parts of the medieval era, towns without charters were treated little differently from those with them.[45] Thus, municipal rights even outside boroughs were real and respected as part of the "law of the land" insisted upon in the Magna Carta. But charters served a crucial role in fixing the bounds of rights and processes. Those who exercised their rights in ways inconsistent with the terms of grant or usage could have those rights abolished—but not without proper definition and inquiry. It is significant, here, that the finders of fact were countryside juries working with itinerant justices and not members of the king's household. The result was increasingly objective enforcement of rights, along with their limits.[46]

Boroughs and ecclesiastical organizations were not the only corporate right-holders in medieval England. For example, the guilds formed in part out of the boroughs asserted rights to self-government that would grow through the early modern era. Guilds were identified closely with their boroughs. Charters might "enforce guild regulations and monopolies . . . and could give the town a trading monopoly in its county." Guilds enjoyed substantial rights of the borough, including freedom from toll, because they often were seen as themselves representing their local municipal corporations.[47]

Economically based corporate groups were slow to develop outside the context of (geographically defined) guilds and boroughs. The first large business corporations in England were the quasi-governmental foreign-trading companies. These corporations were granted the exclusive right to explore, colonize, and trade in particular geographic areas.[48] Trading companies resembled boroughs in that they mixed political, social, and economic concerns. But trading companies' activities and spheres (including geographical spheres) of self-government were significantly larger than those of boroughs.

Trading companies grew around the time of, and perhaps reinforced, growing suspicion of corporate groups among those at the center of English power. By the sixteenth century, it was assumed that a corporation could be created only with the sanction of the state, though such was not openly stated until 1682, in a suit against the London charter. Along with development of this doctrine of state sanction came another important

45. Wang, "Corporate Entity Concept," 499.

46. Cam, *Liberties and Communities*, 207.

47. Reynolds, *An Introduction*, 102.

48. James D. Cox and Thomas Lee Hazen, *Corporations* (New York: Aspen Publishers, 2002), chap. 2, sec. 2.2.

doctrine: *ultra vires*. According to the *ultra vires* doctrine, a corporation could act licitly only when and to the extent that its actions were taken in furtherance of the purpose for which it was created—a purpose eventually required to be stated in its charter. This doctrine was applied to boroughs as well as to business corporations. It was justified as a means by which the sovereign could limit the assumed rights of corporations. Assumed rights were those that corporate groups did not enjoy on account of their charter, but which were deemed necessary for carrying out their purpose.

Outside controls over corporate groups also increased during this period. The role of the visitor (a kind of auditor) was regularized in ecclesiastical corporations and in corporations, such as charitable hospitals, formed to carry out the will of a founding grantor. Such measures merely added to parliamentary actions beginning in the fifteenth century, which gave justices of the peace oversight of ordinances instituted by guilds and similar bodies such as fraternal organizations.[49] Thus by the early modern era, the English state was increasing its control over corporate groups, even as it began exporting the law and practice of such groups overseas.

Municipal Rights in America

Colonists brought with them to America the law of corporations developed in England. And they applied it with vigor to local circumstances. For example, Virginia and Massachusetts—both chartered, incorporated colonies—were very different in important ways. But both began and for decades were treated as corporations, possessing wide latitude for self-government. The colonies took full advantage of this latitude, and of their isolated state, in exercising local autonomy, governing themselves, and making their own laws.[50] In addition, prior to independence the corporate charters of cities such as New York City were regarded as "inviolate grants of privilege and property not subject to the whim of legislative or royal authority."[51] These charters had been granted by the Crown; the vast major-

49. Holdsworth, "English Corporation Law," 383, 386, 394–97.
50. Donald S. Lutz, "Religious Dimensions in the Development of American Constitutionalism," *Emory Law Journal* 39 (1990): 21, 25, 23. Lutz points out that, during the early colonial period, settlers were "usually under the nominal control of a board of directors in London[;] the grant of local control, the impossibility of running any colony from London given the distance involved, and the preoccupation in England with the English Civil War gave the settlers considerable latitude in running their own affairs." Of course, the laws were required to be not inconsistent with the laws of England.
51. Jon C. Teaford, "The Birth of a Public Corporation," *Michigan Law Review* 83 (1985): 690.

ity of American municipalities lacked charters. This did not, however, keep unchartered municipalities from acting and being treated as important corporate groups, with rights analogous to those of English boroughs.

Soon after colonization began, so did broad grants of power from colonial governments to their municipalities. The first "Town Act" was passed in 1636, granting powers far broader than those granted to lesser municipalities in England. These acts "were broad, open-ended mandates for the town meeting to manage local business." Local popular sovereignty was so widespread and valued in colonial America that townspeople resisted chartered incorporation for fear they would thereby lose important rights.[52]

In New England the town meeting enabled citizens to vote directly on matters of economics, taxation, health, education, and morality. Early constitutional documents defined the powers of local elected officials—heads of local corporate groups—as essentially executive functions designed to carry out the will of the town meeting.[53] Before independence, New England towns already had established a pattern of government in which local, self-governing municipalities sent delegates to the colonial legislature to represent them. Rather than the towns' deriving their legitimacy from grants by the colony, the colonial government derived its legitimacy from local assemblies.[54]

But not all Americans were fond of townships and their rights, especially after revolution had separated America from England. For example, James Madison in Federalist No. 10 argued that local majority rule can lead to oppression. Others during this period expressed mistrust for "municipal charters as perpetuating special privileges in derogation of the recently established republican form of government."[55] Nonetheless, the Massachusetts Constitution of 1780 not only recognized towns' claims to self-government, but likened "Massachusetts itself to the smaller corporations within it."[56]

Madison's view won out, in the long run, because municipal rights came to be seen in individualistic terms. Government itself came to be seen as "nothing more than 'a voluntary association of individuals: . . . a social compact, by which the whole people covenants with each citizen, and each

52. Williams, "Invention of the Municipal Corporation," 412, 413.

53. Dorchester Agreement 1633, reprinted in Frohnen, *American Republic*, 31.

54. Joseph P. Viteritti, "Municipal Home Rule and the Conditions of Justifiable Secession," *Fordham Urban Law Journal* 23 (1995): 1, 7–9.

55. Janice C. Griffith, "Local Government Contracts: Escaping from the Governmental/Proprietary Maze," *Iowa Law Review* 75 (1990): 277, 300.

56. Liam Seamus O'Melinn, "The Sanctity of Association: The Corporation and Individualism in American Law," *San Diego Law Review* 37 (2000): 126.

citizen with the whole people, that all shall be governed by certain laws for the common good.'"[57] Thus both the corporation and the state increasingly came to be seen as mere aggregations of individuals. Within a few decades of independence, the *self* in *self-government* increasingly came to mean the individual, to the exclusion of the township or other corporate group.

Of particular importance to the undoing of the nexus between individual and group rights was a distinction central to modern liberal ideology: that between public and private spheres of action. American municipalities lost their rights in large measure because judges and legislators during the early republican period could not or would not understand and accept their mixing of economic, social, and political functions. Early on, there was a demand that municipal corporations be defined as either public or private. In the end, the public classification won out, and municipalities were subordinated utterly to the states. The courts simply rejected the organic, communalist nature of corporate groups in favor of functional distinctions with little basis in law or historical practice.

Soon after independence, American courts began distinguishing between "private" corporations, set up for some self-interested end, and "municipal" or "quasi" corporations, which served the public. During this same era, courts began defining municipal rights according to statutory standards rather than local usage and common-law procedures.[58] A key turning point for American local self-government was reached in 1819 with the Supreme Court's decision in the case of *Trustees of Dartmouth v. Woodward*.[59] It was in this case that the Court established the legal distinction between municipal corporations and corporations set up for business or charitable purposes. In holding that the New Hampshire legislature could not alter Dartmouth College's charter, the Court emphasized its view that that charter was in essence a private contract. It went so far as to define the charter's specific terms as a vested property right of the original grantor (the university's founder). Thus "private" corporations were to be protected as contracts among the parties and enforced as such. "Public" charters, on the other hand, would have no protections. According to the Court, the state legislature had the right to alter "public" corporations such as municipalities because such corporations are mere instruments of government created and properly ruled by the state.

States applied the Court's logic differently, with New England states leading the way in revoking municipal rights. Some municipal rights took

---

57. Ibid.
58. Williams, "Invention of the Municipal Corporation," 421–22.
59. *Trustees of Dartmouth v. Woodward*, 17 U.S. (4 Wheat.) 518 (1819).

longer to undermine than others—courts long respected rights rooted in municipal-service corporations. But erosion was steady and widespread. In 1857 the New York state legislature asserted its utter dominance over municipal governance, proclaiming its freedom to intervene at will.[60] The courts affirmed this power in *People ex rel. Wood v. Draper.*[61] The Supreme Court in that case upheld the state legislature's action abolishing the local police departments of New York City and Brooklyn and replacing them with a state-controlled Metropolitan Police District. According to the Court, the state had the right to do this, even in the face of a provision of the state constitution authorizing local governments to elect and appoint their own officers. Why? Because the state legislature possesses "the whole law-making power of the state."[62] According to the Court, municipalities have, and can be given, no *right* to control their own administration; they have only such control as the state chooses, at any time, to give them.

Today, then, municipalities stand to the states as boroughs stood to the English monarch prior to formalization of *quo warranto* proceedings. Charters, like customary usages, provide no substantive rights either to the municipality as a corporate group or to the local citizens as members of that group. Open to alteration or revocation at will, without cause or due process, the charters are nothing more than statements of current policy. This situation resulted from a decades-long campaign to strip municipalities and their citizens of rights of self-government. Mayors, town councils, and other local leaders lost the right to exercise control over local administration and even to set up and control their own police forces—rights that even heavy-handed kings during the medieval era had ceded to the boroughs. And the citizenry, from having the right to control its own local affairs in a wide range of areas including economic regulations, health, safety, and morality, lost direct control in the town meeting and even the right to meaningful voting rights in the locality as cities increasingly became mere administrative units doing the bidding of the state. As municipalities lost rights necessary for control of their own destinies, so did their citizens.

Gerald E. Frug notes the extent of municipal decline: "It is not simply that cities have become totally subject to state control—although that itself demonstrates their powerlessness—but also that cities have lost the elements of association and economic strength that had formerly enabled

---

60. Hendrik Hartog, *Public Property and Private Power: The Corporation of the City of New York in American Law, 1730–1870* (Chapel Hill: University of North Carolina Press, 1983), 237.

61. *People ex rel. Wood v. Draper,* 15 N.Y. 532 (1857).

62. Viteritti, "Municipal Home Rule," 13.

them to play an important part in the development of Western society."[63] And with that loss of communitarian solidarity and economic power has come the loss of important rights to local control over issues central to citizens' lives, and also the self-expression and group expression intrinsic to the practice of self-government.

Rights of the American Business Corporation

On first blush one might see the public/private distinction as increasing the rights of business corporations. It established the sanctity of "private" corporation charters and agreements as contractual property rights. It brought increased protections for shareholders' investments. And corporations themselves acquired certain new rights. For example, more than a century ago courts in the United States began according corporations a number of constitutional rights previously reserved for individual persons, including rights against unreasonable search and seizure.[64] But the result has not, in fact, been a substantive increase in either the rights of groups or the rights of persons. The business corporation has become less a person than a machine for the generation of income. Business corporations today are defined as structures owning property, acting and in particular having legal existence and liability separate from that of their shareholders.[65] Though its roots lie in corporate groups through which members exercised the right to control important aspects of their lives in common, the business corporation today has reduced shareholders to mere passive investors, as it has reduced managers to mere income maximizers.

Real self-government involves moral decisions beyond technical concerns related to profit maximization. Self-government requires that one make decisions regarding substantive ends, about the kind of life one wishes to pursue with one's fellows, about the kind of person one wishes to be. But the business corporation no longer is considered to aim at such ends. It no longer has the right to be a full moral actor. Corporate shareholders, in effect, no longer are the body of a corporate group with a common good rooted in a substantive purpose, be it settling new territory, operating a charity hospital, or manufacturing potholders. Thus

63. Gerald E. Frug, "The City as a Legal Concept," *Harvard Law Review* 93 (1980): 1119–20.
64. Morton J. Horwitz, "Santa Clara Revisited: The Development of Corporate Theory," *West Virginia Law Review* 88 (1985): 173, 183.
65. Cox and Hazen, *Corporations*, chap. 2, sec. 7.1.

shareholders no longer have the right to pursue moral conduct through their participation in the corporation.

The older understanding of the business corporation as a combination of head and members, incorporating without standing utterly apart from them, was evidenced by corporate names like *The Governor and Company of the Bank of England.* And these corporations had substantive purposes. Trading companies, for example, were to conduct business and organize common life in particular geographic areas. Trading companies' pursuit of their goals afforded purposive self-government for themselves and for the groups involved in trade and settlement. A business corporation may be seen as a corporate group formed with the purpose of securing pecuniary gain for its members. But historically this could be accomplished only through a particular course of action or production of a particular kind of good. Much the same might have been said of a merchants' guild during the medieval era. The substantive purpose, providing the criteria by which the corporation would be judged, was not mere profit, but internal flourishing through self-governing conduct with the goal of achieving excellence in a given craft, trade in a certain region, and so on. The business corporation, despite its many differing ends, was not distinguished early on from municipal, ecclesiastical, or charitable corporations. Indeed, at the end of the eighteenth century, there still was not a well-defined formal classification for business corporations.[66] The reason was simple: differing corporate groups were not all that different.

Like municipalities, business corporations in America grew in large measure out of the trading companies responsible for colonization. Also like municipal corporations, early business corporations combined economic with more public ends. Business corporations began to be formed during the late eighteenth century in England, but generally only to accomplish acts of significant public utility such as railroad and canal construction (deemed necessary for industrialization). Ordinary commercial enterprises were generally organized as unincorporated joint-stock companies, which lacked corporate privileges.[67] Within the colonies, almost all corporations were established for religious and/or charitable, rather than business, purposes. This is not to say that business corporations did not exist, only that the vast majority were local public-service corporations formed, for example, for the purpose of building and running turnpikes, bridges, wharves, or water supplies.[68]

66. Davis, *Essays,* 3.
67. Cox and Hazen, *Corporations,* chap. 2, sec. 2.2.
68. James J. Fishman, "The Development of Nonprofit Corporation Law and an Agenda for Reform," *Emory Law Journal* 34 (1985): 622–23.

The mixed public/private character of business corporations continued after independence. American business corporations commonly focused on providing financial or municipal services. Banks were the most important business corporations during the period immediately following independence, but they soon saturated their markets, reducing profits and, with them, pressure for additional charters.[69] Municipal-service corporations, on the other hand, continued to expand. These corporations provided public improvements without raising taxes. Thus, state governments often sought to encourage their formation by investing in them or guaranteeing corporate-debt instruments, thereby mixing public with private capital.[70]

In addition to supporting their capitalization, states aided business corporations by bestowing monopoly trade status and granting specific tax exemptions, the power of eminent domain, and/or exemptions from military service for corporate employees, and in exchange, the state often received discounted corporate stock or hefty tax payments.[71] Despite substantial opposition to the spread of these specially privileged groups, between 1789 and 1801 more than 270 charters were granted for publicly supported business corporations.[72]

States' support for business corporations created political and economic conflict during the nineteenth century. Moreover, the mixing of public with private functions had changed radically from its medieval origins. Corporate groups during the medieval era had autonomy and purpose of their own—London's rights were linked to its natural end of flourishing as a city. Its guilds aimed at the flourishing of trades, crafts, and so on as part of a flourishing London—and a flourishing England. Nineteenth-century public concerns, on the other hand, were linked to the use of business corporations for particular economic ends. People treated corporations as tools for achieving industrialization rather than as independent sources of legitimate, autonomous common action. And any chance that the municipality-based guilds of the medieval era might become the model for business corporations was eliminated by hostile statutory actions against guild associations during the eighteenth century. Guilds were held to be illegal restraints of trade and essentially stamped out.[73]

---

69. Davis, *Essays*, 295.

70. George F. Carpinello, "State Protective Legislation and Nonresident Corporations: The Privileges and Immunities Clause as a Treaty of Nondiscrimination," *Iowa Law Review* 73 (1988): 324.

71. Ibid.

72. Davis, *Essays*, 8.

73. Charles E. Rice, *Freedom of Association* (New York: New York University Press, 1962), 22.

By the beginning of the twentieth century, states generally refrained from taking any direct financial interest in business corporations.[74] Over the course of the nineteenth century, courts also began to deny any automatic monopoly status to business corporations and to limit the liability of shareholders to the amount of their investment. This latter move officially was aimed at protecting investors from fraud at a time when markets for stocks were becoming increasingly anonymous and prone to speculation and misrepresentation. It succeeded in frustrating the once-common corporate practice of assessing shareholders to make up capital deficiencies—to pay off debt and avoid bankruptcy.[75]

Changing modes of incorporation also reflected and encouraged dissipation of any understanding of business corporations as real corporate groups with common goods tied to the general common good of society. After some initial grants from the English Crown, the vast majority of colonial corporations were formed by grants from colonial proprietors, governors, or assemblies.[76] Incorporation by special statute followed. In 1811 New York began allowing businesses to incorporate by compliance with a general statute, rendering the process much easier in the manufacturing sector in particular. Beginning in 1835 and again in 1888, states raced to increase the number and liberality of general incorporation statutes. Then in 1896 New Jersey enacted what may be regarded as the first permissive modern incorporation act. The New Jersey statute conferred broad powers on corporations, empowered promoters of corporations to set up almost any kind of corporate structure they desired, granted broad powers to corporate directors and managers, and provided great protection against liability for corporate directors and managers. Corporations also began legally holding stock in other corporations.[77]

The era of corporate trusts had begun. And trusts separated corporations from their members, making shareholders owners of something that owned something in its turn. Shareholders were becoming ever more distant from actual participation in the group they formerly would have joined, and whose purpose would have become their own. This limited view of the role of shareholders spawned, as it was furthered by, changes in the means by which corporations might change their purpose and nature. Earlier courts had imposed a requirement of shareholder unanim-

---

74. Carpinello, "State Protective Legislation," 397–98.
75. Cox and Hazen, *Corporations*, chap. 2, sec. 2.3.
76. Davis, *Essays*, 3, 10. This was despite the fact that there was no provision for such methods at common law.
77. Cox and Hazen, *Corporations*, chap. 2, sec. 2.2.

ity for fundamental changes to the corporation. By the 1890s states were passing legislation providing for majority rule in such instances.[78] Also by the end of the nineteenth century, power was centralized in management through limitations on shareholder voting rights, in particular the provision of exclusive statutory powers in managers and the replacement of weighted voting with one share, one vote.[79]

Corporate management for all intents and purposes had become the corporation. It now was a legal entity almost entirely separate from the shareholders. The corporation itself owned property, under the control of its management, leaving shareholders with only a "property interest" in the profits and the distribution of assets upon liquidation. The corporation had the right to sue its own officers over issues of control and financial mismanagement. Shareholders could defend their rights directly only through a class-action lawsuit. And such a lawsuit would be difficult to win, certainly on any grounds other than insufficient profitability. Lawrence M. Friedman observes that, in judging management conduct in such lawsuits, courts "looked to the concept of fiduciary obligation. The officers and directors were trustees for the corporation. This meant that officers could not engage in self-dealing; they could not buy from or sell to the company; they were strictly accountable for any profits they made in transactions with the company."[80] That is, only self-dealing and gross negligence could bring personal liability for the directors. Otherwise, management's "business judgment" would rule.

By the end of the nineteenth century it was clear that management, and not the shareholders, held the decision-making power in large corporations. In 1919 one commentator noted, "It cannot be too strongly emphasized that stockholders today are primarily investors and not proprietors."[81] Thus corporations no longer provided a means by which shareholders/members could become a cohesive moral group with common ends—and no means by which they could control management, other than through the demand that management produce profits. By the beginning of the twenty-first century, scandals would proliferate as more and more managers treated "their" corporations as private bank accounts,

---

78. Ibid. Many of these statutes also enhanced the ability of directors to initiate actions making fundamental changes to the corporation.

79. Lynne L. Dallas, "The Control and Conflict of Interest Voting Systems," *North Carolina Law Review* 71 (1992): 6.

80. Lawrence M. Friedman, *A History of American Law* (New York: Touchstone, 1985), 449–50, 452.

81. Horwitz, "Santa Clara Revisited," 206–7.

maintained in solvency and unrestricted in conduct so long as stock values were (increasingly fraudulently) pumped up.

As to the corporation's charter, it now is a mere off-the-shelf form, a formality with only technical importance. It no longer plays any substantial role in defining the corporation's nature and purpose. Indeed, business corporations no longer are allowed to mix public with private ends. They no longer include even substantive business purposes in their charters—no limits on business conduct that could allow for the development of moral interaction within a specific sector of a particular industry. Shareholders of given business corporations rarely form a cohesive group with a particular moral vision. There no longer exists a meaningful sphere of self-government within which corporation members may control their common actions and pursue goods in common within the corporate form in the realm of economic activity.

Courts today regard the corporate charter as "a contract between the corporation and the individuals who become shareholders or members of the corporation."[82] The charter also can be viewed as a contract between the organizers and the state. The duties and rights flowing from the articles of incorporation and the state incorporation laws can be viewed as forming a "nexus of contracts" that is all there is to the corporation. This analysis concludes that firms, with their hierarchical decision-making structures, exist only to limit transaction costs associated with negotiating and enforcing contracts in the market. On this view, the corporation exists purely as a mechanism for increasing the economic efficiency of transactions.

Daniel J. H. Greenwood notes that corporate managers today commonly are held to be trustees for fictional shareholders whose sole desire is the maximization of profits. Such a view causes corporations to act in ways that this fictional shareholder would desire, but not necessarily in a manner any actual, living shareholder would approve.[83] The rights of actual shareholders—of actual persons—to join together and participate meaningfully in the formulation of substantive goals and in the self-governed pursuit of those goals has become the stuff of fiction.

Conclusion

It would be easy to dismiss the historical record presented here as an ideological attack on the natural development of increasingly individual-

---

82. Cox and Hazen, *Corporations,* chap. 2, sec. 3.11.
83. Daniel J. H. Greenwood, "Fictional Shareholders: For Whom Are Corporate Managers Trustees, Revisited," *Southern California Law Review* 69 (1996): 1022–29.

istic principles of economic and public conduct. As our society has moved from one rooted in status to one structured by individual-to-individual contracts, one might argue, it is only natural that the communal groups that once combined to order transactions and maintain public peace would fade away. Indeed, far better for the individual, it might be argued, to owe nothing to such intermediate groups, with their extreme valuation of custom and precedent, as we pursue our own self-interest in free, national markets and in a nation free from local hierarchies.

One can, of course, choose to value the current nexus of individual, market, and state above the variety and diversity of semiautonomous groups that once made up society. But one should not merely assume—or assert—that such a society does not have its real costs in terms of both group and individual rights. In seeking to grant individuals greater freedom from institutions that limit autonomous, individual choice, our courts and legislatures have denied citizens rights to meaningful participation in a plethora of associations that once made up much of their lives. Courts in particular increasingly forbid people from pursuing a host of goals deemed inconsistent with a system of national markets and uniform pursuit of economic efficiency.

Mandates from the state and federal governments have severely reduced the level of self-government available in our municipalities. The bulk of local government today consists of overseeing administration of policies set at a higher political level. At least as important, local citizens have come to accept their powerlessness, and so spend their time on merely rhetorical gestures (declaring "nuclear-free zones," for example), engage in the petty corruption of negotiations over development rights (which municipalities can tinker with, but not meaningfully shape or prevent), or withdraw from the public square altogether.

Even those business managers and shareholders who might wish to operate morally in the economic sphere, aiming at goods beyond profit maximization, face a series of legal obstacles. Shareholder rights are defined in terms of profit maximization. The only effective limits on management conduct stem from the demand for profit maximization. And, as a result, the assumptions of the vast majority of actors have focused on profit maximization. Those who do not want trouble—to be fired or even sued—had best get with the program of self-interested economic efficiency.[84]

84. This is not to say that the law actually requires corporate management to act in an unethical fashion, or even to ignore moral goods. See for example Leo L. Clarke, Bruce P. Frohnen, and Edward C. Lyons, "The Practical Soul of Business Ethics: The Corporate Manager's Dilemma and the Social Teaching of the Catholic Church," *Seattle University Law Review* 29 (2005).

The result is a loss of individual as well as group rights. It has become extremely difficult for the individual person to influence the institutions in which he or she makes a livelihood, in which he or she works and lives. Not only can one not fight city hall, but even influencing it increasingly requires first influencing the statehouse, the courthouse, or even the White House. And influencing corporate headquarters? Well, it is no wonder that Americans increasingly look to methods of mass publicity and litigation where once their membership in the body of a corporate group afforded them the right to be heard.

We have lost important expressive rights because the groups in which we once exercised those rights have been stripped of their public role by the nation-state. This is no small loss. But it is not the only loss we have suffered. Society has been stripped of the means to ground individuals and their rights in institutions and practices harmonizing diverse interests while protecting persons from political oppression.[85] Neither townships nor business corporations any longer are capable of countering and limiting governmental power. Business corporations may be seen as influencing the central government, but one thing they do not do is limit the nation-state's power to control the lives of people in their constitutive groups. As Bertrand de Jouvenel noted, the total state, having co-opted or eliminated all corporate makeweights limiting its power, has become the sole focus of concern for society's atomistic individuals, who must expend their efforts on influencing that state in order to exert any modicum of control over their own lives.[86] Where once society was composed of a multitude of diverse groups in which people sought to act with one another so as to pursue a variety of common goals, today the model is one of an overarching state protecting the rights of individuals from other individuals, from any group that might attempt to take actions they find offensive, and from the state itself.

But who guards the individual rights so valued in this political society? It is the state that stands alone as both guardian and guarded. A multitude of authorities, aiming at differing ends and engaging in a mixture of political, economic, and purely social acts, once allowed space for each person

---

85. Robert A. Nisbet, "Uneasy Cousins," in *Freedom and Virtue: The Conservative/Libertarian Debate*, ed. George W. Carey (Wilmington, DE: ISI Books, 1998), 50: "It is not liberty but chaos and license which . . . come to dominate when moral and social authorities—those of family, neighborhood, local community, job, and religion have lost their appeal to human beings."

86. Bertrand de Jouvenel, *On Power: Its Nature and the History of Its Growth*, trans. J. F. Huntington (Indianapolis: Liberty Fund, 1993), 395.

to carve out his or her own sphere of licit autonomous action while also pursuing substantive goods in common with his or her fellows. Today, metastructures and the elites who control them, whether in government, business, or the so-called nonprofit sector, vie for control of political machinery to form and protect administrative rules and structures of law serving their own interests.

Before lauding too vociferously the accomplishments of the unitary nation-state and its rights regime, we would do well to consider the rights it has destroyed through its hostility to corporate groups. It is all well and good to point to the undoubted injustices of the past. But one ought not to ignore the dangers of the current state, along with the concomitant loss of variety, social engagement, and moral choice through meaningful rights of association. Whatever the moral enormities of past or present, it would seem more rational to put one's faith in a variety of balancing groups, many of which we can exit if we so desire, than to look to the nation-state as the sole guarantor of our atomistic sphere of voluntary action. Better to find liberty in the space and interplay among a diversity of groups than in the (in principle temporary) absence of governmental rules.[87] Better to live in constitutive communities that can protect and guide than in a chaos of hyperindividualism punctuated by occasional and often arbitrary government action. Better to reinvigorate the group than to continue feeding the Minotaur.

87. As to the danger of intolerant groups' quashing individual autonomy, Kathryn Abrams has pointed out that "[t]he plurality of local communities and the possibility of exit diminish both the likelihood and the impact of coercive politics." Because local polities "control questions of citizenship and inclusion over only a limited domain," citizens who find any particular local polity oppressive, or even uncongenial, have a real opportunity to exit which, while often involving hardship, nonetheless is more real and effective than that provided by larger political units such as the nation-state. Kathryn Abrams, "Law's Republicanism," *Yale Law Journal* 97 (1988): 1591, 1605, 1606.

The Ontology of Rights

Kenneth L. Schmitz

Among the many aspects of the history and concept of rights—natural and positive, moral and legal, universal and specific, individual and institutional—it should be possible to reflect upon the general conception of rights and to indicate the grounds in reality for the notion itself. For the prudent application of any understanding of rights, much more is needed than the concept, but it should serve as a compass. And as in flight more than a compass is needed to bring an airplane safely into port, in law more than a general concept is needed in the application of rights, including correct information regarding a situation, openness to alternative possible solutions, selection of the most promising among them, decision to act on the one selected, and courage and skill to carry it through to its realization: in short, knowledge, judgment, and performance. Although such a general reflection does not directly determine the application of the concept in actual situations, it is an essential requirement of wise decisions and prudent action, and it should disclose both a basis and a centering focus for such application.

I am mindful that the present reflection is too general and metaphysical to address the host of special theoretical and practical issues that bear their own characteristics, both in the particular and in the concrete.[1]

---

1. Although often confused, the particular and the concrete differ in their make-up and in their role. The particular is subordinate to the general or universal, as particular case is to general law, whereas the concrete embodies both the particular and the

Moreover, I do not have the practical experience in either law or politics to fruitfully address particular issues. But as the compass in flight, so too the general concept in the service of the concrete has its indispensable role to play. For the effort to uncover the roots of the concept of making a claim by right serves to focus more particular discussions. It thereby avoids a consideration of rights simply in terms of collective power or arbitrary choice, which construes rights as either exclusively private will or exclusively social construction.[2]

If we seek to ground our expectations and understandings in the reality of our situations, it seems that rights themselves must find their original and ultimate ground in human life, and even more deeply in the texture of being itself. Not all rights are natural rights, of course, and even natural rights have secondary social and cultural components that differ from one group to another. This diversity does not make such rights any less real, however, nor does it permit us to misconstrue them as merely relative constructions not grounded in the very roots of being itself.

False Alternatives

To begin such a general reflection, however, some initial distinctions and corrections are called for, if we are to avoid a cul-de-sac in the face of conflicting views as to the nature of rights. For it is possible to conceive rights simply after the model of property possession: "I have my rights!" If we

---

universal, and contains a richness that the more selective particular-in-the-service-of-the-universal does not contain. Prudence is the virtue par excellence in the order of the concrete, in that it frees judgment from a merely automatic or mechanical application of the particular to the general. Compare St. Thomas Aquinas, *Summa theologiae,* 1–2, q. 94, a. 5c: "The natural law is altogether unchangeable in its first principles. But in its secondary principles, which . . . are certain detailed proximate conclusions, drawn from the first principles, not that [*quin*] the natural law is changed so that what it prescribes be not right in most cases. But it may be changed in some particular cases of rare occurrence, through some special causes hindering the observance of such precepts." I have altered the received translation of *quin* so as to bring out the extreme caution with which Thomas viewed these exceptions.

2. The denial to rights of a foundation in reality (*fundamentum in re*) is part of the widespread inheritance of positivism in law and other fields. In like manner, some anthropologists have recently construed the relation of "paternity" as a purely social construction, denying its foundation *in re.* No doubt, the fuller concept and reality of paternity includes variable cultural and social aspects, but it includes biological and genetic factors as well, and it is surely arbitrary to ignore or dismiss them. While rights claims belong to the social, political, and ethical domain, they, too, have a deeper basis *in re.*

understand a right exclusively in terms of individual possession, however, we are apt to inflate the claim and diminish the obligation, all but conferring an unlimited status upon it.[3] Oddly enough, the gentle Spinoza seems to endorse such a view of rights, inasmuch as he defines a right as the capacity to enforce one's will as far as one's power permits: for the wise man wisely, for the foolish man foolishly.[4] On the other hand, if, in direct opposition, we understand rights to be in the keeping of society and conferred by it alone, we convert rights into obligations and even into commands.

The upshot of these two extreme misconceptions is to find ourselves wavering between anarchy and despotism, between an arbitrary individualism and an oppressive collectivism. Although these extremes are seldom voiced in such bald terms, they are not absent in modified form from public discussions, prompted by the fear of tyranny, on the one hand, or libertinism, on the other.

Either understanding of rights envisages them as claims by one party against another: by the individual against society or by the collective against the individual. The negative and conflictual relation is thus conceived as an external one between a wholly autonomous individual and a separate collectivity that has absorbed the individual—be it a state, a political regime, the law, or some other authoritative institution, so that we are

3. In his *Philosophy of Right*, trans. T. M. Knox (Oxford: Clarendon, 1956), the German philosopher Georg Friedrich Wilhelm Hegel remarks on the connection between personality and rights: "Hence the imperative of right is: 'Be a person and respect others as persons'" (pt. 1, para. 36: "Abstract Right"). He elaborates: "To have no interest except in one's formal right may be pure obstinacy, often a fitting accompaniment of a cold heart, and restricted sympathies. It is uncultured people who insist most on their rights, while noble minds look on other aspects of the thing.... It is not absolutely necessary that one should insist on one's rights, because that is only one aspect of the whole situation" (addition to para. 37), 235.

4. Benedict de Spinoza, *Political Treatise,* chap. 2, secs. 3–5: "[E]very individual has sovereign right to do all that he can; in other words, the rights of an individual extend to the utmost limits of his power as it has been conditioned. Now it is the sovereign law and right of nature that each individual should endeavour to preserve itself, as it is, without regard to anything but itself; therefore this sovereign law and right belongs to every individual, namely, to exist and act according to its natural conditions.... As the wise man has sovereign right to do all that reason dictates, ... so also the ignorant and foolish man has sovereign right to do all that desire dictates" (*The Works of Spinoza,* trans. R. Elwes [New York: Dover, 1951], 1:292, 200). Compare Thomas Hobbes, *Leviathan* 1:14: "[T]he right of nature . . . is the liberty each man hath, to use his own power as he will himself, for the preservation of his own nature" (*Leviathan,* ed. J. C. A. Gaskin [Oxford: Oxford University Press, 1998], 86–87). To be sure, self-preservation is proper to every being, and is present in radically different ways in all beings as the preservation of their given unity, but for its appropriate human context as a human right, see n. 20 below.

forced to opt for one side or the other. This inevitably leaves the issue unre-solved since there is no common ground, no participated identity, for the resolution of potential, if not inevitable, conflict. We are left with rebellion, on the one hand, or repression, on the other—or at best, with an uneasy and precariously calculated so-called moderate compromise somewhere between the extremes.

Given the history of the twentieth century, this compromise is under-standable. For if in the nineteenth century we had an excess of individual rapacity,[5] in the twentieth we have certainly had enough of collective repression, in the form of various totalitarian regimes. In the most recent phase, we have heard the inevitable reaction, leading a postmodern thinker such as Jean-François Lyotard to cry, "Let us make war upon total-ity!" and Jacques Derrida to elevate difference to the supreme value, even creating the neologism *différance* to designate it.[6]

It seems more adequate to recognize that rights imply positive relations more than exclusive possessions (whether by individuals or collectives), indeed, that they are in their essential character relational. Here, unex-pectedly, we touch upon the ontological *fundamentum in re* already men-tioned. But then, as we see in the work of St. Thomas Aquinas, in articulating the texture of being we disclose its structure.[7] Since I will be arguing that rights are founded in the "texture of being," it may be well to visit this complex metaphysical territory.

The Texture of Being

Aquinas begins with the central and capital notion of being (*ens*), that which designates any and every individual entity, including ourselves, and that expands to include the whole community of beings. But to call something, considered in its totality, a "being" is to highlight its actual

---

5. I have in mind here the so-called robber-baron capitalists, such as Lytton Strachey wrote of in the first part of the twentieth century.

6. See Jean-François Lyotard, *The Postmodern Condition: A Report on Knowledge*, trans. Geoff Bennington and Brian Massumi (Minneapolis: University of Minnesota Press, 1984), 82. Jacques Derrida, *Of Grammatology*, trans. G. Spivak, corr. ed. (Baltimore: Johns Hopkins, 1997); original French edition, *De la Grammatologie* (Paris: Seuil, 1967); and other writings. For a fuller discussion of *différance*, see Derrida, *Margins of Philoso-phy*, trans. A. Bass (Chicago: University of Chicago Press, 1982), 1–28. See also my "Postmodernism and the Catholic Tradition" and "An Addendum to Further Discus-sion," with replies by Thomas R. Flynn and James L. Marsh, *American Catholic Philo-sophical Quarterly* 73, no. 2 (Spring 1999).

7. St. Thomas Aquinas, *De veritate*, q. 1, a. 1 (vol. 3, Turin: Marietti, 1942).

existence or at least its relation to actual existence (*esse actu, actus essendi:* the activation or actualization of the fundamental energy of existence). It is this that determines the most radical divide between being and not-being. Now, each being has its own character, or nature, which Aquinas terms "essence" and which constitutes the being as a thing (*res*), under-standing the term in the most general way, as a being of one kind or another, and from which we get our notion of "reality." This uses the term in a broader sense than our current English usage, which tends to confine the central meaning to physical things.[8] The inherence of both the actual-ity (*esse*) and the essence (nature or kind) seals the unity of each being: *ens qua unum.* Yet, because the unity of each being is not an island unto itself, its unity is engaged in a tissue of relations in community with others; and this Aquinas terms "aliquid." Now, while this term can be rendered liter-ally as "something other," or even as "otherness," I think that it is appro-priately understood as "relationality," confirming the relatedness of all beings in the community of beings (*communitas entium*).[9]

The relationality of being expands into several cardinal, transcendental relations—"transcendental" insofar as they are constitutive of all beings and are not simply confined to one or another category or type of being. As he proceeds to unfold the texture of being, Aquinas presents that which affirms the intelligibility of being, and which we call "truth" (*verum*). To affirm the radical intelligibility of being is not to boast that everything in reality is as clear to us as a sunny day, but to affirm that being itself in its very constitution makes sense. Many aspects of being may remain myste-rious to us, who are finite, limited knowers; but the mystery of being is not a dark obscurity, hovering like an impenetrable cloud. If we do not see all, it is because of an excess of light, because of an inexhaustible and endless fullness of meaning. For us, the distinctive character of truth is grounded in the response that being (in its many forms) presents to our intelli-gence—the truth that we now consider, as well as that which is forgotten and that which awaits discovery. More deeply still, the intelligibility of being is open to Mind, inasmuch as it flows from the Mind of God, the Creator of finite being. *Verum* is the affirmation of the intelligible charac-ter of being—might I say, "the mind-friendly" offering of being, no matter

8. For an extended reflection on the difference between objects and things, see my book *The Recovery of Wonder: The New Freedom and the Asceticism of Power* (Montreal: McGill-Queen's University Press, 2005).

9. While it lies beyond the capacity of the unaided human intelligence, through revealed faith Aquinas was aware that such relationality is operative at the highest level of being, in the very Trinitarian Godhead itself.

how difficult its yield. It is an affirmative expectation that every seeker—scientist, scholar, and ordinary searcher—acts upon.

The relationality of truth may be adumbrated through analogy with light, so that coming to understand some aspect of being is like "coming into the light." Then, a second transcendental relation in being—that is, one that holds for every instance of being—leads us to acknowledge the attractive allure of the good (*bonum*). For being is not simply an inert presence, a bare fact, but that which invites us in a variety of ways, including that of communion with it, and sometimes of outright possession. Because we are limited beings of definite proportions, not all being is good-for-us.[10] One has only to see a tiger to acknowledge that the beast is better seen through the bars of a cage. Still, even there, we recognize the presence of power, agility, and sheer existential energy (Aristotle's *energeia*, Aquinas's *esse actu*), a root-energy that exhibits a kind of goodness of being. And this may lead us on to an admiring appreciation of its beauty (*pulchrum*), its radiance, proportion, and integrity. If the good may be described as that which is to be desired in union with it, beauty may be thought of as that which we admire (*admirabile*), as it were "from a distance," without implicating the desire of possession or union.

The Relationality of Rights

Now, if, after this presentation of what I have called "the texture of being," rights are said to be relational, we need to ask more precisely about the nature of that relation as it bears upon our understanding of rights. Suppose, then, that we explore the relation as involving both the individual and the group in a more positive fashion. This is to recognize that every right implies an obligation, indeed, even entails reciprocity.[11] But in

10. "This intelligible good is, of its very nature, inexhaustible. A doctrine of Natural law that has such a good as the term of man's moral activity [the perfection of his being] is open to an ever-deepening understanding of man's moral potential. Thomas' theory of Natural law is a doctrine of this kind. For Thomas, Natural law is not [merely] a formal set of prescriptions governing human conduct. Rather, it provides the ground for the morally good life. . . . It is for this reason that the first principle of Natural law—that good is to be done (*bonum faciendum*)—is normative with respect to every human act. . . . Thus the ontological good emerges in man as moral good, in as much as it is willed." James P. Reilly, *Saint Thomas on Law*, Étienne Gilson Series 12 (1988) (Toronto: Pontifical Institute of Mediaeval Studies, 1990), 15.

11. The German term *Recht*, as in *Rechtslehre* (jurisprudence), retains something of this relational character, since it incorporates both *right* and *law*. The Latin *jus* (from a Sanskrit word meaning "to join," often translated in Church documents as "right") is also relational, as are its derivatives *justitia, jus civile*, and *jus gentium*.

clarifying the nature of that reciprocity, we need to press further to confirm the character of the two terms of the relation.

If we understand the relation entailed in freedom as internal to both parties, then we will understand that both the individual and the group participate in the relation as part of their own identity, that is, as internally constitutive and not simply as an externally conditioned relation. But this requires us to inquire into the nature of the two parties and the foundation in them for the possibility of such a participation and mutual co-identification. We need to ask, who, after all, are these two participants? As already indicated, it seems to me fruitful to redefine the terms of the relation and to distinguish the individual from the person,[12] and the collective from the community. That is, it would seem more fruitful to set the terms of the relation as between person and community, rather than between individual and collective.

But then we must ask, what in the person and the community positively grounds the relational character of rights and obligations? And here we are thrust into a new dimension of energies that—I fear I must say it—are not simply transactions of physical power. Given the way in which the study of physical nature and the development of technological power has dominated the past four or five centuries in the West and provided the prevalent model for rational investigation and discourse, it is not easy to find our way into a dimension that is governed by laws other than the laws of physical energy and motion; it is difficult to acknowledge the laws of the spirit as distinct from the laws of motion and matter. In calling this dimension "spirit," I am in danger of creating the impression that I refer exclusively to religion. But there is a natural domain of the spirit as well, and it is to this that I now refer.

Trans-physical Relations

We have every right to ask whether there is any experienced evidence of such a spiritual domain. If it is not simply identifiable with religion, is it identifiable with morality? It is certainly open to religion, and it includes moral concerns; but it is not restricted to the religious or the moral, since it includes other forms of creativity and freedom, as in science, art, tech-

---

12. See Jacques Maritain, *The Person and the Common Good*, trans. J. J. Fitzgerald (Scribner's Sons, 1947; reprint, Notre Dame, IN: University of Notre Dame Press, 1966), for his distinction between the individual as a physical part of society and the person as both a member of society, yet also transcending it.

nology, economics, social action, and political organization. It is difficult to find a convincing name for it, but it expresses itself in many ways: in law and decision making, that is, in the actualization of responsive and responsible freedom; in artistic creativity and technical innovation; in manifestations of deep human concern, in friendship and love as well as in unprecedented deformities of cruelty and recklessness. It is the distinctively human: the *humanum*.[13]

It is not easy to find a foothold for entry into such a domain. The most promising is to begin with our quest for knowledge. The German philosopher Hegel remarks that what is distinctive about the human mind is its ability—and here he resorts to metaphor—to "go out" to an object, identify with it, and return to itself without undergoing a physical change in itself or causing one in the object.[14]

Of course, in this "going out to" and "returning from" the object, there are physical changes in the apparatus of vision and the chemistry of the brain; but in their role as "carriers" they do not define or determine the essential character of the activity of knowing. Indeed, by their very nature they cannot, since, even when they move through space and set up reverberations and waves of energy, they and their results are confined to spatiotemporal locations in the way that knowledge is not. For to know something is not the same as to ingest it or to absorb it or simply to receive it as one receives an electric shock or a pat on the back. We need to draw a distinction between the carriers as instrumental causes and the character of the knowledge-relations themselves that essentially constitute the activity and effects of knowing. Just as a messenger is not the message, so these excitations of the brain cells are not the activity of knowing in its proper nature.

---

13. As Terence (ca. 185–159 BC), the Roman poet and playwright, put it: "I am a man: nothing human is alien to me" (Homo sum: humani nil a me alienum puto) (*Heauton Timorumenos*, 77, as cited in *The Anchor Book of Latin Quotations*, ed. N. Guterman [New York: Doubleday, 1966, 1990], 34). And today we speak of human rights, as in "the Universal Declaration of *Human* Rights."

14. Without embracing the central notion of the Hegelian Absolute System, I find this description of knowing suggestive: "True scientific knowledge, on the contrary, demands abandonment to the very life of the object [*erfordert . . . sich dem Leben des Gegenstandes zu übergehen*], or, which means the same thing, claims to have before it the inner necessity controlling the object, and to express this only. Steeping [*vertiefend*] itself in its object . . . being sunk into the material in hand, and following the course that such material takes, true knowledge returns back into itself [*in die Materie versenkt und in deren Bewegung fortgehend, kommt es in sich selbst zurück*], yet not before the content in its fullness is taken into itself [*sich in sich zurücknimmt*]. . . . this thinking is not an activity which treats the content as something alien and external; it is not reflection into self away from the content." Georg Friedrich Wilhelm Hegel, preface to *Phenomenology of Spirit*, trans. G. Bailey (London: Macmillan, 1955), 112–13.

The carriers are necessary for the realization of human knowledge because it is the human being who knows (and not just the mind), and the human knower is a physical being; but something else is at work as well within the human composite. Without the carriers, sensory knowing does not occur—the blind person does not see, the deaf person does not hear. But these carriers are not integral parts of the relation that constitutes the knower's identification with the object, for this is not a physical identification. By "not integral" I mean that the carriers do not determine the intrinsic character of the knowing relation; something more, something different is required. That is, the carriers serve as sign-vehicles and indicators of the object, but they do not establish the distinctive character by which we know it; nor can they.[15] However much it goes against the contemporary presumption in favor of material forces, we need to concede that there is another dimension of human reality at work here, a dimension situated within the human complex with its material forces and energies, but also a dimension that is not identical with them.

Now, this identification with the object need not be total. I may know very little about the object, but if what I "bring back" with me as my knowledge is not something of the *real thing*, then I have no knowledge of it. If that is the case, then knowledge of rights and of any other relation is simply impossible. At best I will have assembled merely the materials of what I claim to know, rather than the object itself, as though I were to claim to have a house, when I have only a pile of lumber.

The above language seems to fit best with our knowledge of things, such as trees and rocks and solid, substantial things. But it holds as well for relations that are embedded in things; it holds for the smile on the face of a friend, and for even more elusive, ideal relations, such as rights, which are founded in substantial realities. One might say that I know the thing only as it appears to me, and it is certainly true that at this direct and immediate level of knowledge it must appear to me. It must appear to me in some fashion if I am to have first-order knowledge of it. Since I am part of or party to such a relation, I must be involved in it. But the requirement is that *it* appear to me (however incompletely) and not simply that I appear to it, or that brain waves occur in the cranium or that some bodily function take

---

15. For a further elaboration of the distinctive character of spiritual activity, see my "First Principle of Personal Becoming," *Review of Metaphysics* 47 (June 1994): 757–74, in particular 768–72: "The spiritual factor in the human person lives by its own law . . . [which, unlike physical motion is] communication without loss. . . . [The movement of the human spirit in the activity of knowing] is not a natural movement in the sense of a physical transaction [though it has physical accompaniments and conditions]; it is the movement of the human spirit."

place somewhere else; I need to encounter the house and not simply the lumber.

The skeptic may still argue that we are mistaken in our claim to know anything at all, and that we live in a cloud of illusion, but his claim runs counter to conviction based in experience; and more importantly, it runs counter to our instinctive behavior. If someone shouts "Look out!" I duck, and then check to see whether the warning was fraudulent or real. This is the living body's tribute to the incorporeal reality of knowledge within it. Anyone who has faced imminent death refutes the skeptic. These same conditions are operative, though not so dramatically, whenever we claim to know anything. This is not to say that I know only such directly confronted objects, since there are many things that I claim to know on the testimony of others, whom I consider to be trustworthy witnesses. But somewhere along the chain, we rest our knowledge claims upon such witnesses and such encounters.

The introduction of a new dimension, a new set of relationships other than brain waves, need not reintroduce the unfortunate dualism of mind and body. If we ground the distinction in the integrity of the person, we have distinction within unity.[16] I say distinction, and not separation,[17] for it is the whole unitary person who enters into the community as constituting and contributing to its membership, since the unity and integrity of the person *as a being* overrides and governs the complexity of his aspects or parts, and in particular overrides any separation between mind and

---

16. Aquinas, *Summa theologiae*, 1, q. 11, a. 1c: "[Ontological unity (*unum*)] does not add any reality to *being*, but is only the negation of division; for *one* means undivided being [*ens indivisum*]. This is the very reason why *one* is convertible with *being*. For every being is either simple or composite. But what is simple is undivided, both actually and potentially; whereas what is composite does not have being while its parts are divided, but after they make and compose it. Hence it is manifest that the being of anything consists in indivision; and hence it is that everything guards its unity as it guards its being."

17. The prevalent nominalistic tendency in much of modern thought tends to conflate the difference between distinction and separation, converting the former into the latter. Yet the complex and composite nature of the human person, as well as of other things, discloses real (and not merely conceptual) differences that are not separations. This is true of even the simplest distinction, such as between the surface and the quantity of a rock, a distinction that is not merely a mental distinction made for our convenience, nor yet a separation in the way in which in the laboratory the rock may yield separable elements under chemical analysis. The very possibility of recognizing distinctions that are real yet not physical separations is the primary condition for a realist metaphysics such as that which governs the present analysis. Compare my "Analysis by Principles and Analysis by Elements," in *Graceful Reason: Essays in Ancient and Mediaeval Philosophy,* ed. Lloyd Gerson, presented to Joseph Owens, CSSR, as Papers in Mediaeval Studies 4 (Toronto: Pontifical Institute of Mediaeval Studies, 1983), 315–30.

body.[18] We need to acknowledge the distinction-filled and complex yet unitary ontology of the human person. And indeed, there is plenty of evidence regarding the unified coordination of the many factors, elements, and levels that enter into the constitution and experience of the individual person. This composite structure, taken in its characteristic totality and unity (*ens et res*), is what (as our human nature) differentiates us from other animals and other beings on the level of species, while individuating factors seal our incomparable unity from other persons in the concrete order of singular existence. The unique signature of each being (*suppositum entis qua unum*) makes it, literally, "one of a kind."

Freedom More Complex than Choice

Now, it is just this complex ontological character of the human person as a being that is ignored or downplayed by the liberal emphasis on choice, once choice is isolated, not only from the complexity of the human person and in potential conflict with the community, but also when it is withdrawn from the complexity of the reality within which each person takes his or her place as the unique embodiment as a very special kind of being. And it is here that metaphysics has a word of its own to speak of in recovering human freedom from the impoverished concept of liberal liberty.[19]

For the disregard of the metaphysical texture of being alters the meaning of freedom, dissociating it both from the complexity of the human being within which it actively resides and from the universe in which it strives to play out its energies. In earlier thought, which still has a word to say to us, freedom was viewed as rooted in being, whereas in the modern liberal view, it has tended to be founded in itself. The metaphysics of being, on the other hand, understands freedom as properly relative to other aspects of the human person. Within the limitations of the human composite, and in the larger environment of the world of beings, human freedom puts these other aspects or factors into play, so that we can say that they are in an important sense part of the constitution of a fuller freedom than that of the element of choice.

18. The Thomistic formula "*Omne ens est unum*" (Every being is one) expresses the singular unity of every existential supposit or subject of being, including the human person. Compare, e.g., *De veritate*, q. 1, a. 1.

19. See my "Liberal Liberty and Human Freedom," *Chesterton Review* 20, nos. 2 and 3 (May–August 1994): 213–27. See also my "Is Liberalism Good Enough?" in *Liberalism and the Good*, ed. R. Bruce Douglass, Gerald M. Mara, and Henry S. Richardson (New York: Routledge, 1990), 86–104.

I do not mean, of course, that the modern libertarian does not acknowledge the limiting role of these other factors, as though he might sprout wings if he wished it. But the modern understanding of liberty does not endow these factors with the inherent value they have for human freedom. They remain extrinsic and not intrinsic to it. Now, it is these other factors that in their turn have a value-role in the play of freedom. Indeed, they give to freedom a received direction and guidance as to the human good, much as coworkers help in the fulfillment of a project. Except for physically determined processes, such as digestion, blood circulation, and the like, or such as infections, these factors do not compel one's freedom; but neither are they neutral with regard to it. They *oblige* us but do not *compel* us; they put us under obligation, that is, under a necessity that (within limits) we can choose to ignore. Yet, given the human structure and its dynamics, we are not left without an internal "map."

Moral philosophers call this guidance system "natural law," that is, a set of directives (or principles) that lies at the foundations of human action. Neither neutral toward nor in conflict with freedom, but consonant with it and even ingredient in these principles and general directives, these directives need not compel us. Moreover, they admit of diverse cultural variations that fine-tune them, adapting them to one another to form an interrelated cultural context. This *fuller freedom* is shaped to the contours in which the members of a culture live. Yet, just as the variable factors cannot be ignored, neither do the basic principles admit of infinite diversity or mutability.[20] They are heuristic *inclinations,* pointing human agency in certain ways toward the discovery of right action, such as organizing the food supply and its distribution, protecting vulnerable life, educating the young, and so forth.[21] I use the word *heuristic* in the sense that these inclinations

20. At *Summa theologiae,* 1–2, q. 94, a. 5, Aquinas asks, "Whether the Natural Law can be Changed?" While insisting that, "as to its first principles, the natural law is altogether unchangeable [*omnino immutabilis*]," he replies: "A change in the natural law may be understood . . . by way of addition [we might say: by development]. In this sense, nothing hinders the natural law from being changed, since many things for the benefit of human life have been added over and above the natural law, both by the divine law and by human laws." Compare n. 1 above.

21. Compare Jacques Maritain, *The Rights of Man and Natural Law,* trans. Doris C. Anson (New York: Scribner's Sons, 1943). See also Aquinas, "Treatise on Law," *Summa theologiae,* 1–2, esp. qq. 90–97. In particular, q. 90, a. 1 and 1m: "Since law is a kind of rule and measure, it may be in something in two ways. First, as in that which measures and rules; and since this is proper to reason, it follows that, in this way, law is in the reason alone.—Secondly, as in that which is measured and ruled. In this way, law is in all those things that are inclined to something because of some law; so that any inclination arising from a law may be called a law, not essentially, but by participation as it were." Compare q. 91, a. 2c.

function within the complex human being so as to help the person to discern the appropriate action in a given situation.[22]

Aquinas points out the guiding nature of law:

> There is in man, first of all, an inclination to good in accordance with the nature which he has in common with all substances. Inasmuch, namely, as every substance seeks the preservation of its own being, according to its nature; and by reason of this inclination, whatever is a means of preserving human life, and of warding off its obstacles, belongs to the natural law. Secondly, there is in man an inclination to things that pertain to him more specially, according to that nature which he has in common with other animals; and in virtue of this inclination, those things are said to belong to the natural law *which nature has taught to all animals,* such as sexual intercourse, the education of offspring and so forth. Thirdly, there is in man an inclination to good according to the nature of his reason, which nature is proper to him. Thus man has a natural inclination to know the truth about God, and to live in society; and in this respect, whatever pertains to this inclination belongs to the natural law.[23]

This inner "map" or "guidance system," which traditional philosophers call "human nature," is more delicate than we might like. For it can be affected by our relations with others and the values of the society in which we live. This is of especial importance in our formative years. It may be called our "conscience," but we must not think of it as invincible to all influence, like an impermeable lodestone, since we do speak of "malformed" consciences. And just as there can be more or less healthy individuals, so too can there be more or less healthy societies.

The Properly Human Good

The norm by which we adjudge individuals and societies is neither obvious nor beyond dispute, but at their most basic level both may be measured by the norm of the human good (*bonum humanum, bonum honestum*), both personal and communal. Societies that have a high level of

---

22. Aquinas, "Treatise on Law," *Summa theologiae,* 1–2, q. 94, a. 3c: "Not all virtuous acts are prescribed by the natural law. For many things are done virtuously, to which nature does not primarily incline, but which, through the inquiry of reason, have been found by men to be conducive to well-living."

23. Aquinas, "Treatise on Law," *Summa theologiae,* 1–2, q. 94, a. 2c.

instability and violence, of distrust and internal conflict, do not realize the full measure of the human good. Too much energy is dispelled in mistrust and avoidance, as a heavy hand dampens healthy motivation. Other societies that oppress factions of their members also fall below the measure of a healthy society, since there are no justifiable grounds in human nature for the radical preference of one race or class over another. Then, too, a society that does not nurture its young or respect its old or that aborts its future will not likely survive, or deserve to do so. I have just touched upon what Aristotle called the "strengths" or virtues of social life: civil peace, love of neighbor, equal dignity (which his own society fell short of), or again: patience, fraternity, justice.

The inculcation and observance of these values among the citizenry of a society requires an appropriate balance between individual interests and the common good, a balance not easily attained or maintained, yet engrained in the optimum condition for both person and community. I would describe these values and the principles that seek to realize them as shelters of humanity in the city of being—houses built out of the "bricks and mortar" that have been provided by the very texture of being, in the ways it offers itself to us. Yet these houses do not build themselves; rather, they are in a special way our preeminent human task, the task of integrating the many facets of our complex being—our persons and our societies—fashioned from received "lumber" into well-built homes where the past can be remembered, the present lived, and the future cared for. It is the task of human synthesis. In this process, education has a particular contribution to make with respect to the individual, and law—both natural law and positive law—has an indispensable contribution to make in the continuing development, maintenance, and reformation of society.

The Web of Causes

In this way, we may hope to develop, build, and maintain an ordered liberty. For freedom is not simply liberty of choice—the *conatus* so exclusively promoted by modernity—but a composite of other causes as well. Indeed, the traditional doctrine of the four causes speaks to the character of freedom. (1) The material cause (*causa materialis,* our physical dimension, subject to the laws of physics) contributes conditions with respect to which our freedom must address itself and incorporate. (2) The aspect that modernity has laid such stress upon, namely, choice and decision (*conatus*), provides the impetus that sets the whole process of selection, deliberation, decision, and execution under way. It is the voluntary energy of institution that is the effective cause (*causa efficiens*). (3) The formal cause (*causa formalis*) provides the guidance system mentioned above, and at its root is nothing less than our human nature. (4) But in seeking the good—one hopes the real human and social good, but sometimes only what is immediate or apparent—the final cause (*causa finalis*) comes into play as well.

It is this web of causes—and not only *conatus* or impetus modeled on physical force—that is the composite seat of human freedom in its fullness. And it is the context in which freedom is meant to be exercised. As much care and respect is to be given to each of these factors in the discharge of a free act as is to be given to the factor of choice, or *conatus*. And so the task of integration is not only the social integration of each person's action for the good of the community (the common good), but more intimately it is the personal task of the integration of the several factors of human freedom within the person (the personal good), so that an integrated freedom might become fruitful for both person and community.

Personal Integration and Community Participation

Indeed, Pope John Paul II—in his earlier incarnation as a philosopher—makes much of the task of the human person as precisely the call to integrate the various internal dynamisms—such as our physical processes, our emotional life, our subconscious drives, our intellectual awareness, and our desires—into the wholeness of the life to which we are called. And he underscores this as the work of each person's freedom. Thus, in his discussion of sexuality in *Love and Responsibility*, after acknowledging the natural character of the sexual urge and the promptings of affection between a man and a woman, he calls for these to be brought under what he terms "the personalistic norm,"[24] that is, under the free and responsible activity of the person as a whole. For an ordered freedom resonates with the broader and deeper rhythms of our participation in the dynamisms of our being, a participation that is situated within the broader and deeper context of the community of beings.[25] Indeed, this is to be said of all our actions, in which we have the task of integrating the physical, empirical,

24. See Karol Wojtyla, "The Commandment to Love, and the Personalistic Norm," in *Love and Responsibility*, trans. H. T. Willetts (1981; reprint, San Francisco: Ignatius Press, 1993), 40–44.

25. For the English translation of the first edition of *Osoba i Czyn*, see Karol Wojtyla, *The Acting Person*, trans. A. Potocki, ed. A.-T. Tymieniecka (Dordrecht: Reidel, 1979), pt. 4, "Participation," 261–300. For the bilingual edition (with the Polish text of the third revised edition), see *Persona e Atto*, ed. G. Reale and T. Styczen (Rome: Rusconi Libri, 1999).

intellectual, and value dimensions of our personal being. It may be said that we are our own "work in progress."[26]

It is, then, with personality and the capacity for responsible freedom that the concept of rights emerges from the more general ontological context of the good of existence.[27] It is then appropriately addressed as *value*. Natural law is thereby situated within the ontological constitution of the person and within the community of beings. This gives to rights their deepest and broadest grounds in the texture of being itself, since the person is an integer within the human and cosmic community of beings.

If rights are considered in terms of person and community rather than of individual and collective, we can see the grounds in both person and community whereby each may lay claims upon the other. The reciprocal right-of-claim begins with the manner in which the human person comes-into-being. For a person comes into being as a member of a group: a family, tribe, nation, political society. The person comes into being not only *out of*, but also *in and within*, a group, to which he or she belongs in fact and by right as a member. The relation, from the beginning, is not merely an external one, but is constitutive and internally rooted in the very being and identity of the person. That is, it is a relation not only of origin, but also of make-up or identity. For the origin establishes an abiding context in which we continue the being we have received. More accurately, we are distinct both from other members and from the group as such, but not by external difference alone. It is obvious that as individuals, we are spatially, that is, materially and physically, separate from one another, but that does not undermine the accompanying *internal* character of the nonspatial relations intrinsic to the whole person—relations that bind each of us to the several groups in which we participate.

These nonspatial relations are rooted in the primary and secondary existential and formal aspects of the person (*ens et res*): in family membership, as children, siblings, and parents (unless one is to deny the *reality* of one's brothers, sisters, father, or mother!), and in other relations, such as our culture and society; all of these form part of our identity. If we consider materiality as the source of local separation, we are entitled to acknowledge these other formally distinct relations as nonmaterial, or "immaterial," however strange the term may strike us.[28]

---

26. For a discussion of integration, including its bodily and mental aspects, see Wojtyla, *The Acting Person*, pt. 3, "The Integration of the Person in the Action," 189–258.
27. Compare n. 10.
28. In accepting this usage, we need to distinguish the immaterial from the spiritual, inasmuch as the spiritual forms a certain type of immateriality, namely, one that is capable of existence and activity transcending material conditions and, in some

Internal, Constitutive Bonds

In saying that each person has "constitutive" ties to the other members and to the group as such, I mean that the ties are part of the person's constitution, or make-up, including (in an important sense) his identity. Most obviously, this includes the genetic make-up, but also the inception into the family, whatever form it may take in different cultures, and then later on the induction into a specific language and culture, with its values and institutions. But these ties are so intimate, so much a part of personal identity, that they may truly be said to be constitutive of the being and identity of the person.[29] Can we not infer, then, that from the beginning, the context of emergence is such that there are mutual claims brought into play, bearing upon both the person and the group?

Such an understanding of the mutual interrelation of person and community acknowledges a tension-filled expansion of the understanding of both unity and difference. We cannot retain the simple opposition of the one and the many, as though the individual is one and the many are simply many individual ones, a collective rather than a community. First of all, the singular person is already and internally a composite of many parts, aspects, dimensions, and powers, all sealed by the concrete—if ever-changing—unity of his or her personal identity. And the community is not simply a collection of many isolated or externally related ones. Traditional philosophers give to these terms, *one* and *many*, analogous meanings as they are found in different contexts—analogous but not equivocal or unrelated.[30] That is, in all their diversity, they share in the unity that constitutes

---

instances at least, independent of them. In this sense, the human person is not simply spiritual nor simply material, but a composite of both, and the immateriality of form is the medium that seals the unity of the two dimensions of the person. Compare the Thomistic formula *"forma dat esse"* (form begets being). See Aquinas, *Summa theologiae*, 1, q. 75, aa. 2 and 6. See also my "Immateriality Past and Present," *Immateriality: Proceedings of the American Catholic Philosophical Association* 52 (1978): 1–15.

29. Here it is important to insist upon the whole person, in his or her entirety, to avoid reducing the person simply to the substantial unity of the existent *supposit*. The *supposit* (*ens per se*) instantiates the central and supporting existence of the person in the concrete order (*suppositum entis* [the substantive subject of being]); but it by no means exhausts the full being and identity of the person, which includes the various accidental characteristics—of differing stability, interiority, and importance—throughout which the *supposit* maintains the core unity of the person (*ens indivisum*).

30. I have in mind the long tradition of philosophical writers on analogy, taking its origin from Aristotle, and receiving extended development in the thought of Aquinas and his interpreters. From an abundant scholarly literature, see Étienne Gilson, *The Christian Philosophy of St. Thomas Aquinas*, trans. L. K. Shook, CSB (New York: Random House, 1956), 105, with references at 457. By way of revelation, theology refers to the "mystical body" of Christ, calling the multitude of the faithful to the participated dig-

a community.[31] For the person is, in some real sense, many, that is, complex; and the community is, in some real sense, one, as the very term *community* implies. By extension and in an economic and social context, business law has come to speak of "corporate personality." To the latter are assigned certain rights and obligations in the commercial and financial field, after the manner of personal rights.

The Ontological Omnipresence of Values

If we follow the present labyrinthine reflection upon the general meaning of rights, we come at last to a final point of analysis. For what is implied in the mutual and intrinsic relation of person and community, understood as a relation of being, is the rejection of the distinction between fact and value,[32] that is, between a purportedly value-neutral objective domain and a subjectively constructed value-sphere. The distinction is widely held but is open to question, or at least to restricted usage. Denying it does not diminish the importance of the spirit of objectivity, which—far from being disinterested in values—takes a serious interest in their truth-value.

For the interrelation of person and community is ingrained in their shared being, so that the good secured by rights is already anticipated in the very coming-to-be and be-ing of both person and community. Being is not simply a matter of fact, but is pregnant with values. As I have tried to show, recalling the text of Aquinas's *De veritate*, the traditional doctrine of the transcendental properties of being speaks to this.[33] For in recognizing

---

nity of the person of Christ, a participation received through the sacrament of baptism that forms an intimate unity of fellowship (*ecclesia*). See Pope Pius XII, Encyclical *Mystici Corporis* AAS 35 (1943), which draws upon the teaching of St. Paul (1 Cor. 12:12 and Eph. 1:18–23), a teaching reiterated by *Lumen Gentium*, n. 7 (Vatican II Council, "*Lumen Gentium*: Dogmatic Constitution on the Church," in *The Documents of Vatican II*, ed. Walter M. Abbott [New York: Guild Press, 1966]).

31. For a contemporary discussion that accommodates both the modern recognition of subjectivity and the traditional foundation of the person in the community of beings, see Karol Wojtyla, *The Acting Person*, pt. 4, chap. 7, "Intersubjectivity by Participation"; and *Persona e Atto*, 612–93, esp. 647–61. See also Karol Wojtyla, "The Person: Subject and Community," *Review of Metaphysics* 33 (December 1979): 273–301, as well as essays in *Person and Community*, trans. and ed. T. Sandok, OSM (New York: Peter Lang, n.d.).

32. Although the term *value* is often used in a subjective sense, I use it here as equivalent to the transcendental good.

33. Once again, see Aquinas, *De veritate*, q. 1, a. 1, but also *Summa theologiae*, 1, q. 5, "On the good in general," particularly a. 1, ad 1m: "Viewed in its first [i.e., substantial] being, a thing is said to be absolutely [*simpliciter*], and to be good relatively [*secundum quid*] [i.e., insofar as it has being]; but viewed in its complete actuality a thing is said to be relatively, and so to be good absolutely. . . . Because regarded in its first actuality, a

the difference between the true and the good, to which we respond in knowledge and freedom, the transcendentals are said to be distinct in conception (*secundum rationem*) but one in reality with being (*idem in re*). What holds the true and the good together is acknowledged as unity (*unum*), but also as relation (*aliquid*). The relationality (*aliquid*) rooted in the character of being itself forms a communal principle within being that far exceeds the human community, so that the very concept of rights implicating the good is rooted in the relationality of being and not simply in human subjectivity or sociality.

Conclusions

˙ What, then, is the ultimate site of rights? There seem to be three contenders. First, there are those who find the ultimate ground and justification for rights in an implicit or explicit contract, an agreement of wills. Underlying this contractual agreement (the social contract) is a certain understanding of freedom as grounded in human decision (*conatus*). This is played out in an exaggerated and popular form in the counsel heard during election campaigns: "It does not matter how you vote, as long as you vote." Or again: "Just do it!" One finds such a view in Thomas Hobbes's contractual understanding of the founding agreement that raises human society above the warring state of nature.[34] This view is so plastic, however, that it would seem to permit—in principle—justified rights claims to be determined by the perceived requirements of society at any given time, to be decided by those in power, whether parents deciding the fate of a defective infant or the state deciding the fate of a particular group. In this sense, the realization of contractual theory may run counter to the more deeply grounded demand for human rights.

A second site locates the source and justification of rights at a deeper level, in the specific nature of being human. Natural law is often expressed

---

thing is a being absolutely; and regarded in its complete actuality [*ultimum*], it is good absolutely, though even in its first actuality, it is in some way [*quodammodo*] good, and even in its complete actuality, it is in some way being."

34. Hobbes, *Leviathan*, 2:17. The contractual notion of values has been differently conceived, but the common thread is the elective agency of the individual in the establishment of social conventions. In modern times some form of contractualism has been held by Hobbes, Locke, Rousseau, Wolff, Kant, and more recently by John Rawls. Values are arrived at by some form of consensus (even if by practical reason in Kant), rather than by inscription, as in natural law theories. For a general treatment in the context of the history of philosophical thought and with pertinent references, see F. Copleston, *A History of Philosophy*, vols. 4 and 5 (New York: Doubleday, 1963–1964).

in these terms, in which the basis for rights claims is rooted in the universal and specific character that we share with all other human beings. This has the advantage over the contractual view in that it stabilizes the basis for such claims and generalizes them to all members of the human species. In grounding rights in a natural base it is possible to set limits to contractual alterations and to provide an intelligible and objective norm for the determination of rights claims. Without explicitly endorsing any metaphysical claims to a shared essential nature, the Universal Declaration of Human Rights rests ultimately on this normative basis.[35] For the most part, such a standard works well enough, insofar as it acknowledges a shared human nature and provides an objective norm for the determination of rights claims.

A third site probes more deeply, and seems to me stronger. It finds grounds for value in the concrete human person within the very texture of being itself. This is a radical move, since—while it situates the human species within the transcendental character of being and its properties—it requires a more sweeping understanding of the embedment of the good in the universal texture of being, and may seem too metaphysical for some. It is here, as I have argued, that the traditional doctrine of the transcendental properties of being comes into play and bears fruit in the practical order, lending depth and stability to a doctrine of rights. For in such a view, being is not simply a fact, but rather the context from which values of the first order take their rise. There is, first of all, the value of actuality itself (*esse actu*), since all specific essentials and all relations are embedded in actual being. Aquinas understood this principle as the root of all other principles, telling us that all that which comes before the mind presents itself as being.[36]

Now, for Aquinas, as we have said, the term *being* (*ens*) stands for actually existing being and all that is related in any way to such actuality, since even images of nonexistent things stand before the mind as participating

35. I situate this second site within the debates on the UN Universal Declaration of Human Rights, insofar as it appeals to a formal and abstract consideration of rights. It is fully coherent with the third site (to be mentioned), but in some versions it can avoid an explicit commitment to the metaphysical grounding argued for in this essay. Jacques Maritain (see his *Rights of Man and Natural Law*) attends to the directive power inherent in human nature. At the same time, his thought probes more deeply into what I refer to below as the third site, i.e., human nature grounded in the existential texture of being itself. Compare Maritain, *Existence and the Existent,* trans. L. Galantière and G. Phelan (New York: Pantheon, 1948).

36. Aquinas, *De veritate*, q.`1, a. 1: "Now that which the intellect first conceives as inherently its most intelligible object, and to which it reduces all conceptions, is being [*ens*], as Avicenna says in the beginning of his *Metaphysics* (tract 1, bk. 2, c. 1)." He tells us, further, that being as existential is most actual and most intimate within all things: *Summa theologiae*, 1, q. 4, a. 1, ad 3m: "Being itself is the most perfect [i.e., complete] of

in some minimal way in their actual presence to the mind. Each of these presences, however, possesses some kind of form and identity; that is, they are things (*res:* "reities," I would call them) and unities (*unum*). Yet insofar as they are all being, they form part of the community of beings and stand in relation to one another (*aliquid*, understood as relationality). With the emergence of intelligence and freedom within this community, new relations are instituted: relations of truth or intelligibility (*verum*), of the good or value (*bonum*), and of natural as well as man-made beauty (*pulchrum*), with its admirable clarity, harmony, and proportion.[37] These transcendental terms unfold the texture of being that is the original and ultimate ground of rights.

Such a radical and sweeping view of existential reality provides the broadest context and deepest basis for the concept of rights, since it does not rest legitimacy upon particular willed agreements (contractual theory), nor even upon the restricted sense in which they rest upon human nature without further explicit grounding in the texture of being itself, that is, without bringing the texture of being and web of causes into explicit relation with the presence of rights. For the complete intelligibility and rationality of rights is complicit within the very structure of being itself as we encounter it in affirmative ways. This permits the further specification and determination of *human* rights within an intelligible and value-laden community of being, and—where appropriate—further determination through variant cultural situations and even through contractual agreements, where these are appropriate. It does not leave rights to the potentially arbitrary wills of participants or even to the narrow demands of immediately perceived human goods, but situates rights within the broadest and deepest context of the community of beings, calling upon us to recognize rights sanctioned by the intelligibility and the value of being itself. So that authentic rights are concordant not simply with the agreement of human wills, nor do they rest upon human nature alone, but they are more deeply in tune with a universe that, in its most intimate depths and on it most exalted heights, is not indifferent to human persons and their aspirations.

---

all things, for it is compared to all things as that which is act; for nothing has actuality except so far as it is. Hence being is the actuality of all things, even of forms themselves." And *Summa theologiae,* 1, q. 8, a. 1: "Being is innermost [*magis intimum*] in each thing and most fundamentally present [*inest*] within all things, since it is formal in respect of everything found in a thing." By "formal" he does not mean "natural" but "actual," elsewhere saying that actuality is most formal (*formalissime*), i.e., trans-formal.

37. Once again, Aquinas, *De veritate,* q. 1, a. 1c, and *Commentary on the Divine Names.*

The Historical and Communal Roots
of Legal Rights and the Erosion of the State

Paul Gottfried

A question that arose in European jurisprudence after World War II concerns the relation between positive law and moral absolutes. Significantly, this project has not stood still. Since the 1940s the absolutes in question have been interpreted in varying ways, whether in terms of natural law going back to Aristotle or, more recently, as an accretion of human rights. It should therefore be no surprise that existing laws have been measured against competing or incommensurable absolutes. To judge laws forbidding sodomy against conventional moral standards, for example, would not be the same as evaluating them in terms of a right to self-expression or to emotional satisfaction. In the postwar period, European traditionalists more often than not stressed the nexus between positive law and traditional morality, and the defenders of this morality often appealed to religious authority. Expressive rights were not yet in fashion, nor did they provide the ultimate standard for evaluating the laws under which Western peoples lived.

Schmitt on Savigny's Legal Theory

It is worth noting that German legal theorist Carl Schmitt (1888–1985) examined European legal codes and the possibility for a shared European law independently of any of the above perspectives. Schmitt took into account neither the belief in unchanging moral standards (or human rights) nor self-justifying codifications that depend on popular ratifica-tion. In a wartime essay, composed in 1943–1944 and delivered in French and Spanish as well as German, "Über die heutige Lage der europäischen Rechtswissenschaft" (On the current condition of European legal science), Schmitt relates European jurisprudence to a uniquely European legal mind.[1] A host of glossators and legal commentators had paved the way for the reception of Roman law into late medieval and early modern Europe. They had also prepared the adaptation of this law to the European state system, a process that Schmitt explores most thoroughly in his postwar writings dealing with the development of European international law since the Middle Ages.

Schmitt cites as the standard-bearer for the kind of jurisprudence he has in mind Friedrich Carl von Savigny (1779–1861), the German legal histo-rian and father of the nineteenth-century Historical School. An expert on property and Roman law, rector at the University of Berlin, and Prussian royal minister in the 1840s, Savigny stood out as one of the most widely respected jurists of his age.[2] Yet, as Schmitt tells us, by the late nineteenth century, Savigny's reputation had plummeted and his commentaries on the evolution of law, as a process informed by the language and traditions of the people among whom it took shape, had been largely discarded. A new legal positivism, one that differed from Savigny's conception of "pos-itive law," seen as a gradual historical accretion, had triumphed in West-ern Europe. In contrast to "the way students of law who were defending inherited right once thought," "the later positivism," according to Schmitt,

does not recognize a place of origin or a homeland. It recognizes neither causes nor any hypothetically posed legal norm. It seeks the opposite of a non-deliberate right [absichtlos], and what it intends to advance are control and calculated interest. A word like source is from the standpoint of such positivism a non-binding metaphor for an occasion that requires an ordinance. Indeed for the practitioners of such positivism it would be senseless and even comical to give any thought to the "source" of a law.[3]

---

1. Carl Schmitt, *Verfassungsrechtliche Aufsätze aus den Jahren 1924–54: Materialen zu einer Verfassungslehre* (Berlin: Duncker and Humbolt, 1958), 392–97. My first published essay, "German Romanticism and Natural Law," *Studies in Romanticism* 4 (Summer 1968): 231–42, written before I encountered Schmitt's study, covers much of the same ground as his commentary on Savigny.

2. See Franz Schnabel, *Deutsche Geschichte im neunzehnten Jahrhundert: Die vormärz-liche Zeit* (Freiburg: Verlag Herder, 1964), 206.

3. Schmitt, *Verfassungsrechtliche Aufsätze*, 411.

Certain details about this statement must be explained to clarify its context. Schmitt was writing at a time when the Third Reich had abandoned any serious sense of right, except as a cover for a terrorist regime that had plunged Europe into a general war. Although Schmitt had initially tried to accommodate Nazi leaders, he had fallen out of favor by the mid-thirties and was thereafter kept under SS surveillance. His pointed comments about the replacement of *Recht* (legal right) by *Anordnung* (executive directive or order) referred *inter alia* to Hitler's aberrant government, although not until his postwar tracts did Schmitt make this point entirely explicit.[4] In the 1947 essay "Zugang zum Machthaber" (Access to the one who exercises power), he extends his critical remarks about a modern government that operates exclusively by orders to what he had witnessed in Germany between 1933 and 1945.[5] The stress on true law and true right as operating without deliberate design is a feature of Schmitt's critique of the present notion of right that he traces back to Savigny's jurisprudence. According to Savigny's theory of cumulative law, which pervades his examination of Roman codifications, an organic unity can be found in the way that self-conscious peoples formulate the rules guiding their institutions. The forces of habit and shared traditions give to such laws what Schmitt's fellow jurist Johannes Popitz had called "relative eternity."[6] This sense of one thing leading to another in an unbroken tradition animates Savigny's well-known polemic of 1814, *Vom Beruf unserer Zeit für Gesetzgebung und Rechtswissenschaft* (On the calling of our age for legislating and legal science). Here the author contrasted to the legal codes reflecting the influence of the French Revolution the older view that "all right develops first through custom and established belief, until defined by jurists, through quietly operating forces as opposed to any legislator's arbitrary will."[7] The legal historian, Savigny explained in 1840, should "recognize that a living combination of circumstances binds the present to the past."[8]

Schmitt singles out for praise Savigny's opinion that jurists must locate and then interpret "a living right that establishes itself by means of habituation." Through this exercise the "concrete level-headedness that is present among youthful nations can be joined to a high scientific learning."

---

4. Agostino Carrino, *L'Europa e il futuro delle costituzioni* (Turin: G. Giappichelli Editore, 2002), 155–56.

5. Schmitt, *Verfassungsrechtliche Aufsätze*, 430–39.

6. Quoted ibid., 412.

7. Friedrich Carl von Savigny, *Vom Beruf unserer Zeit für Gesetzgebung und Rechtswissenschaft* (Heidelberg: Mohr and Zimmer, 1814), 3.

8. Savigny, quoted in Schmitt, *Verfassungsrechtliche Aufsätze*, 415.

Savigny hoped that he would "produce not a weak, anachronistic imitation of Roman learning but a modern type of learning. We shall thereby have something to show that is more solid than a sure, quick administration of justice." Schmitt sees in this passage a statement of Savigny's belief, which was also his own, that "the study of right is precisely its source." Having surveyed the legal and judicial practices of three countries, England, France, and Germany, Savigny believed *Rechtswissenschaft* (legal science) had a special importance for the German people. While the British had created a case-law tradition rooted in society and history and while the French operated with established written procedures and with judges who were essentially public administrators, the Germans needed jurists who would clarify how their laws had evolved. Savigny, explains Schmitt, was essential for his age and attracted disciples because he searched for the sources of the legal practices that had been adopted by particular peoples. He did this by looking for the unity of tradition that had shaped and bound together nations. Unlike the advocates of "universal rights," this jurist did not believe that the same political or institutional shoe fit every nation's foot.[9]

Schmitt appeals to Savigny's legal theory in the course of criticizing "motorized legislation"—a mechanized creation of executive or administrative directives—and rule that goes forward on the basis of orders. In the midst of a trend stretching back for several generations marked by the "mechanization of right," it seemed appropriate to recall someone who "represented the European mind at a truly magnificent moment."[10] It was he who had warned against the "multiplication of laws" and who had defined legal studies independently of both theology and a purely technical craft. Savigny had opposed the rise of natural right theory as a substitute theology, one that smuggled "secularized" religious doctrine into modern legal codes. And he had properly feared the codifications that had accompanied the spread of the French Revolution and its dominant ideas. Savigny viewed such ideas as a secularized theology, one designed to justify written laws, which were grafted onto societies that had no historic relation to these pieces of paper. One can imagine what Savigny would have thought of our present American "conservative" project of exporting our present political life to the rest of the globe.

Despite his explicit admiration for an earlier jurist, Schmitt denies that he is seeking a "return to Savigny" in any technical sense. At this point he makes his famous dictum "an historical truth is true only once." Schmitt

9. Ibid., 413, 419–20.
10. Schmitt, *Verfassungsrechtliche Aufsätze*, 421.

is telling us that what had made his predecessor pertinent to his contemporaries was no longer our historical situation. Thus Savigny's ideas could not be viewed any longer in the way in which they had presented themselves to his disciples. In a similar situation, the mid-nineteenth-century Swiss-German historian Johann Jacob Bachofen had traced the emergence of patriarchy out of an older matriarchy as the pivotal event for later legal developments. But Bachofen's exploratory efforts eventually ran up against countervailing evidence concerning the nonexistence of a matriarchal society before the supposed turn toward patriarchy had taken place. Likewise Savigny's attempt to trace Roman legal precedents and precepts back to the early Roman Republic might have overreached in searching for unbroken chains. Like Bachofen, Savigny might have been looking into the distant past for what had not existed in the form in which he had imagined it.[11]

Moreover, Savigny's career as president of the Prussian cabinet of ministers in 1847–1848, under King Frederick William IV, ended in a series of frustrations. As a royal administrator, the jurist had tried too hard to put his bookish notions into practice as state policy. Savigny had urged his king not to grant a legislative assembly, for this would have resulted in destroying the traditional unity of powers vested in the Prussian state. In political matters, his sights were turned backwards, and so he never came to accept a *Rechtsstaat*, a government marked by uniform legal procedures and the separation of powers, in what was becoming a bourgeois society. The revolution in Berlin in 1848 drove Savigny out of government, and the sorely disappointed Alsatian nobleman never returned to political service, outside of a few diplomatic missions. In 1855, he turned down an honorific position from the restored monarchy to sit in the Prussian upper house.[12]

Questions can be raised concerning Savigny's legal theory that Schmitt only hints at or simply disregards. First, the notions of "customary right" (*Gewohnheitsrecht*) and "a living context" can be made to stand for either too little or too much. If "customary right" refers to legal or constitutional

---

11. Ibid., 416; and E. W. Böckenförde, "Die Historische Rechtsschule und das Problem der Geschichtlichkeit der Rechts," in *Staat, Gesellschaft, Freiheit,* ed. E. W. Böckenförde (Frankfurt am Main: Suhrkamp, 1976), 9–41.

12. See the short sketch of Savigny in *Lexikon des Konservatismus,* ed. Caspar von Schrenck-Notzing (Graz: Stocker Verlag), 476–77; for a comprehensive examination of his life and effect, see Adolf Stoll, *F. C. von Savigny: Ein Bild seines Lebens mit einer Sammlung seiner Briefe,* 3 vols. (Berlin: C. Heymann, 1927–1939); and Karl Mannheim's brilliant examination of Savigny and other nineteenth-century classical conservatives, *Konservatismus. Beitrag zur Soziologie des Wissens* (Frankfurt am Main: Suhrkamp, 1984), esp. 187–97, 200–205, and 213–23.

practices in which precedents are sought (or artfully invented), then it may be possible to justify as a living tradition whatever resourceful jurists come up with. When Senator Charles Schumer of New York insists that he cannot vote for an anti-abortion candidate for a judgeship because that nominee "threatens the constitution that I learned to revere from my father," the senator may not be duplicitous. The document that he and his father respect is indeed a "living" tradition that has been adapted to current circumstances (in this case a woman's right to dispose of her fetus). It is not only traditionalists who can evoke a "living connection of circumstances," by quoting Edmund Burke or Savigny. In the United States the social-engineering Left has its own well-rehearsed argument for a living history.[13]

But if Savigny meant by *customary right* or *tradition* what he undoubtedly did, a moral and normative link between generations that takes the shape of law, he was examining what has been greatly weakened or irreversibly disfigured. Schmitt had observed the results of a shattered understanding of law in 1944, decades before the rise of feminism, the drive for gay marriage, and the accelerating role of the central state as an engine for social reform. A widely displayed sign on American public buildings in 1989, "Two-hundred Years of the Bill of Rights," left out the fine print about how thoroughly transformed in meaning that bill had become, as a result of judicial construction. What we are asked to do is to stop worrying about a constant meaning for our founding document so that we can celebrate a continuity of phraseology together with the work of creative custodians. Herein supposedly can be located the *Ununterbrochenheit* (tradition) that is to be held up as an ideal. Partly but not fully bridging the gap between constant meaning and expediential adaptation is what Schmitt calls "legality," which designates the worship of law in modern liberal regimes. As long as certain legal procedures are observed, and citizens do think they are being heeded, there will be a general inclination to accept otherwise unsettling changes. But such changes cannot be ascribed to the force of a living tradition, and certainly not in the sense in which Savigny understood that term.

Second, the Historical School seems to be crying out for moral absolutes, although not necessarily for a doctrine of human rights. Although *Gewohn-heitsrecht* conduces toward a stable society, it does not suffice to give a convincing moral sanction to all legal usages. Some traditions—for example,

---

13. This view of law as an evolving good, based on the gradual emergence of "rights," underlies Ronald Dworkin's *Law's Empire* (London: Fontana Press, 1986). As should be amply clear from his argument, Dworkin has no interest in preserving social traditions as the basis of rights.

burning witches, owning slaves, binding the feet of Chinese girls, and widows committing suicide in Hindu suttee—are now mercifully gone, and there seems no need to weep over these vanished traditions. Even allowing for the principle that hard cases make bad laws, one has to notice that what is customary is not always self-justifying. Possibly such a problem did not dawn on Savigny, a personally devout Christian, who did not identify custom specifically with things that he found outrageous. But the examples of dubious habitual practices can be multiplied and justify the at-least-minimal link made by Aristotle between *nomos* (law) and *logistikon* (human rationality). Sound laws show reason—or what Savigny attributes to youthful peoples, which is "level-headedness" (*Besonnenheit*). This may be the view of Schmitt when he praises jurisprudence "as the first-born child of the modern European mind, that is, modern Western rationalism."[14]

Having noted the flaws in Savigny's legal-historical theory, it might be equally helpful to note its considerable merits. Despite his forced examples, imprudent counsels to his monarch, and overly broad generalizations, Savigny the legal theorist was remarkably perceptive about social forces. There is much in his understanding of human nature that recalls the timeless insights of Aristotle. In Aristotle's *Nicomachean Ethics*, attention is paid to the role of habituation in molding character and citizenship. We are told, for example, that

> it is necessary for a habit [*ethos*] to exist that is suitable for excellence [*arete*], which is [a habit] to love beauty and to scorn what is disgraceful. For the young it is difficult to arrive at this proper path toward excellence unless there are laws to educate them. Living moderately and tenaciously is not agreeable to the multitude and especially to the young. . . .
>
> . . . Nor is it likely that the young will come across the proper nurture and diligence, except insofar as it is possible for them to pursue and become accustomed [*ethizesthai*] to them, and thus we need laws for such things that extend throughout life.[15]

Aristotle does not exaggerate the capacity of most men to find moderation on their own. Neither *logos* nor *didaxē* (instruction) will suffice to implant that avoidance of extremes that is necessary for communal life. And while for the more promising dispositions, gentle habituation will

---

14. Aristotle, *Ethica Nicomachea*, Oxford Classical Texts (Oxford: Oxford University Press, 1970), secs. 1139a, 24 and 25; 1180a, 21; Schmitt, *Verfassungsrechtliche Aufsätze*, 415.

15. Ibid., secs. 1103a, 17–22; 1180a, 8; 1148b, 17.

serve as the "nurturing soil" (*gē trephousa*) into which the "seed" of reason can be placed, others will need something more dramatic to restrain their violent natures. Ordinary people live by sensation (*kata pathos zoēn*), which "is more likely to yield to force than persuasion."[16]

The regard that Aristotle exhibits for the relation of ethos to civic life is not meant to disparage Reason. Rather he is underscoring the importance of habit and custom as the nurturing soil without which *koinonia* is unattainable. In *The Politics* he goes beyond these prescriptions for individual character development by speaking of the *ethē* that operate in particular regimes. The effect of custom is to be found not only in those who are educated for public service but also in the types of government under which human beings have flourished. All *ethē* are culturally specific, and thus if one population is replaced by another, the corresponding form of government will also likely change. The *ethos tēs politeias* is a culturally specific way of life, and it does not take the same institutional form wherever applied. This distinction must be borne in mind lest we identify classical reason with a faculty that demands the implantation of the same political institutions everywhere.[17] This was no more the view of Aristotle than the one embraced by Savigny or Burke. And the opposite of ethical rationalism need not be an escape from morals, but recognition of the necessary relation between custom and the common life. The attempt to show the operation of human intelligence in established social institutions is equally apparent in Aristotle's conception of *aretē*, the manifestations of which are shaped by specific relations. The excellence suitable for a servant or a son does not require the same skills for a master or a father. Note that Aristotle does not deny excellence per se, but he treats this quality in relation to a social context. Isolated individuals may engage in speculative thought but do not achieve *aretē* in its highest form unless they are divine.[18] Others have to work toward this end through a network of connections depending on habit and deference.

Another function of custom is to make community possible, and while bad traditions are conceivable, it is hard to imagine a form of social life that can persist without custom. Whence the Rabbinic dictum "custom has the force of law," for without the former there can be no community at all. Custom may be compared to food. Though not all nutrients may be appropriate for a particular person, the total absence of them will lead to death.

16. Ibid., sec. 1179b, 20–25.
17. Aristotle, *Politica,* Oxford Classical Texts (Oxford: Oxford University Press, 1957), sec. 1337a.
18. Aristotle, *Ethica Nicomachea*, secs. 1103a, 17–22; 1180a, 8; 1148b, 17.

The same applies for tradition. Citing what is harmful or distasteful about a particular tradition does not disprove the value of tradition generally for those living together over generations.

In such a setting, individual choice or preference cannot result in predictable and responsible connections among those separated by ages, dispositions, and capacities. As observed by political theorist Michael Walzer, "involuntary associations" are the unifying glue of societies, even if some continue to think otherwise.[19] In line with this understanding, Savigny looked to historical communities, their language, and their customs to understand the laws that they had conferred on themselves. And he believed that there were patterns of thought that formed the basis of communal laws. The jurist therefore had to be involved in anthropological research when he examined legal codes but not as the investigator of what is primitive and obsolete. It was rather to confirm what he thought was true of communal life that he studied the conceptual patterns inherent in lawgiving. Only "once we have been imbued" by the enduring past, notes Savigny, can we venture forth as jurists for the present age.[20]

Toward an Ahistorical Super State in Modern Europe

Italian legal scholar and professor at the University of Naples Agostino Carrino has examined the very different premises about social life than the ones we have considered in the evolution of the European Union—and in the movement toward a European super state. Carrino turns a critical eye toward those jurists who constructed the EU Charter of Human Rights in 2000 and who are now promoting an EU constitution. These lawgivers, in whose work Carrino himself had once actively participated, are fashioning a structure of law that can be superimposed on national regimes. They are carrying out this task, moreover, as celebrants of "modernity." Within this "historic time frame" self-conscious modernists demand

> a release from traditions, from religious, economic, social, and political chains, from community of every type, whether personal or professional. This liberation will be translated into the recognition that every single individual enjoys a circle of rights, including the right to form voluntary

19. Michael Walzer, *Politics and Passion: Toward a More Egalitarian Liberalism* (New Haven: Yale University Press, 2004), 15–16.

20. See the introduction to Savigny's *Geschichte des römischen Rechts im Mittelalter*, vol. 1 (Heidelberg: Mohr and Zimmer, 1814).

associations. He holds these rights, which are different from and superior to all involuntary associations of a traditional kind to which one accedes by birth. This self-determining premise is the basis for the ascription of duties and obligations that derive from the juridical status of a citizen.[21]

Despite Carrino's association with the internationalist socialist Left and his longtime commitment to the EU project, he ridicules what he thinks is the last gasp of a liberal worldview. The roots of that view lie in that part of the Enlightenment, taken as a universalist political framework dissociated from any group's collective past, that makes little sense to the present inhabitants of Europe. According to modernist wishful thinking, the "empty throne," from which older authorities had been driven, will soon be filled with a new "founding myth." This contrived truth will be a *"carta costitutiva"* (constituent charter), and out of that will spring a spanking-new political society.

Carrino compares this mythical legitimation to the recycling by papal authorities in the Middle Ages of the legend of the Donation of Constantine. He brings up the questionable claim, fictitiously traced back to the Emperor Constantine, by which the Roman Catholic Church had tried to establish for itself a right to Central Italy. But while the medieval Church was an institutional force and exercised real authority, the trust bestowed on constitutional texts and invented peoples, Carrino insists, is delusional. The new founding documents are "pedagogical postures" and "rationalist exercises." They incorporate the fantasy of a future world of autonomous individuals, one that will seek self-realization outside of established communities and families. To whatever extent this project remains unrealized, the EU constitution, we are assured, will help push it along.[22]

Carrino scorns the idea of constitutionally creating a social-cultural sense, a vagary that among the Germans has spawned "constitutional patriotism." This artificial sentiment, which progressives work to detach from any specific national loyalty, can only succeed in a country that is afflicted with self-rejection. Elsewhere it would not be likely to gain much ground. Carrino's frame of reference is that of nineteenth-century conservative critics of constitutionalism typified by the jurisprudence of Schmitt. Carrino quotes Schmitt on the subject of the motorized directives that administrative governments resort to—without regard to traditional legal authorities. Driving this leap into the dark, he suggests, are the interests of international capital and moralizing jurists. Given its insubstantial foun-

21. Carrino, *L'Europa e il futuro delle costituzioni*, 47.
22. Ibid., 37, 43, 44.

dation, we are told, the EU has no serious chance of becoming the general European government.[23]

Carrino assumes this government will not develop beyond its current point of progress. Although he might in the end be shown to be right, he also overlooks the palpable signs of EU health. Despite the evidence of incompatibility between the constitution, the common law, and the judicial supremacy of Parliament, the British have adapted their legal practices to EU courts and the EU Charter of Human Rights. Carrino notes this but also disparages the "abstract," ahistorical character of what is being done in England. He likewise assures us that these changes are happening in the face of the impending "collapse of constitutionalism" (*tracollo della costituzione*). In the wake of economic globalism, Westerners have labored under the illusion that constitutions can be written for countries that will then be able and willing to mold themselves to what they have been given. Supposedly that illusion is now yielding to the reasonable supposition that "every constitution preserves a sense of significance only to the degree that it can be found to exist in a vital relation to a social and historical context, with an environment from which it necessarily depends and with which it interacts."[24] Carrino cites the American case in which a constitution has taken roots and survived because of its relation to a historic nation.

Although Carrino is correct that the Enlightenment project he criticizes has been under attack, what he overlooks is how well it has fared, despite its recent setbacks by French and Dutch opponents of the EU constitution. As late as July 1995, Carrino himself, in a lecture on EU sovereignty and the postwar Italian constitution at Saarbrücken, had looked forward to Italy's present constitutional regime's being superseded by a European government, and proposed ways by which Articles 10 and 11 of the Italian constitution, which envisaged Italian membership in world organizations set up to promote peace, could be revised to deal with the transfer of power to a European state under the Maastricht Treaty.[25] Even more relevant, the world's only superpower endorses with equal vigor the political homogenization of Europe, and the American regime that now routinely ties political morality to global democracy is widely imagined to be Christian and conservative. In any case the individualist perspective that values autonomy and excludes historic Western communities continues to hold sway. It permeates our mainstream political culture in the United States

23. Ibid., 46–56.
24. Ibid., 22–26.
25. Ibid., 32.

and Europe, which is precisely why its human-rights agenda may be the least controversial aspect of the proposed EU super state.

More divisive about the new consolidation of power are the financial arrangements, particularly price-setting and currency unification. And the reason for this may not be mere inattention to "human rights" in contrast to the EU's commercial and monetary stipulations. Those who persist in speaking inappropriately about Islam, homosexual relations, or the received account of the Holocaust are subject to criminal prosecution in EU courts—or in subordinated national courts. Since the Treaty of Schengen in June 1990, the seven signatory European countries, and those who have since joined them, have accepted, beyond open borders for themselves, a new international criminal law. Expressions of hostility to other races and to foreigners have become criminal offenses, and those who express such sentiments, as well as those who commit more than thirty other internationally prosecutable crimes, are extraditable to EU courts.[26] The outcry against violations of what in the United States are called "civil liberties" and against the loss of national sovereignty has been less than deafening across the Atlantic. By contrast, the possible effects of EU economic policies on the standard of living and a growing concern about the crime rates among immigrants have been far more likely than trampled freedoms to generate second thoughts about the extent of EU jurisdiction.[27] Part of this may be traced to the fact that multiculturalism and the punishment of its critics are already taking place in managerialized European nation-states. The EU does not really pose the greatest threat to European nations or to their customs. That threat is now coming from within.

The Effects of Long-term Liberalism

One may speculate as to why traditional loyalties have broken down, and the answers that emerge are not mutually exclusive. Some political theorists, exemplified by Pierre Manent, view this breakdown as the long-term effect of "liberal" ideas. These ideas, going back to Machiavelli and more remotely, to the late medieval nominalists, aim at constructing a political society without regard to religious morality or any nonmaterial sense of the good. Although liberalism came in varied forms, from an

---

26. Ibid., 165–91.

27. For an exhaustive study of the Treaty of Schengen, which may be in the process of being translated, see Vendelin Hreblay, *Les accords de Schengen: Origine, fonctionnement, avenir (pratique du droit communautaire)* (Paris: Bruylant, 1998).

authoritarian version that appeals to fear to an anarchist one based on individual pleasure, what unified these versions were a constructivist view of society, a skeptical approach to religious belief and to premodern authorities, and an excessively high value placed on individual will and individual gratification.[28]

Despite certain attempts to mix liberalism with restraining influences, for example, Protestantism, Victorian morality, and constitutional checks and balances, its momentum proved unstoppable. And that momentum pushed liberals, as we learn from Catholic social theorist James Kalb, into constructing "a pervasive system of control—necessarily hierarchical and irresponsible—that passes itself off as a neutral system of freedom and equality. . . . The fundamental irrationality of liberal modernity, foreshadowed by Emerson and Dewey, today characterizes PC and postmodernism." According to Kalb, the jump from material and verbal freedom to expressive freedom and then administrative manipulation was always implicit in the liberal assault on authorities. Without communal standards of the good and the acceptance of social leadership founded on the family, public administration and universal rights had to "present themselves as neutral methods for arbitrating hopelessly inconsistent preferences and understandings."[29] The "irrational Left" has become the champion of the expressive possibilities of postmodern society but also the guarantor of civil order in the chaos it has helped unleash.

Other criticisms about the plunge from hyperindividualism into a politics of behavioral control focus attention on the contemporary scene. My own work, for example, stresses the firmly established friendship between the managerial state and a denatured Christian theology. Out of the establishment of a secular theocracy in alliance with public administration has come, among other results, the present "politics of guilt." The state instills group self-esteem and group shame in terms of the victim or victimizing status assigned to members of society. The majority, white Christian population

---

28. See Pierre Manent, *Histoire intellectuelle du liberalisme* (Paris: Calmann-Lévy, 1987), 7–15, 43–50; and by the same author, *Naissance de la politique moderne* (Paris: Payrot, 1977).

29. James Kalb, "Liberalism, Tradition, and Faith," *Telos* 128 (Summer 2004): 136. Kalb is particularly helpful (see 138–39) in explaining why selective appeals to "tradition" and bourgeois virtues cannot rein in the dynamics of modern liberalism. Even more relevant is Kalb's forthcoming book, *The Tyranny of Liberalism: Understanding and Overcoming Administered Freedom, Inquisitorial Tolerance, and Equality by Command* (Wilmington, DE: ISI Books, 2008). See also my work *After Liberalism: Mass Democracy in the Managerial State* (Princeton: Princeton University Press, 1999), 135–42, for a parallel argument.

acclimates itself to these rankings, which public education, the media, and government all work to reinforce. Unlike the investigation of a liberal starting point at the end of the Middle Ages pointing toward later ills, my own account of present ills begins by looking at social changes in the nineteenth century. That is as far back as I find it necessary to trace the current moral revolution and the alteration of social behavior to which it has given rise. At the end of the predominantly predemocratic bourgeois age, the advocates of social engineering and cultural transformation came together in a new political formation, a democratic public administration that claimed to be both "scientific" and concerned about promoting equality. Unlike Kalb, I have no serious quarrel with traditional liberalism. Rather, I argue that such liberal thinking belonged to a bourgeois society that had lost its social and political hegemony before later "liberalisms" came to prevail.[30]

My work also elaborates on certain distinctions among "liberalisms," distinguishing a form of liberalism that was concerned with religious and academic freedom and the right to own property from one that empowers public administrators to redistribute income and socialize the young. In its most recent form, the radicalized liberalism has promoted homosexual marriage and in Europe the accommodation of militant Muslim immigrants. The term *liberal* loses fixed meaning in proportion to its use in justifying a growing assortment of antibourgeois directives, all of which have been pushed by contemporary democratic public administration. Unlike the French Revolution or the American civil rights movement, developments that became radicalized in relatively short time periods, the unfolding of liberalism's eternal essence as conceived by Catholic traditionalists assumes a much, much longer time frame.

These critics view liberalism as an internally consistent development that has extended over many centuries, going from the weakening of late medieval society and the erosion of the once-prevalent Christian Aristotelian synthesis down to certain late modern arrangements. The investigators attach long-range, portentous consequences to some highlighted conceptual first step into outer darkness.[31] Whence comes their very negative views of late medieval nominalism or of the Protestant Reformation,

---

30. *After Liberalism*, 3–48. I continue to discuss the thesis expounded here in my *Multiculturalism and the Politics of Guilt: Toward a Secular Theocracy* (Columbia: University of Missouri Press, 2003).

31. See my "Reply to James Kalb" in *Telos* 122 (Winter 2002): 120–26, which was in response to Kalb's review of *After Liberalism* in *Telos* 120 (Summer 2001): 186–92. My comments in *Telos* 122 come directly after Kalb's restatement of his interpretation of liberalism in the same issue (111–19).

which are presented as early stages in the attack on medieval organic or ecclesiological ways of thinking and conceptualizing reality.

What must be granted even by those with strong reservations about this perspective, however, is that certain interests and values have long remained embedded in the liberal project. And once separated from relatively traditional social contexts, liberal ideals assumed a succession of lives under new users. Schmitt was obviously aware of this fact. He observed that states and the state system were postmedieval developments and presupposed the subordination of ecclesiastical authorities to political power in Catholic as well as in Protestant countries. Nation-states came into existence in the early modern period, and they enjoyed the support of "political scientists," most notably Thomas Hobbes and Jean Bodin, and of legists who served at the disposal of royal administrations.

In no way could the state be described as an ecclesiastically conceived invention. Its success depended on sovereigns who were justifying their newly acquired authority. Without this inventive enterprise, it would have been harder to subdue social and religious violence, particularly after the Protestant Reformation had given rise to sectarian division. "The modern state," Schmitt famously points out, "moved from a preoccupation with practical technique [*Sachtechnik*] to the building of political order."[32] Schmitt here is not considering the prospects for returning to a premodern setting; rather, he is speculating about what can be done to save the system of political authority that arose with modernity. By the post–World War II period, he believed that the European nation-state system was tottering. This glorious achievement of modern Europe gave the appearance of being about to join medieval Christendom on the junk heap of history.

The reason for this crisis was a constellation of unfavorable circumstances, from revolutionary global ideologies to modern warfare. Schmitt notes the transfer of politics beyond the European chessboard, on which the fortunes of nation-states had been decided in previous centuries. Besides the escalation of conflicts among European states, two other situations had contributed to the disintegration of the "European order." One was the consolidation of what Schmitt calls the "quantitative total state," a regime characteristic of the postwar West.[33] Schmitt found that this

32. Carl Schmitt, *Die Diktatur: Von den Anfängen des modernen Souveränitätsgedankens bis zum proletarischen Klassenkampf* (Berlin: Duncker and Humblot, 1994), 12.

33. See my *Carl Schmitt: Politics and Theory* (Westport, CT: Greenwood Press, 1990), 74–80; the introduction by G. L. Ulmen to his annotated translation of Schmitt's *Nomos der Erde im Völkerrecht des Jus Publicum Europaeum* (New York: Telos Press, 2003); and my critical review in *American Outlook* (Fall 2003).

consolidation was the result of two grave developments that had occurred simultaneously in political life, "the socialization of the state" and the "politicization of society." The two poles of human interaction had grown less independent as they had interpenetrated and infected each other. This perception about the confusion of the political and social spheres was carried forward in the work of Schmitt's student Ernst Forsthoff, who examined the erosion of traditional state authority in the democratic welfare state; at the same time, the Italian political scientist M. Nigro fruitfully applied the same insight to an analysis of political socialization and the practice of pluralism in public administration.[34] These interrelated circumstances, maintains Schmitt, allowed the observer to note with equal certitude, depending on where he turned, either an "impotent state" or a "state-controlled society."

The second situation that had contributed to this disintegration was the loosening of judicial standards. Schmitt contends that the system of European nation-states had been anchored in a specific system of law, developed on the continent by legists steeped in the Roman corpus. Their modified Roman system could not work any longer once administrators and legislators began to produce motorized directives to please their subjects or constituents. In France, renowned professor of public law Simone Goyard-Fabre observes that criminal procedures have turned into the same kind of theatrical performance that courtroom pleading has become in the United States. The Code Napoléon, derived from Roman law, on which French civil and criminal procedures are still technically based, was until recently applied rigorously in courtroom judgment, and those pleading a case had to offer "demonstrative" arguments by making steady reference to the relevant procedure or statute. Now, explains Goyard-Fabre, French judges feel free to apply "values" considered fashionable, while the courtroom has been thrown open to "dialogues" and the "ethic of discussion." This "paradigm shift" has also involved the introduction of other American innovations, for example, "class action suits" by groups that claim to be aggrieved and the straying of public prosecutors away from what used to be understood as state interest, into the accommodation of grievances in a self-advertised pluralistic society.[35]

It might be asked why Schmitt, who saw the beginning of this legal debacle, did not look for an alternative in a return to natural law. This

---

34. M. Nigro, "Carl Schmitt e lo stato amministrativo," in *Rivista trimestrale di diritto e procedura civile* (Milan: Giuffré, 1986), 793.

35. Simone Goyard-Fabre, "Quelques réflexions philosophiques," *Krisis* 25 (November 2004): 18–32; and *Les embarrass philosophiques du droit national* (Paris: J. Vrin, 2002).

question was posed twice in the German Catholic periodical *Hochland*, once in 1924, in an essay by Hugo Ball about Cartesianism in politics,[36] and the second time in 1950, in a far more abrasive manner, in F. A. von Heydte's tract "The State of European Jurisprudence." In his essay, Heydte scolds Schmitt, who was then being tarred with his connections to the Third Reich, for his "fear to speak the name of God as a legal theorist."[37] But Heydte might have gone too far in his invective when he attributed Schmitt's avoidance of Thomistic categories to professional agnosticism. Schmitt's work abounds in theological references: Italian scholar Michele Nicoletti devotes almost seven hundred pages in *Trascendenza e Potere* to the intricacies of Schmitt's theology as revealed in his political tracts. Although a learned commentator on Scholastic thought, Schmitt was not a Thomist. His theological inclinations, which affect his historical speculations and even his understanding of the state, were Augustinian and neo-Platonic.[38] His critics on the left and the German Straussian Heinrich Meier attack Schmitt not as an atheist, but as a religious fatalist, a judgment that seems to be at least partly correct.[39] From Schmitt's perspective, the choice of legal conceptions in his day was not between Christian Aristotelian natural law and something else. It was between the quantitative total state and motorized directives, on the one side, and, on the other, workable legal standards that could keep those developments in check.

What had offered itself as an alternative to both came from the Austrian liberal jurist Hans Kelsen (1881–1973), who as a refugee in the thirties carried his ideas to the United States. Kelsen taught an explicitly ahistorical doctrine, which turned away from the inconvenience of state sovereignty toward a universal order built on self-referential legal principles. This normativist model could be traced back to Immanuel Kant, who sought perpetual peace in a world order that presupposes individual equality and a constructivist, universally extendible polity.[40] Supposedly rational beings,

36. Hugo Ball, "Carl Schmitts Politische Theologie," *Hochland* 21 (April 1924): 261–86.

37. F. A. von Heydte, "Heil aus der Gefangenschaft? Carl Schmitt und die Lage der europäischen Rechtswissenschaft," *Hochland* 43 (1950–1951): 288.

38. See Michele Nicoletti, *Trascendenza e Potere: La teologia politica di Carl Schmitt* (Brescia: Morcelliana, 1990).

39. Schmitt's obsession with human depravity, which supposedly turns him into a defender of war to the knife, is a basic theme in Heinrich Meier's *Carl Schmitt, Leo Strauss und der Begriff des Politischen: Gespräch unter Abwesenden* (Stuttgart: Metzler, 1988); see 59–68.

40. For Kelsen's presentation of his concept of sovereignty, see his *General Theory of Law and State,* trans. Anders Wedberg (Cambridge: Harvard University Press, 1945), particularly the appendix on natural law. An early illustration of Kelsen's attempt to

who were not fixated on internal state sovereignty and were averse to war, would recognize the wisdom of this plan, one that Kelsen had already unveiled in German-speaking lands before World War I.

In an astute comment on Kelsen's interwar work *Der Wandel des Souveranitätsbegriff* (1931), Carrino observes that one finds here

> the unity of a juridical image of the world rather than the substantial unity of human relations. The unity of the juridical order appears artificial, hypothetical and probabilistic and is an imagined unity. The effort of the Viennese to tie together what he clearly sees as being dissolved, after the juridical historicism and the plurality of national rights theorized from nineteenth-century juridical positivism, is a tragic effort [*sforzo tragico*], which only a cultured man educated in the last international empire . . . would desperately undertake, while appealing to the instruments of scientific rationality, to mathematical formalism, and to the ultimate "value" of liberal intellectuality.[41]

It is not hard to discern in the passage just cited the ideal of constitutional patriotism. This ideal wears the trappings of a "scientific ideal," but although its "myth of scientificality" has grown less and less credible, according to Carrino, its outlines continue to show a remarkably long shelf life. Kelsen's utopia can survive even without a self-referential universal code of law. This scheme for a constructivist regime is now the EU project, conceived as an administered world without war. And this scheme is succeeding, both because of interlocking economic interests and because of the growing rejection among Europeans of their national communities and of any traditional religious sense.

Kelsen epitomized for Schmitt the abstract liberal universalism that he examined in his major writings of the twenties and early thirties. The Viennese jurist blithely assumed that a critical mass of human beings would put aside the limited blessing of living in sovereign states to become world citizens. And once shown this happy future, they would then consent to living under the legal procedures and human rights that they had bestowed on themselves. This world republic would, moreover, function, without the ambitious trying to impose their arbitrary power on the more docile. Though I will not attempt here to do full justice to Schmitt's critique

---

apply a neo-Kantian epistemology to the reconstruction of legal norms is *Hauptprobleme der Staatslehre entwickelt aus der Lehre vom Rechtssatz* (Tübingen: J. C. Mohr, 1911).

41. Agostino Carrino, *L'ordine delle norme: Stato e diritto in Hans Kelsen*, 3rd ed. (Naples: Edizioni Scientifiche, 1992), 284–85.

of Kelsen, which would require an entire volume to present, there is one part that bears directly on this essay. It concerns Kelsen's deliberate disregard of historical circumstances, starting with the improbability that human beings could be persuaded to live together permanently in a rational, humanitarian manner.[42]

For Schmitt, there was no way back to a medieval European world, one in which political power rested on ecclesiastical authority. But what had taken its place was another hope for unity through world planning. Progressive intellectuals reconceptualized the *res christiana* as a rationalist project that might be extended to embrace the entire world. What Schmitt found in Roman law, in contrast to what he rejected, was a longtime, proven source of stability. It was a means of establishing relations within and among European states, and within the Catholic Church through canon law, which had worked for many centuries. It avoided the utopian temptation of forcing patterns of social existence into an ideal direction.[43] Schmitt praised the operation of this historical positivism in Savigny, who searched for the historical fit between how communities lived and how they embodied their sense of the good in legal institutions.

Renouncing National Consciousness

Since what has been alluded to is a historically based conservatism, it might be useful to note its present obsolescence. Historical positivism offers no guidelines for a situation in which historical and institutional continuities have broken down or have been emphatically jettisoned. How exactly does one apply the perspective of Savigny to societies that wish to break from their own pasts? The German case comes readily to mind, for it involves the demonization among politicians and journalists of the German national culture that had existed before May 1945—and even before the Nazis' accession to power. Germans do not mince words in their self-condemnation, and

42. Carrino (ibid., 366–72) notes that Kelsen gingerly avoids the problem of activist judges' being allowed to interpret legal norms. He also points to the American experience, in which judges have been permitted to become the de facto authors of laws rather than the mere interpreters of constitutional texts. Kelsen did respond to Schmitt's charge that his theories contributed to the powerlessness of the Weimar government in the face of the Nazi threat in *Wer soll der Hüter der Verfassung sein?* (Tübingen: J. C. Mohr, 1931), 8–10, 44–46, and 54–56. See also Giovanni Sartori, "The Essence of the Political in Carl Schmitt," *Journal of Theoretical Politics* 1 (July 1989): 70; and Lee Congdon, "The Other God That Failed," *Chronicles* (July 1990): 41–42.

43. Carrino, *L'Europa e il futuro delle costituzioni,* 149.

Foreign Minister Joschka Fischer points proudly as well as contritely to the fact that the "founding myth of the present German republic is Auschwitz."[44]

But less masochistic examples also come to mind about the tendency of Western countries today to reject the idea of national specificity. In the United States the "conservative" side of the electoral spectrum has undertaken to spread global democratic revolution; and one of the conservative movement's most honored spokesmen, American Enterprise Institute for Public Policy Research senior scholar Michael A. Ledeen, calls for promoting world revolution, spearheaded by the American government and American economic expansion, against traditional cultures. Ledeen is jubilant about the prospect of cosmic upheaval: "Creative destruction is our middle name, both within our own society and abroad."[45] Secretary of State Condoleezza Rice, on a visit to France in February 2005, dwelled on the supposed overlap between French Jacobinism and the founding ideas of her own country. Such a happy accident, we are told, ensures a shared moral purpose between the two democratic countries, whose governments were founded in a kindred revolutionary mission.[46]

The fact that journalists, intellectuals, and voters are not aware of this contradiction may indicate, according to Bruce Frohnen, how thoroughly "conservatism has lost its mind."[47] It also underlines the difficulty of setting apart the historic Left, to which American "conservatives," whether they admit it or not, now adhere, from what passes for the respectable Right. The overlaps between the two allowable "nonextremist" sides of the spectrum have become truly striking—for example, when both sides assume the validity of whatever past social-engineering American courts engaged in to remedy past inequalities.[48] On both immigration and the

44. This revealing statement about the German Republic as a form and vehicle of contrition, which Fischer made to the French Jewish antinationalist Bernard-Henri Lévy, is in a report by Michael Kleeberg in the *Welt* (May 22, 1999) and is reprinted in Heinz Nawratil's *Der Kult mit der Schuld* (Munich: Universitas, 2000), 23–24.

45. Michael A. Ledeen, *The War against the Terror Masters* (New York: St. Martin's Press, 2002), 212–13. For a thesaurus of quotations about America's destiny and duty to revolutionize the world from leading "conservative" spokesmen, see Claes G. Ryn, *America the Virtuous: The Crisis of Democracy and the Quest for Empire* (New Brunswick: Transaction Publishers, 2003).

46. See the *Wall Street Journal*, February 9, 2005, A10; and Justin Vaïsse, "Condoleezza et la démocratie: cinq pistes de réflexion," in *Le Monde*, February 11, 2005, A1.

47. Bruce Frohnen, "Has Conservatism Lost Its Mind? The Half Remembered Legacy of Russell Kirk" *Policy Review* 64 (Winter 1994): 62.

48. Books that make this argument well are Robert Nisbet, *The Present Age: Progress and Anarchy in Modern America* (New York: Harper and Row, 1988); and Forrest McDon-

celebration of the American civil rights revolution, the politically effective American Right strikes generally the same notes as its opposition. Both sides now invoke a revolutionary legacy, and, although their timetables for change may differ, both look toward implementing American feminism and other progressive Western movements outside the West. One may of course welcome this consensus as expressive of universal morality and a universal standard of "human rights." Nonetheless, it is misleading to treat the American establishment Right any more than the American establishment Left as a custodian of the antirevolutionary past.

It is equally misleading to view the EU project or other variations on Kelsen's international legal order as mere pie in the sky. Carrino's dismissive treatment of the European super state as a figment that will not win the hearts and loyalties of its intended subjects has ceased to be convincing. Ironically, these expressions of skepticism come from someone who not only once missionized for this project but (as far as I know) is still identified with political groups supporting it. Carrino never addresses the hard questions that could be raised in response to his skepticism. Why should Europeans move decisively in a different direction, given their previous accommodations to Eurocrats and to international human-rights courts and given the weakened condition of national and familiar bonds? Present arrangements will likely remain in place, whether or not Europeans vote, or are allowed to vote, for the EU constitution.

Carrino also underestimates the degree to which the clients in modern welfare-state democracies are willing to put up with manipulation. Once public administrators control income and pensions and obtain the power to socialize the young, what difference should it make in which country the issuer of pensions resides? A check issued from Brussels is as good as one coming from a former national or provincial capital. And as long as someone pays for government programs that are thought to go to retired yuppies, with few or no offspring, why should those who receive them care whether the taxpayers happen to be third world Muslims or European Christians?

Arguably the reason that Germans can be taught to hate themselves as much as they do, and as much as I demonstrate in my book on multiculturalism, is not that their inherited sins are necessarily worse than those of other nations. Russians committed equally inhumane acts under Lenin and Stalin and ran a far more politically repressive society than that of Germany before

---

ald and Ellen Shapiro McDonald, *Requiem: Variations on Eighteenth-Century Themes* (Lawrence: University Press of Kansas, 1988), particularly the concluding section.

Hitler. But, unlike the Germans who read intimations of the Third Reich back into every phase of their national history, the Russians, like the Japanese, who also perpetrated horrible wartime crimes, continue to resonate with national pride.[49] Russian leaders set about rigging the last presidential election in Ukraine, with no apparent regret that Stalin's regime had murdered millions of Ukrainians in the thirties. Such past misconduct has not elicited any apologies from the Russian government, and even less has it generated a cult of guilt among the Russians like that that thrives among the Germans.[50]

Russians behave differently from their Western counterparts, who seem to luxuriate in collective guilt, because they possess a different group consciousness. Despite the Soviet plunge into state socialism, the Russian Revolution, unlike the postwar German reeducation, did not try to expunge all traces of national identity. As Richard E. Pipes has pointed out in his studies of Russian history, the Soviets found ways to combine Marxist internationalism with reverence for the Russian motherland.[51] And they did this while remaining relatively immune from attacks by the internationalist Left, because of what was seen as the successful marriage between the Russian government and workers' socialism. For those who were sympathetic toward the Soviet experiment, it seemed natural that one should indulge Russian imperialism.

Equally important, the socialist homeland and its conquered satellites remained poor. They therefore lacked the material preconditions for the social and cultural innovation that has marked the contemporary West. A combination of prosperity and cultural upheaval with a growing dependence on a post-national state is a development that Eastern European socialist countries have yet to go through. Those Europeans who scorn the idea of national community and who look to the state (which means any state) to provide them with creature comforts can easily despise what they

49. For the extraordinary forms of German self-loathing, as manifested in German politics and German culture, see my book *The Strange Death of Marxism: The European Left in the New Millennium* (Columbia: University of Missouri Press, 2005). The same theme is widely discussed in my introduction to *Multikulturalismus und die Politik der Schuld* (Graz: Leopold Stocker Verlag, 2004).

50. See the discussion of Vladimir Putin's geopolitics in *Belgravia Dispatch*, December 16, 2004, www.belgraviadispatch.com/archives.

51. See Richard E. Pipes, with F. C. Barghoorn, *Soviet Russian Nationalism* (Oxford: Oxford University Press, 1956); and Richard E. Pipes, *Formation of the Soviet Union* (New York: Atheneum, 1968). Although Pipes may go too far in looking for national patterns characteristic of Russia in Soviet Communist behavior, his interpretations do explain how Soviet Communists turned overnight into right-wing nationalists after the implosion of the Soviet Union.

no longer are. The politics of guilt might have helped shape this observable collective self-rejection, but there are nonideological reasons for it as well. Fevered expressions of regret about one's ancestral past come easily to those who have no national culture and who have renounced a traditional community.

Conclusion

The recent growing repugnance in the West for the Western past and for the nations that belong to it has a social source. It affects preeminently those who look to public administration to guide their lives and to care for their needs. Such people generally do not care about the revolutionary impact of motorized directives any more than they do about the problem of lost national continuity. The National Democratic Party, which is associated in Germany with the Far Right, has sprung up in the least politically correct part of the old German Fatherland, indeed in that part that was formerly Communist. One alleged proof of the NDP's extremism was its stated wish to commemorate the Allied bombing of Dresden in February 1945. Party members were engaging in this commemoration as self-described German patriots, without public expressions of remorse over the Holocaust. The comparison by NDP deputies in Saxony between Nazi crimes and the firebombing of Dresden evoked media outcries. Outraged demands came from the leaders of the national party blocs to ban what is considered a "neo-Nazi" front. All of this coincided with demonstrations by tens of thousands of German youth, mostly coming from Western Germany, the purpose of which was to underscore their conviction that the helpless civilians wiped out in Dresden fully deserved to be destroyed.[52] But this utter lack of sympathy for German civilians killed in wartime firebombing may tell us less about the callousness of young Germans than about their growing detachment from any national past. It is easier to pour contempt on those who have ceased to be one's family or nation than to disavow those to whom one still feels connected.

In this situation, and in that of other uprooted Western societies, one wonders what continued relevance there is in the teaching of Savigny or in Schmitt's reformulation of this teaching. Perhaps one might respond that the historicism of these venerable gentlemen throws light on why historical positivism has ceased to be pertinent. Schmitt's observation that

52. On the reactions evoked by the commemoration of the Dresden bombing, see the *Daily Telegraph,* February 10, 2005, A1.

"an historical truth is true only once" does not prescribe a relativistic moral view. It is a warning not to attach excessive importance to what is historically variable. Note that much of Schmitt's work after World War II focused on the possibilities of a global division of spheres of influence after the withering away of the European state system. Despite his predilection for the European order and its legal framework, Schmitt was willing to think beyond it historically.

While the *jus europaeum* and the political structure to which it was bound have faded almost entirely, Europeans are still waiting to find their replacement. Europeans are facing an interregnum characterized by social breakdown and successive attempts at political reorganization. In the meantime they and we are awash in abstract universals flowing from the Enlightenment and the Communist Revolution, but there is no reason to assume that such pieties or an American world policeman will establish permanent solutions to the search for a new political order. Given the way the human race has lived until now, which may be partly biologically programmed, the multicultural experiment in creatively reconfigured family patterns, without traditional gender and national identities, cannot go on and on.[53] In the end, people may return to families and even kin-based communities, whatever they may call these arrangements, thereby confirming the observation of Joseph de Maistre: "I have certainly found Frenchmen, Germans, and Italians but never simply a man." Human predicates and their attendant cultures will likely stage a comeback in a Europe that has tried and then moved beyond multiculturalism. Whether that West will still be recognizably Western is of course far from certain.

---

53. Two monographs that treat the constant features in family and communal organization and relate them to a partly biologically shaped "human nature" are Thomas Fleming, *The Morality of Everyday Life: Rediscovering an Ancient Alternative to the Liberal Tradition* (Columbia: University of Missouri Press, 2004); and Steven Goldberg, *The Inevitability of Patriarchy: Why the Biological Difference between Men and Women Always Produces Male Domination* (New York: William Morrow, 1973).

Reintegrating Rights

Catholicism, Social Ontology, and Contemporary Rights Discourse

Kenneth L. Grasso

In my beginning is my end.

—T. S. Eliot, "East Coker"

Since a theory of rights, like "all legal and political systems of thought," will "depend on some premise from outside the system itself," as Brian Tierney reminds us, it follows that rights doctrines are not freestanding conceptual frameworks.[1] Inasmuch as we cannot even begin to sort out the order of rights and responsibilities until we are clear about the nature of the subjects to which they attach, a theory of rights will necessarily presuppose an anthropology (including an account of the human good) and a social ontology encompassing an account of the relationship of the individual to society and the character and role of the whole range of institutions to which human nature gives rise (including the state). Different

This is a revised and considerably expanded version of "The Rights of Monads or of Intrinsically Social Beings?" which appeared in the *Ave Maria Law Review* 3 (Spring 2005): 233–57. Reprinted by permission.

1. Brian Tierney, *The Idea of Natural Rights: Studies on Natural Rights, Natural Law, and Church Law, 1150–1625* (1997; reprint, Grand Rapids, MI: Eerdmans, 2001), 193.

anthropologies and social ontologies, in turn, will result in different accounts of the nature of the juridical order and in divergent understandings of the nature, scope, and foundation of the order of rights.

Here I want to explore two different models of society and their implications for our thinking about rights. My argument is divided into three parts. The first will examine some of the problematic features of contemporary American rights discourse, arguing that these features are a function, at least in part, of the flawed ontology of social life implicit in this discourse. The second will provide an overview of the very different ontology of social life that emerges in Catholic thought, an ontology, I will suggest, that allows us to bring into sharp focus the social (as opposed to economic or political) dimension of human existence. The third will seek to show how these two different ontologies point toward very different theories of rights, and will argue that Catholic social thought points us toward a way of thinking about rights that is more consistent with the demands of both social life and the principle of limited government than the type of rights discourse that dominates contemporary America's civil conversation.

Contemporary Rights Talk, Enlightenment Liberalism, and the Voluntarist Theory of Society

While rights claims have long been a staple of our political discourse, over the past half-century American public life has been transformed by the ascendancy of "a new" and highly problematic "version of rights discourse." What is striking about contemporary America's "rights talk," as Mary Ann Glendon points out, is "its starkness and simplicity, its prodigality in bestowing the rights label, its legalistic character, its exaggerated absoluteness, its hyperindividualism, its insularity, and its silence with respect to personal, civic, and collective responsibilities."[2] In the form it has assumed in the work of its most influential academic theoreticians, this new brand of rights talk holds that the right of individuals to choose their own values, goals, and lifestyles "trumps" the claims of competing social goods such as the commonweal, public morality, and communal solidarity.

---

2. Mary Ann Glendon, *Rights Talk: The Impoverishment of Political Discourse* (New York: Free Press, 1991), x. It should be noted that this dialect is not as novel as Glendon sometimes seems to claim. As her argument suggests, its roots lie within certain influential currents in modern thought.

The ascendancy of this new doctrine has had far-reaching and extremely destructive social and political consequences. Insofar as contemporary rights talk, in Jean Bethke Elshtain's words, "correlates rights, wants and preferences," it has produced an environment in which every strongly felt desire tends to be elevated to the status of a right, and issued in a seemingly endless multiplication of rights with, as Glendon notes, little or no "consideration of the ends to which they are oriented, their relationship to one another, to corresponding responsibilities, or to the general welfare." By virtue of its radically individualistic thrust, its deployment of the idea of rights to, in Elshtain's apt formulation, "institutionalize the autonomy of the [individual] will,"[3] the rights revolution of the past half century has impoverished our political discourse by obscuring a wide array of important human and social goods and precluding a careful balancing of the claims of individual freedom against other goods.

Through the revolution in law and public policy it has wrought and the legalistic, adversarial, and rights-oriented mentality it has fostered in American culture, our rights dialect, as Richard E. Morgan has shown, has acted "to marginally disable major American institutions, both governmental and private," by privileging individual autonomy over the goods these institutions serve and the conditions of their effective functioning. It also has prompted what William A. Donohue describes as a far-reaching "unraveling of the social fabric" and engendered an "unprecedented level of social pathologies." Through what George W. Carey terms its subordination of the "basic principles upon which our constitutional system was founded," such as "republicanism, separation of powers and federalism" to the protection of rights, the dominant form of rights talk has issued in a massive transfer of power from elected legislatures to unelected judges, and from state and local governments to the federal judiciary.[4]

Perhaps the most ironic consequence of contemporary rights talk concerns its effect on the scope of government. Historically, rights had functioned in American political culture primarily as a means of limiting the institutions and activities of government; the provisions of a bill of rights

---

3. Jean Bethke Elshtain, "Persons, Politics and a Catholic Understanding of Human Rights," in *Recognizing Religion in a Secular Society*, ed. Douglas Farrow (Montreal: McGill-Queen's University Press, 2004), 72; Glendon, *Rights Talk*, 14.

4. Richard E. Morgan, *Disabling America: The "Rights Industry" in Our Time* (New York: Basic Books, 1984), 3; William A. Donohue, *The New Freedom: Individualism and Collectivism in the Social Lives of Americans* (New Brunswick: Transaction Publishers, 1990), 4, 8; George W. Carey, *In Defense of the Constitution*, rev. and exp. ed. (Indianapolis: Liberty Fund, 1995), 4–5.

were understood as cumulatively establishing a boundary that government may not cross, a zone or sphere of life that was off-limits to the state. A number of features of contemporary rights talk, however, have combined to sever the connection between rights and limited government. These include an increasing emphasis on entitlements (on "positive" as opposed to "negative" rights, or "social" or "economic" as opposed to "political" rights); what Tierney terms the "almost absurd inflation of rights language" to encompass an ever more "luxuriant array of rights" of all kinds; an insistence on the primacy of individual autonomy over other human and social goods; and what Russell Hittinger calls the "open-ended" and "under-specified" character of contemporary rights claims.[5]

Indeed, the type of rights discourse that now dominates our civil conversation has issued in a massive expansion in the scope of government because it authorizes the state to intervene ever more aggressively in an ever-increasing number of spheres of social life in the name of vindicating an ever-expanding catalog of rights. As a result, we have witnessed "the conversion of once-traditional, once-autonomous, once-social relationships into those of the law and the courts" and the transformation of more and more social relations and institutions into "the handmaiden of legislature, law office, regulatory agency, and courtroom."[6]

Whose Rights Talk? Which Social Ontology?

Confronted with this flawed and destructive brand of rights talk, several thoughtful observers (most notably Alasdair MacIntyre) have suggested that we would be better off abandoning the language of rights talk altogether.[7] Although it is difficult not to sympathize with the frustrations that prompt this suggestion, it also is difficult to avoid the conclusion that what is being proposed here is something akin to throwing out the baby with the bathwater. On the one hand, rights talk is so deeply ingrained in contemporary political discourse that it is difficult to see how it could simply be abandoned or what might replace it. Languages, after all, cannot be created *ex nihilo*. Likewise, there is the fact that the abandonment of rights

5. Tierney, *The Idea of Natural Rights*, 345–46; Russell Hittinger, *The First Grace: Rediscovering the Natural Law in a Post-Christian World* (Wilmington, DE: ISI Books, 2003), 129, 133.

6. Robert A. Nisbet, *The Twilight of Authority* (1975; reprint, Indianapolis: Liberty Fund, 2000), 219.

7. MacIntyre is perhaps the leading critic of this language. See his *After Virtue: A Study in Moral Theory*, 2nd ed. (Notre Dame, IN: University of Notre Dame Press, 1984), 66–70; and "Community, Law and the Rhetoric of Rights" *Listening* 26 (1991): 96–110.

language would conceptually impoverish our political discourse. If rights language has been embraced by so wide an array of intellectual traditions and political perspectives, it is because this language provides us with an extraordinarily powerful tool for limiting the powers of government and/or specifying the ultimate ends of law and public policy, specifying the content, as it were, of the commonweal. Enabling us to articulate a variety of important norms and goods more precisely than would otherwise be the case, rights language in principle represents a real advance in our political vocabulary. Indeed, a case can be made that the idea of natural rights represents one of Western civilization's most precious political achievements.

Finally, there is what Tierney terms the "adaptability" of the idea of rights, the fact that a plurality of different theories of rights is in principle possible. This means that there is no necessary linkage (either logically or historically) between rights talk and an "atomic individualism," and that the problems besetting contemporary rights talk are not inherent in rights talk as such, but are instead a product of the particular type of rights talk that dominates our civil conversation. As Tierney notes, the old adage holds here: "*abusus non tollit usum*" (abuse does not take away rightful use). The "abuses" that pervade contemporary rights talk do not mean that the concept cannot "be of very great value" in our political discourse.[8] Contrary to what is sometimes suggested, in short, what our circumstances require is not the rejection of rights talk, but the development of a new and better way of thinking and talking about rights. To paraphrase MacIntyre, the real question we confront is not whether to abandon the idea of rights, but whose rights doctrine—and thus which social ontology—we are to embrace.

The first step in the forging of a better understanding is the identification of the source of the problems besetting contemporary rights talk. As is now widely recognized, the answer is to be found in the model of human nature and society implicit in it. Contemporary rights discourse takes its bearings from an anthropology that views human beings as "unencumbered" selves, as "free and independent selves" who are "unbound by moral ties antecedent to choice," unbound by "ends we have not chosen—ends given by nature or God, for example, or by our identities as members of families, peoples, cultures, or traditions."[9] Our concern

---

8. Tierney, *The Idea of Natural Rights*, 345, 347, 97.

9. Michael J. Sandel, *Democracy's Discontent: America in Search of a Public Philosophy* (Cambridge: Harvard University Press, Belknap Press, 1996), 12.

here, however, is less with this anthropology as such than with the social ontology with which it is linked.

The hallmarks of this ontology are essentially twofold. The first consists in a particular map of human social life. Contemporary rights discourse sees social life through the prism of what Glendon has aptly termed the "individual-state-market grid."[10] It sees social life, in other words, through a lens that allows it to discern only three realities: the individual (understood as an unencumbered self); the state (understood as the guardian of rights—above all, the right of each individual to self-definition and self-determination—and creator of a framework of order within which each individual is afforded the maximum possible freedom to pursue his or her self-chosen goals consistent with the exercise of that same freedom by others); and the market (understood as a realm of autonomous individual activity in accordance with a utilitarian calculus of self-interest and thus as the institutional embodiment of the sovereignty of the individual). In this vision, all human groups must be conceptualized either as "more or less arbitrarily fashioned creatures of mere Positive Law" or through the prism of market models, as "arbitrary institutions sustained [solely] by the private desires of individuals."[11]

This map of social life, of course, is simply untenable. It ignores the whole realm of "nongovernmental, nonmarket relations and institutions."[12] It ignores, in other words, nonutilitarian forms of community, what Glendon terms "communities of memory and mutual aid," groups like "families, neighborhoods, workplace associations and religious and other communities of obligations" that collectively constitute "civil society."[13] These groups are organized and operate according to a very different logic than that which informs the world of the market: possessing a highly personal character, they are united by ties that are solidaristic rather than instrumental and contractual. This grid obscures not just the distinctive nature of these groups and the delicate social ecology on which they depend, but their irreplaceable contributions to human flourishing, self-government, and ordered liberty. At the same time, it reduces the basic issue of political theory to the relationship of the state and the individual,

10. Glendon, *Rights Talk*, 143.

11. Otto von Gierke, *Political Theories of the Middle Ages,* trans. Frederic William Maitland (1900; reprint, Boston: Beacon Press, 1958), 100; Stanley Hauerwas, "Symposium," *Center Journal* 1, no. 3 (1982): 44–45.

12. James W. Skillen, *Recharging the American Experiment: Principled Pluralism for Genuine Civic Community* (Grand Rapids, MI: Baker Books, 1994), 70.

13. Glendon, *Rights Talk*, 119, 120.

and the basic question of public policy to the drawing of the line between the jurisdiction of the market and the sphere of the state.

This truncated map of society, in turn, is rooted in a particular understanding of the nature of human social relations that Charles Taylor has dubbed "atomism," which refers to a conception of social life that involves "a purely instrumental view of society," a view that insists that society is "in some sense constituted by individuals for the fulfillment of certain ends which . . . [are] primarily individual." Implicit in atomism is a rejection of "the view that man is a social animal" in favor of an affirmation of "the self-sufficiency of man alone or, if you prefer, of the individual."[14] Atomism thus involves the denial of a "strong, constitutive" conception of community in which society is understood as "an ingredient or constituent" of the identity of individuals rather than a "possible aim of antecedently individualized selves."[15]

Here again, this vision of social life is simply untenable. On the one hand, it ignores the fact that men and women are not "monads" but "essentially social beings," the fact that "people do not 'enter' society; they are constituted in part by society and in turn constitute it."[16] Reinhold Niebuhr has ably formulated the essential point:

> The highest reaches of individual consciousness and awareness are rooted in social experience and find their ultimate meaning in relation to the community. The individual is the product of the whole socio-historical process, though he may reach a height of uniqueness which seems to transcend his social history completely. His individual decisions and achievements grow into, as well as out of, the community. . . . Even the highest forms of art avail themselves of tools and forms, of characteristic insights and styles which betray the time and place of the artist . . . [even when] they rise to very great heights of individual insight . . . [and] achieve a corresponding height of universal validity.[17]

On the other hand, atomism ignores the ways in which human beings, as MacIntyre so forcefully reminds us, are dependent creatures, and thus are

14. Charles Taylor, *Philosophy and the Human Sciences: Philosophical Papers 2* (Cambridge: Cambridge University Press, 1985), 187–89.

15. Michael J. Sandel, *Liberalism and the Limits of Justice,* 2nd ed. (Cambridge: Cambridge University Press, 1998), 151, 64.

16. Glendon, *Rights Talk,* 74.

17. Reinhold Niebuhr, *The Children of Light and the Children of Darkness* (New York: Scribner's Sons, 1944), 50.

beings naturally situated within a complex matrix of relationships of care-giving and dependency, as well as ignoring what Jacques Maritain terms "the radical generosity"—the natural orientation to self-giving and communion—"inscribed within the very being of the person." As Elshtain notes, this vision of atomism is "so 'weightless' it would evaporate were it not for the fact that . . . it has become dogma."[18]

The Hegemony of Enlightenment Liberalism

As to how the atomistic vision has acquired this status, the answer is found in the hegemony of a particular intellectual tradition that provides what Roberto Unger terms the "deep structure of thought" underlying both our academic theorizing and our civil conversation, namely, Enlightenment liberalism. For its "true nature" to be understood, as Unger has shown, this structure "must be seen all of a piece, not just as a set of doctrines about the disposition of power and wealth in society," but as a "metaphysical system."[19] Although their full implications were only worked out slowly over the course of several centuries, Enlightenment liberalism's metaphysical commitments have profound implications for its understanding of human nature and society. The nominalism and rationalism that lie at its metaphysical core, for example, entail what two recent writers describe as "the rejection of teleology," the rejection of "the claim that there is a discoverable excellence or optimal condition . . . which characterizes human beings" as such.[20]

This denial has momentous consequences. It pushes liberalism relentlessly toward the denial of the existence of an order of natural or God-given human or social ends, and thus toward a view of human beings as sovereign wills free to make of themselves and the world whatever they choose. It pushes liberalism relentlessly toward the rejection of the very idea of a knowable and substantive human good, and thus toward a com-

---

18. Alasdair MacIntyre, *Dependent Rational Animals: Why Human Beings Need the Virtues* (Chicago: Open Court, 1999); Jacques Maritain, *The Rights of Man and Natural Law*, trans. Doris C. Anson (1943; reprint, New York: Gordian Press, 1971), 5; Jean Bethke Elshtain, "The Liberal Captivity of Feminism," in *The Liberal Future in America*, ed. Phillip Abbott and Michael B. Levy (Westport, CT: Greenwood Press, 1985), 73.

19. Roberto Mangabeira Unger, *Knowledge and Politics* (New York: Free Press, 1984), 8, 6, 11.

20. R. Bruce Douglass and Gerald M. Mara, "The Search for a Defensible Good: The Emerging Dilemma of Liberalism," in *Liberalism and the Good*, ed. R. Bruce Douglass, Gerald M. Mara, and Henry S. Richardson (New York: Routledge, 1990), 258.

mitment to what George F. Will terms "the moral equality of appetites."[21] It pushes liberalism relentlessly toward an understanding of freedom as "radical indetermination,"[22] as simply the power to choose between alternatives independently of all causes except freedom itself, and thus toward both the denial that freedom possesses an intrinsic orientation toward an inscribed good or set of goods and, as Kenneth L. Schmitz notes, an insistence that freedom finds fulfillment "not simply [in] the power to choose," but "equally, even primarily, [in] the power to *unchoose*."[23] It pushes liberalism toward "an unrelenting subordination of all allegedly objective goods to the subjective good of individual choice,"[24] toward the elevation of choice to the status of the highest human good.

Most important for our purposes here, however, are the implications of the rejection of teleology for Enlightenment liberalism's understanding of social life. As Francis Canavan points out, since "to the nominalist mind only individuals are real," its metaphysics of the person "makes it hard" for liberalism "to entertain the notion of relations as natural." The result is a wholly voluntarist conception of social relations. The individual, in this view, "is an atom, motivated by self-interest," rather than an essentially "social being from whose nature flow relations to his family, neighbors, fellow workers, the community, and the political order." Far from being understood as rooted in our dynamic orientation toward perfection, the fulfillment of our human nature, social relations are instead seen as "the essentially contractual" products of the self-interest, the subjective preferences, of naturally autonomous individuals. Social relations are thus something "external, accidental and adventitious," not "consequences" of the very structure of human nature.[25] We thus arrive at what we earlier termed "atomism," at what Niebuhr describes as "the illusion that communities . . . are created by the fiat of human will" as "instruments" employed by "atomic individuals" in the pursuit of their purposes.[26]

21. George F. Will, *Statecraft as Soulcraft: What Government Does* (New York: Simon and Schuster, 1983), 158.

22. Servais Pinckaers, *The Sources of Christian Ethics*, trans. Mary Thomas Noble, OP (Washington, DC: The Catholic University of America Press, 1995), 245.

23. Kenneth L. Schmitz, "Is Liberalism Good Enough?" in *Liberalism and the Good,* ed. Douglass, Mara, and Richardson, 90.

24. Francis Canavan, SJ, *The Pluralist Game* (Lanham, MD: Rowman and Littlefield, 1995), 76.

25. Francis Canavan, SJ, "From Ockham to Blackmun: The Philosophical Roots of Liberal Jurisprudence," in *Courts and the Culture War,* ed. Bradley C. S. Watson (Lanham, MD: Lexington Books, 2002), 23; Canavan, *Pluralist Game,* 121, 131.

26. Niebuhr, *Children of Light,* 53.

This voluntarist conception of social relations has far-reaching implications for an understanding of the institutions and groups that individuals create. On the one hand, by reducing them to nothing more than the "artificial . . . products of the will and interests of individuals,"[27] it deprives these institutions of a determinate nature, a natural structure. By depriving us of "given natural norms by which institutions can be judged as more or less in harmony with the needs of mankind's common nature," Enlightenment liberalism's voluntarist vision of society effectively "makes all institutions arbitrary."[28] On the other hand, it compels us to understand all social groups (and compels all social institutions to understand themselves) through the prism of market models. It thus reduces them to nothing more than what Carl Schneider terms collections "of individuals temporarily united for their mutual convenience and armed with rights against each other."[29] The intellectual universe of Enlightenment liberalism, in short, has no room for solidaristic institutions, binding commitments, relations other than market relations: "society" is absorbed into the world of the market. We thus arrive at the world of the individual-state-market grid, a world of atomic individuals united only by contracts and the sovereign will of the state.

Where does the state fit into this vision of social life? On the question of the proper scope of government, contemporary liberal theorists move in two conflicting directions. The proponents of classical liberalism or libertarian liberalism "defend the market economy and claim that redistributive policies violate people's rights" to "the fruits" of their "own labor," and seek to sharply circumscribe the role of the state in the overall economy of social life. In contrast, the proponents of "egalitarian" liberalism rely less on the market in the ordering of social life and advocate a more active state charged with fostering equality in all spheres of social life and vindicating "certain social and economic rights—rights to welfare, education, health care, and so on."[30] Whereas classical liberals tend to embrace the ideal of what is sometimes called the nightwatchman state, the proponents of egalitarian liberalism champion the cause of the welfare state.

If contemporary liberal theorists differ on the scope of the state, they nevertheless tend to share a common political morality in which the idea

27. Unger, *Knowledge and Politics*, 81.
28. Canavan, "From Ockham to Blackmun," 22.
29. Carl Schneider, "Moral Discourse and the Transformation of American Family Law," *Michigan Law Review* 83 (1985): 1859. Schneider is speaking specifically of a certain view of the family here, but what his formulation aptly captures is the effect of liberalism on all human communities.
30. Sandel, *Democracy's Discontent*, 11.

of rights plays a central role. There is, of course, nothing surprising in this fact. If, as Tierney has demonstrated, the idea of rights long predates the seventeenth and eighteenth centuries, the fact is that from Enlightenment liberalism's inception the idea of rights has figured centrally in the political theories it has spawned. "From its beginnings," as Canavan notes, these theories have "tended . . . to limit the powers of government by guaranteeing the rights of individuals."[31] Likewise, from its inception, they have tended to insist that the primary goal of state power is reducible to the protection of the rights of the individual, that the powers of government are simply "implications" of "antecedent rights claims."[32] What is new in contemporary liberal theory is less a matter of its emphasis on rights than its understanding of them, the idea of rights toward which its model of human nature and society inexorably pushes it.

As Canavan observes, in viewing the individual as "an atom . . . to whom violence is done if he is subjected to a relationship he has not chosen" (or, it might be added, to which he no longer consents) and in insisting that individual freedom takes "precedence over any other human or social good that conflicts with it," liberal rights doctrines center on what Gerard V. Bradley terms the "megaright" of individual autonomy, the right of the individual to self-definition and self-determination.[33] "At the heart of liberty," as Justices O'Connor, Souter, and Kennedy affirmed in their opinion in *Planned Parenthood v. Casey*, "is the right to define one's own concept of existence, of meaning, of the universe, and of the mystery of human life." Each individual thus has the right to act on his or her subjective preferences so long as they are compatible with the equal right of others to do the same. Existing to protect this right in all its manifold forms, government is limited to the pursuit of "general goods" that "all persons could reasonably accept as all-purpose conditions of pursuing their aims, whatever they are."[34]

Today, it is widely recognized that the better way of thinking about rights we so badly need is impossible without a model of social life decisively richer and more complex than that which is possible on the premises of Enlightenment liberalism. Nevertheless, we have experienced great

31. Canavan, *Pluralist Game,* 138.
32. Hittinger, *First Grace,* 127, 128.
33. Canavan, *Pluralist Game,* 76, 121; Gerard V. Bradley, "Shall We Ratify the New Constitution? The Judicial Manifesto in *Casey* and *Lee,*" in *Benchmarks,* ed. Terry Eastland (Washington, DC: Ethics and Public Policy Center, 1995), 121.
34. *Planned Parenthood of Southeastern Pennsylvania v. Casey,* 112 S. Ct. 2791 (1992); David A. J. Richards, *Toleration and the Constitution* (New York: Oxford University Press, 1986), 244, 259.

difficulty in articulating the "thicker" model of social life we seek. This is due not only to the pervasive influence of Enlightenment liberalism on the contemporary intellectual scene, but to the tendency of certain dangers that frequently accompany thicker social ontologies. While the classical tradition certainly provides a thick conception of social life, for example, it does so at a considerable cost: the absorption of the social into the political and of the individual into the social whole, the absorption of both the whole range of human social relations and the individual human person into the compact, undifferentiated unity of the polity. If Enlightenment liberalism is blind to the depth of human sociality, traditions encompassing thick understandings of social life are frequently blind to the nature and dignity of individual human beings as persons; and if the former dissolves solidaristic social institutions into the market, the latter frequently absorb them into the body politic.

Communitatis Communitatum: *Normative Pluralism and the Catholic Vision of Human Social Life*

It is against this backdrop, I would suggest, that the possible contribution of Catholic social thought can be seen. Catholic social thought begins with a moral and metaphysical realism set in the framework of the Christian idea of a created universe. Man, as the Second Vatican Council affirms, is subject to "a law which he has not laid upon himself which he must obey,"[35] a law which, in Pope John Paul II's words, is "inscribed in our humanity," in the very "teleological structure" of human nature itself.[36] Inasmuch as there exists an order of human and social ends that binds us prior to, and independently of, our consent to pursue them, the moral order is not a mere human construct. On the contrary, its imperatives are embedded in the very structure of human nature.

Likewise, Catholic social thought affirms the naturalness of political life and a thick conception of the common good. Political authority is natural, it insists, because without it the "individuals, [the] families and the various groups which make up the civil community, are aware of their inabil-

---

35. *Gaudium et Spes*, in *Vatican Council II: The Conciliar Documents*, ed. Austin Flannery (Collegeville, MN: Liturgical Press, 1977), 916 (sec. 16). Because they often are available in multiple editions, official Church documents will be cited both by page number in the edition being employed here and by section number in the document itself. Hereafter *Gaudium et Spes* will be cited parenthetically in the text as *GS*.

36. Pope John Paul II, "Marriage: A Natural Reality, Not a Cultural Construct," *The Pope Speaks* 46 (July–August 2001): 226.

ity to achieve a truly human life by their own unaided efforts." It is natural, in other words, because it is necessary to the achievement of "the common good," which it defines as "the sum total of all those conditions of social life which enable individuals, families, and organizations to achieve complete and efficacious fulfillment" (*GS*, 980–81 [sec. 74]). As Maritain points out, the common good in question here consists of nothing less than the "communion" of its members "in the good life." If it encompasses the "progressive liberation" of the human person "from the bondage of material nature," this good is "above all" concerned with the development of "conditions of life in common," which foster "in a positive manner . . . the flowering of moral and rational life."[37]

Finally, and most importantly for our purposes here, Catholicism affirms a deeply social vision of the person. "Life in society is not something accessory to man" (*GS*, 926 [sec. 25]), as the Second Vatican Council affirms, because man "by his innermost nature . . . is a social being" (*GS*, 913 [sec. 12]). In this view, "human beings" are "creatures essentially, not contingently, related to others."[38] Inasmuch as man can only be himself in and through community, it follows that he "is by nature as much a social being as he is an individual being."[39]

In part, the human person's nature as a social being is rooted in his lack of self-sufficiency as an individual. Without society, "man can neither live nor develop his gifts" (*GS*, 913 [sec. 12]). Most fundamentally, however, it is rooted in what John Paul II terms "the capacity and responsibility" for "love and communion" inscribed on the very being of the person. Created in the image of a Triune God, love thus constitutes "the fundamental and innate vocation of every human person."[40] Indeed, it is "only in a sincere giving of himself" that "man can fully discover his true self" (*GS*, 925 [sec. 24]). Hence our humanity demands a life of interpersonal self-giving and receiving.

If the Catholic vision of social life, however, is thick, it is also pluralistic and personalistic. To begin with the former, Catholic social thought embraces what is sometimes called institutional or normative pluralism, insisting, as John Paul II maintains, that "the social nature is not completely fulfilled in the State, but is realized in various intermediary groups

---

37. Maritain, *The Rights of Man*, 8, 43, 45.

38. Jean Bethke Elshtain, "Catholic Social Thought, the City, and Liberal America," in *Catholicism, Liberalism and Communitarianism: The Catholic Intellectual Tradition and the Moral Foundations of Democracy*, ed. Kenneth L. Grasso, Gerard V. Bradley, and Robert P. Hunt (Lanham, MD: Rowman and Littlefield, 1995), 104.

39. Johannes Messner, *Social Ethics* (St. Louis: B. Herder, 1949), 99.

40. Pope John Paul II, *Familiaris Consortio* (Boston: St. Paul Editions, n.d. [1981]), 22 (sec. 11).

beginning with the family and including social, political and cultural groups."[41] As Heinrich Rommen puts it, the social nature of the human person gives rise "to a plurality of social forms and . . . cooperative spheres that . . . serve independent ends in the order of the common good." These groups are no more creations of the state than they are purely conventional products of contractual agreements among naturally free individuals. Rather, they "stem from human nature itself" (*CA,* 21 [sec. 13]). Thus, "however adaptable" their specific "forms" may be in "different states of historical development and national culture," the fact remains that "with regard to their specific ends," these social forms "are irreplaceable."[42]

They are irreplaceable, to begin with, because each discharges a distinctive function that is essential to human flourishing, which is essential in equipping individuals to realize their humanity. Likewise, they are irreplaceable by virtue of their status as the principal sites, as it were, wherein human beings fulfill their vocations as persons. "It is only through the free gift of self that one truly finds oneself," as John Paul II declares. "One cannot give oneself . . . to an abstract ideal," but only "to another person or to other persons." These groups thus constitute the principal location where we enter into and live out those relationships of "solidarity and communion with others" for which God created us and through which we discover ourselves (*CA,* 58–59 [sec. 40]).

Insofar as the social ties in which our nature finds expression include relations of both an instrumental and solidaristic character, this pluralist understanding of the structure of social life takes us decisively beyond the horizon of the individual-state-market grid. Indeed, it highlights what this grid obscures: the existence of a complex matrix of institutions that differ dramatically in their organizing principles from both the state and the market. And if, from the Catholic perspective, the state and the network of social relations constitutive of the marketplace play indispensable roles in the overall scheme of social life, it is nevertheless principally in and through nonstate and nonmarket institutions, in and through the institutions of civil society, that individuals enter into those relationships of "solidarity and communion with others" that lie at the heart of our vocations as persons. Without these communities, John Paul II argues, society would become "an anonymous and impersonal mass," and the individual, by

41. Pope John Paul II, *Centesimus Annus* (Boston: St. Paul Books and Media, n.d. [1991]), 21 (sec. 13). Hereafter this document will be cited parenthetically in the text as *CA.*

42. Heinrich Rommen, *The State in Catholic Thought* (St. Louis: B. Herder, 1945), 143, 144.

being treated as "only . . . a producer and consumer of goods, or . . . an object of state administration," would "be suffocated between the two poles represented by the state and the marketplace" (*CA*, 70–71 [sec. 49]). For Catholic social thought, the groups and institutions of civil society, rather than the state or market, constitute, as it were, the center of social gravity.

Thus, for Catholic social thought, "society is a unity composed of member communities that are relatively independent, or autonomous, since they have their own social ends, their own common good, and consequently their own functions."[43] This vision of society as a *communitatis communitatum* (community of communities), in turn, has profound implications. It means that "the common good" of society "is necessarily pluralistic in character," that it necessarily "includes the particular goods" of the whole range of institutions issuing from the social nature of the human person.[44] Only if those communities are able to be themselves, only if they can effectively pursue their particular ends, their distinctive common goods, can human beings "enjoy the possibility of achieving their own perfection in a certain fullness of measure and also with some relative ease."[45]

It means that although a natural institution, the state is neither the only nor necessarily the most important institution in which the social nature of the human person finds expression. (Indeed, Catholic social thought, as Messner notes, affirms "the primacy of the family among social units including the state.") The state, therefore, must share the stage of social life with the whole range of social institutions and communities that issue from human nature. In Rommen's formulation, precisely because these other social institutions "have their intrinsic values and objective ends," precisely because they make indispensable contributions to human flourishing, the state does not make them "superfluous," and may neither "abolish" them nor "take over" their functions and purposes.[46]

From this it follows that the basic question of political theory cannot be reduced to the proper relationship between the sovereign state and the sovereign individual. It also follows that the state's role in the overall economy of social life is a limited one. The state is limited by the fact that only certain limited aspects of the common good have been entrusted to its care.

---

43. Messner, *Social Ethics*, 140.

44. Jonathan S. Chaplin, "Subsidiarity as a Political Norm," in *Political Theory and Christian Vision* (Lanham, MD: University Press of America, 1994), 86.

45. Pope Paul VI, *Dignitatis Humanae*, in *Religious Liberty: An End and a Beginning*, ed. John Courtney Murray, SJ (New York: MacMillan, 1966), 177 (sec. 7).

46. Messner, *Social Ethics*, 30; Rommen, *The State in Catholic Thought*, 301.

The remainder have been entrusted to the care of other institutions and communities—institutions and communities that are "original entities and original social organizations" in their own right rather than mere creatures of the state existing at its pleasure and exercising functions delegated to them by it.[47] The state is thus limited by the limited character of its functions relative to the overall economy of human social life, and thus by the responsibilities, the distinctive functions, of the other institutions with which it shares the stage of social life. Society "is organized as the state, but only for certain purposes and for the performance of certain functions relative to those purposes."[48]

The Subjectivity of Society

Catholicism's ontology of social life combines this commitment to institutional pluralism with a personalist understanding of human nature and society. Man, it affirms, is a person, a being "endowed with reason and free will and therefore privileged to bear responsibility."[49] This personalist anthropology, it should be stressed, should not be confused with Enlightenment liberalism's view of man as a sovereign will. While affirming the reality of human freedom, Catholicism also affirms man's capacity to recognize and order his life in accordance with a moral law inscribed on the structure of his humanity by its Creator. Indeed, far from being opposed to freedom, Catholic doctrine maintains that it is only through the realization of the goods inscribed on its very structure that human freedom finds its fulfillment. Implicit in our personhood, therefore, is a task and a grave responsibility. As a person, each human being has what Pope Pius XII described as "the entirely personal duty to . . . order to perfection his material and spiritual life."[50]

"The sublime dignity of the human person," in turn, has profound implications for our understanding of social life and its proper ordering. It means that social life must reflect and promote our dignity as persons. Precisely because they exist for the sake of persons, it follows that all forms of social life have what Rommen describes as "a service character." The

47. Rommen, *The State in Catholic Thought*, 256.
48. Francis Canavan, SJ, "Religious Liberty: John Courtney Murray and Vatican II," in *John Courtney Murray and the American Civil Conversation,* ed. Robert P. Hunt and Kenneth L. Grasso (Grand Rapids, MI: Eerdmans, 1992), 168.
49. Pope Paul VI, *Dignitatis Humanae,* 167–68 (sec. 2).
50. Pope Pius XII, "The Anniversary of *Rerum Novarum,*" in *The Major Addresses of Pope Pius XII,* vol. 2, ed. Vincent A. Yzermans (St. Paul: North Central, 1961), 31.

cardinal point of Catholic teaching on social life, as Pope John XXIII affirms, "is that individual men are necessarily the foundation, cause, and end of all social institutions."[51] Indeed, insofar as only "individual persons are substantial beings," a society is not a substance, but a unity of order (*unitas ordinis*) encompassing "a multitude of families, individual persons, and groups."[52]

As Maritain points out, the fact that society consists of persons means its common good is more than "the collection of the individual goods of each of the persons who constitute it," but neither is it like "the proper good of a whole, like the species with respect to its individuals or the hive with respect to its bees, [which] relates the parts to itself alone and sacrifices them to itself." As the common good of a society of "human persons," this good is "a good received and communicated" by the members of society. Accordingly, "it is . . . common to both *the whole and the parts* into which it flows back and which in turn, must benefit from it," and thus "requires by its very essence . . . redistribution to the persons who constitute society" and "respect for their dignity."[53] Thus, the common good takes "priority over" particular goods, over the goods of individuals and social groups, "only in the sense that . . . what is contained in the common good" is necessary to their attainment.[54]

By virtue of our personhood, moreover, the common good has an inherently limited character. On the one hand, as Maritain explains, "the human person is ordained directly to God as to its ultimate end," and by virtue of this "ordination . . . transcends every created common good," including "the common good of the political society." Thus, "the person is engaged in its entirety as a part of society, but not by reason of everything that is in it and everything that belongs to it."[55] Precisely because the person possesses a destiny transcending all temporal societies, the common good of the political community possesses an inherently limited nature.

From our nature as persons, it also follows that social activity has a subsidiary character. Precisely because man is a person, Messner observes, his "self-realization" is "not something given" him "from without," but "implies personal responsibility" and involves "the exercise of freedom."

---

51. Rommen, *The State in Catholic Thought*, 44; Pope John XXIII, *Mater et Magistra* (Boston: Daughters of St. Paul, n.d. [1961]), 219, 63.
52. Rommen, *The State in Catholic Thought*, 36–37, 254.
53. Maritain, *The Person and the Common Good*, trans. J. J. Fitzgerald (New York: Scribner's Sons, 1947), 50–51, 61.
54. Chaplin, "Subsidiarity as a Political Norm," 86.
55. Maritain, *The Person and the Common Good*, 15, 72.

Accordingly, "any social grouping, including the state, can assume merely an ancillary role in this process."[56] It is thus no accident that, as we have seen, Catholic social thought identifies the common good of society as conditions in which individuals, families, and other intermediary groups *"enjoy the possibility* of achieving their own perfection in a certain fullness of measure and also with some relative ease."[57]

Taken in conjunction with Catholicism's commitment to normative pluralism, personalism grounds the affirmation by Catholic thought of the existence of an order of human rights that must be respected by the state and whose protection and promotion are an essential element of the common good. In John Paul II's words, "[T]he common good that . . . the State serves is brought to full realization only when all the citizens are sure of their rights."[58] "Universal and inviolable," these rights flow from our "very nature,"[59] from the demands of human dignity and the responsibilities inherent in this dignity.

Thus, as John Courtney Murray contends, man's dignity as a person confers upon "him certain immunities, and . . . endows him with certain empowerments. He may make certain demands upon society and the state which require action in their support and he may also utter certain prohibitions in the face of society and the state."[60] On the one hand, the rights of the person include "access" to the various material and cultural resources "necessary for living a genuinely human life" (*GS*, 927 [sec. 26]). On the other hand, insofar as the quest for truth and goodness must proceed in a manner in keeping with our dignity as persons, which requires us "to act of conscious and free choice . . . not by blind impulses or mere external restraint" (*GS*, 917 [sec. 17]), this dignity demands an inviolable sphere of personal freedom within which individuals can confront the responsibilities inherent in their personhood in a manner in keeping with their nature as persons. It also demands that the state and other institutions in which our social nature finds expression respect the legitimate limits of their jurisdictions.

From the fact that the institutions and groups of civil society are communities of persons, it follows that they too are the subjects of rights. The case of the family illustrates the essential principles involved. "Just as the

---

56. Messner, *Social Ethics,* 574–75.
57. Pope Paul VI, *Dignitatis Humanae,* 173 (sec. 6; emphasis added).
58. Pope John Paul II, *Redemptor Hominis* (Washington, DC: U.S. Catholic Conference, 1979), 63 (sec. 17).
59. Pope John XXIII, *Pacem in Terris* (Boston: St. Paul Books and Media, n.d. [1963]), 71 (sec. 38).
60. John Courtney Murray, SJ, *We Hold These Truths: Catholic Reflections on the American Proposition* (1960; reprint, Lanham, MD: Rowman and Littlefield, 2005), 89.

person is a subject," John Paul II affirms, "so too is the family since it is made up of persons who joined together by a profound bond of communion form a single *communal subject*." As such, it possesses both responsibilities rooted in the ends it exists to serve and a very real dignity. From these responsibilities and this dignity flow "certain proper and specific rights" that transcend the rights of the individuals who compose it. Precisely because "the family is *much more* than the sum of its individual members," it follows that "the rights of the family are not simply the sum total" of the rights of its individual members. Like the rights of individuals, furthermore, the rights of the family encompass both the right to access the economic and cultural resources required to discharge its mission and the right, as "in a certain sense" a "sovereign society," to a large measure of autonomy and self governance.[61]

Although "the family is more of a subject than any other social institution," all such institutions "possess a subjectivity" that is "proper" to themselves and that they "receive" from the "persons and families" that compose them.[62] Thus, as Messner notes, the rights of communities "are rights in themselves, just as individual rights are, and not only an appendix to the latter," and include the right of these communities to exist and perform the responsibilities proper to them. And, inasmuch as human nature gives rise to a plurality of communities each with its own distinct ends, functions, and common good, there exists "a plurality of categories of equally fundamental rights, none of which can simply be derived from another."[63]

Nor does this order of rights exhaust the implications of Catholicism's normative pluralism and personalism. Inasmuch as the dignity of the human person "requires that every man enjoy the right to act freely and responsibly," as John XXIII notes, it demands that "in social relations man should exercise his rights, [and] fulfill his obligations . . . chiefly on his own responsibility and initiative." This means that nonstate groups "must be considered the indispensable means to safeguard the dignity of the human person."[64] It also means that freedom is elevated to the status of a foundational principle in the ordering of social and political life, that "the freedom of man [must] be respected as far as possible and curtailed only when and insofar as necessary."[65] This commitment to the method of

61. *Letter to Families from Pope John Paul II* (Boston: St. Paul Books and Media, n.d. [1994]), 51 (sec. 15); 62 (sec. 17); 65 (sec. 17).
62. Ibid., 15, 51.
63. Messner, *Social Ethics*, 178, 177.
64. Pope John XXIII, *Pacem in Terris*, 13–14 (sec. 34); 12 (sec. 24).
65. Pope Paul VI, *Dignitatis Humanae*, 178 (sec. 7).

freedom, of course, encompasses the freedom not merely of individuals but of social groups as well. By virtue of their dignity as communal subjects, they too must have the freedom "to act . . . on their own initiative and on their own responsibility in order to achieve their desired ends."[66]

Taken together, Catholic social thought's commitments to pluralism and personalism issue in a recognition of what John Paul II terms "the 'subjectivity' of society" (*CA,* 21 [sec. 13]). From this recognition, in turn, follows a commitment to what Canavan calls the "self-organization of society." Given the creative subjectivity of society, "the energies of society" should flow "from below upwards, not from the top down,"[67] as "persons freely organize themselves to pursue a wide variety of goals" in a multiplicity of associations.[68] As society develops, in other words, it naturally articulates itself into a wide array of communities and institutions. The Catholic vision of the human person and society thus issues in "a steady bias toward decentralization, freedom, and initiative."[69]

The Subsidiary State

What emerges here is a distinctive vision of the state and its role in the overall economy of social life. The state, in this view, is neither the only institution in which the social nature of the human person finds expression nor the most important. Its jurisdiction, moreover, does not extend to directly managing or controlling the whole of social life any more than it extends to "the direct and positive actualization of the private good of individual citizens."[70] The state, in short, does not exist to supplant the array of institutions and groups in which the social nature of the human person finds expression, to absorb their functions, or to micromanage their affairs. For it to attempt to do any of these things would be an affront to the dignity of the human person and a transgression of its rightful jurisdiction. As we have seen, moreover, the state does not create "the sum total of conditions" necessary to human flourishing, "the sum total of conditions" constitutive of the common good, unilaterally. Rather, it collaborates in the creation of these conditions with the full range of institutions

66. Pope John XXIII, *Pacem in Terris,* 11 (sec. 23).

67. Francis Canavan, SJ, "The Popes and the Economy," *Notre Dame Journal of Law, Ethics, and Public Policy* 11, no. 2 (1997): 440.

68. Francis Canavan, SJ, "The Image of Man in Catholic Thought," in *Catholicism, Liberalism and Communitarianism,* ed. Grasso, Bradley, and Hunt, 24.

69. Canavan, "The Popes and the Economy," 437.

70. Heinrich Pesch, *Heinrich Pesch on Solidarist Economics,* trans. Rupert J. Ederer (Lanham, MD: University Press of America, 1998), 22.

that issue from the social nature of the human person. As Maritain observes, although the common good is its "final end," the state's "immediate end" is that particular segment of this good that might be called "the public order and welfare."[71]

In what does the public order and welfare consist? It consists in the creation of "an order of tranquility, justice and peace" that will enable the full range of institutions in which our nature as social beings finds expression to freely and effectively pursue its own particular ends.[72] As Chaplin notes, the state establishes such an order primarily through the construction of a framework of public law "recognizing and protecting the various rights and duties pertaining to each [institution or group] and, in the interests of the common good, adjudicating between them when conflicts of rights and duties arise."[73] It is the responsibility of the state, in short, to coordinate social activity so as to enable these groups to be themselves, and thereby to make their essential contributions to human flourishing, to coordinate social activity so as to create conditions in which individuals and groups can "pursue freely and effectively the achievement of man's wellbeing in its totality" (*GS*, 983 [sec. 75]). Messner, in fact, goes so far as to argue that "to make possible for the families which form the political community the fulfillment of their natural functions is *the primary function of the state*."[74] With regard to the groups and institutions of civil society, Franz H. Mueller observes that "the functions of the state are essentially subsidiary."[75]

What this means, to begin with, is that the state must acknowledge the right of these institutions to exist and to discharge their distinctive functions, as well as their right, as communities of persons, to a large measure of autonomy and self-governance. The state, furthermore, must take account of these groups and seek to facilitate their activities. Toward this end, for example, it must provide them with a secure foundation in its public law and recognize them as the subjects of social rights and obligations. This means, in turn, that the state must recognize and respect the natural structure—in John Paul II's phrase, "the proper identity"[76]—of each of these institutions and communities. It is thus the nature of these institutions "that [must] control the legal forms, not vice versa." Likewise,

71. Maritain, *Man and the State* (Chicago: University of Chicago Press, 1951), 12, 14.
72. Rommen, *The State in Catholic Thought*, 270.
73. Chaplin, "Subsidiarity as a Political Norm," 95.
74. Messner, *Social Ethics*, 289 (emphasis added).
75. Franz H. Mueller, *The Church and the Social Question* (Washington, DC: American Enterprise Institute, 1984), 81.
76. Pope John Paul II, *Sollicitudo Rei Socialis* (Boston: St. Paul Books and Media, n.d. [1987]), 59 (sec. 33).

the state not only must put into place the infrastructure necessary to social unity and the proper functioning of nonstate institutions (for example, roads, a common currency, a legal system, etc.), but also must seek to create conditions in which all of these groups have "ready access" to the material and cultural resources they need to prosper. It thus must seek to safeguard the "social ecology" upon which each depends, to assure, in other words, that none of these groups, in Rommen's phraseology, is allowed to prevail "hypotrophically over the others." Rather, the state must seek to interrelate the various communities in which our social nature issues so as to enable them to collaborate as "balanced parts of a well-organized unity in order" so as to secure conditions in which each can make its proper contribution to human flourishing.[77]

What emerges, in short, is a conception of government's role that is neither statist nor libertarian, that makes neither the state nor the market the center of social gravity. In sharp contrast to the welfare state of contemporary liberalism, to what John Paul II calls "the Social Assistance State," the subsidiary state would respect the identities and legitimate autonomy of the various institutions and groups to which human nature gives rise, as well as their right to discharge their functions (*CA*, 71 [sec. 48]). In equally sharp contrast to the nightwatchman state of classical liberalism, however, it would not simply leave these groups to fend for themselves, but would intervene in the impersonal workings of the market to assure that the institutions of civil society have access to the resources they need to flourish and to protect the social ecology on which they depend.[78]

Rights, Civil Society, and the State: Two Visions

Catholic social thought, in short, begins from an ontology of social life that differs fundamentally from those that inform the dominant traditions in both modern and classical thought. It offers us a thick vision of social life that does not absorb the individual into society or the social into the political, and an affirmation of the dignity of the individual human person that does not degenerate into a sterile and corrosive individualism. What is important for our purposes here is the way in which these two different

77. Rommen, *The State in Catholic Thought*, 143, 253.
78. For a more developed account of this understanding of man, society, and the state, see my work "The Subsidiary State: Society, the State and the Principle of Subsidiarity in Catholic Social Thought," in *Christianity and Civil Society: Catholic and Neo-Calvinist Perspectives*, ed. Jeanne Heffernan (Lanham, MD: Lexington Books, 2008).

models of social life point us toward two very different approaches to the whole subject of rights. Enlightenment liberalism's thinking on rights takes shape against the backdrop of an ontology of social life whose defining attributes are its atomism and reductionist understanding of all social groups as aggregations of individuals temporarily united for reasons of mutual utility. Rejecting a strong or constitutive conception of social life, this ontology understands human beings as contingently rather than essentially social creatures, and social relations as essentially external, conventional, and voluntary rather than products of our nature as social beings.

Asocial Rights

Liberal rights doctrines thus take their bearings from a vision of human beings as autonomous individuals, monads existing outside of any structure of social relations. From the individual so conceived, such doctrines proceed to deduce or derive a whole order of rights. Thus, these rights "have a clearly defined independent existence predating society." Only after these rights have been specified is the individual then inserted into society. These rights are thus "lexically prior" to social life, which must operate "within the limits they set." To these rights, in other words, society and its institutions "must bend."[79] Just as social relations and the goods they instantiate do not enter into the very constitution of human nature, so these relations and goods do not enter into the very constitution of rights, but remain external to them. Social life comes after rights ontologically as something rights-bearing individuals (motivated by self-interest) voluntarily choose to establish, and it possesses an instrumental and contractual character. It leaves the nature of these rights essentially untouched.

These rights doctrines are thus characterized by a commitment to what Charles Taylor terms "the primacy of rights." In this view, whereas rights—in particular, the "freedom to choose one's own mode of life"—are ascribed to individuals "as binding unconditionally," our "obligation . . . to belong to or sustain society, or a society of a certain type, or to obey authority, or authority of a certain type" is "seen as derivative, as laid on us conditionally, through our consent, or through its being to our advantage." "The individual and his or her rights," therefore, take "priority . . . over society."[80]

79. Alexander M. Bickel, *The Morality of Consent* (New Haven: Yale University Press, 1975), 4.
80. Taylor, *Philosophy and the Human Sciences*, 187.

Given this starting point, it is no accident that one of the most striking features of the rights doctrines spawned by Enlightenment liberalism is their hyperindividualistic, one is tempted to say asocial or even antisocial, character. The rights such doctrines champion, as Marx observed, are the rights of man "regarded as an isolated monad." "Founded . . . upon the separation of man from man," they are ultimately the very "right of such separation."[81] Furthermore, inasmuch as the atomistic rights doctrines spawned by liberalism cause any constraint on individual choice to be perceived as suspect, the "important and troubling questions that arise as one evaluates the writ over which individual rights and social obligation, respectively, should run are blanked out of existence." Their effect is thus to give "over everything, or nearly so, to the individualist pole in advance."[82]

The hyperindividualistic, asocial character of these rights doctrines manifests itself in many ways. It manifests itself in the denial that the institutions of civil society are subjects of rights that transcend the rights that their members possess as individuals, in the reduction of the rights of these communities to "only an appendix" to the rights of the individuals who compose them.[83] It manifests itself in the reduction of the task of government to the protection of the rights of the individual (as it understands these rights), and thus the denial to government of any responsibility for promoting the goods proper to nonutilitarian forms of social life or of recognizing and protecting the institutions of civil society and the social ecology on which they depend. It manifests itself in the insistence that the right of individuals to self-determination trumps not only the claims of social institutions to preserve their integrity, but all other human and social goods save the right of other individuals to that same freedom.

Not surprisingly, given their hyperindividualistic character, liberal rights doctrines have a profoundly destructive impact on the groups and institutions of civil society. They erode these groups and institutions through both the disintegrative effects of legal order they establish and the ethos they embody and implicitly inculcate. To begin with, these doctrines preclude efforts to provide a secure foundation for these institutions in public law, to recognize their rights in this law, and to safeguard through law and public policy the delicate social ecology on which their well-being depends. Indeed, while the welfare state of egalitarian liberalism undermines these groups and institutions by absorbing their functions and

---

81. Karl Marx, "On the Jewish Question," in *The Marx-Engels Reader,* ed. Robert C. Tucker (New York: Norton, 1972), 40.
82. Elshtain, "The Liberal Captivity of Feminism," 67.
83. Messner, *Social Ethics,* 178.

micromanaging their operation, the nightwatchman state of libertarian liberalism leaves them to fend for themselves in the face of the impersonal workings of the market.[84]

Simultaneously, liberal rights doctrines enshrine in both culture and law the liberal understanding of the institutions of civil society as nothing more than temporary aggregations of individuals united for reasons of mutual utility, and the normative conclusions about their proper ordering that liberalism draws from this understanding. In fact, they invest individuals with rights that make it difficult for these institutions to sustain their distinctive identities and solidaristic character, and for society to maintain the social environment on which their flourishing depends. The cumulative effect of this is to destabilize these institutions and to place them under relentless pressure (both cultural and legal) to refashion themselves in accordance with liberalism's atomistic vision of social relations.

The Sovereign Individual and the Omnicompetent State

Against this backdrop, what is perhaps the central irony of liberal rights doctrines begins to emerge. If the idea of limited government long predates the modern world, the fact is that since its emergence in the seventeenth century, Enlightenment liberalism has been closely associated with the cause of constitutionalism. Indeed, it has provided what are beyond any question the modern era's most influential accounts of, and most influential justifications for, the institutions and practices of constitutional government. As we have seen, moreover, one of the distinctive features of liberalism's approach to constitutionalism has been its invocation of individual rights as the primary principle defining the limits of state power.

As Stanley Hauerwas points out, however, it has gradually become apparent that "there exists a fundamental tension between our commitments to the rights of the individual, [the] preservation of intermediate associations, and the ability to retain a limited state."[85] Liberal rights doctrines do not just undermine solidaristic institutions—they simultaneously threaten limited government. Indeed, their ascendancy must be numbered

---

84. For perhaps the classic discussion of the destructive impact of the modern state on what are often called intermediary institutions, see Robert A. Nisbet, *The Quest for Community* (London: Oxford University Press, 1953; reprint, San Francisco: Institute for Contemporary Studies, 1990). For a helpful discussion of the destructive impact of the workings of the market on these institutions, see Andrew Bard Schmookler, *The Illusion of Choice* (Albany, NY: State University of New York Press, 1993).

85. Hauerwas, "Symposium," 44.

among the factors responsible for the far-reaching expansion in the size and scope of government over the past several centuries. To begin with, as Alexis de Tocqueville foresaw, the inevitable result of the social and psychological vacuum created by the progressive disabling of the institutions of civil society has been a massive expansion in the size and scope of the state. In part, this expansion has been a function of the state's self-aggrandizing tendencies. "It is in the nature of every government," Tocqueville remarks, "to continually wish to increase its sphere of action."[86]

This expansion also has stemmed from the fact that in an atomized society, the state is the only possible candidate to fill the vacuum created by the erosion of civil society and to respond to the social pathologies spawned by this erosion. Political life, like nature, abhors a vacuum, and when other institutions are disabled, the functions that they can no longer fulfill will necessarily tend to fall to the state by default. In an atomized society, as Tocqueville points out, the "needs" and "longings" of individuals "naturally" come to center on "that huge entity which alone stands out above the universal level of abasement" and "alone has both some stability and some capacity to see its undertakings through," namely, the state. Indeed, the very expansion of government to compensate for the weakening of these institutions creates "a vicious circle of cause and effect" by weakening them still further and thereby triggering a further expansion in the scope of government.[87] Individualism and statism thus prove to be mutually reinforcing: as other social institutions decline, the state expands, and, as the state expands, other social institutions decline still further. Thus, "the absolutely sovereign and omnicompetent state is the logical correlate of a society which consists of atomic individuals."[88]

This vacuum, however, is not the only factor at work here. Liberal rights doctrines have a logic of their own, a logic that operates at cross-purposes with liberalism's commitment to limited government. On the one hand, there is the movement from classical liberalism to egalitarian liberalism. When liberalism's embrace of social and economic rights (in the name of equalizing the opportunity of individuals to live the lifestyle of their choice) is combined with its single-minded focus on the market and state (at the expense of other social institutions), the inevitable result is a massive increase in the size and scope of government as the state is charged with providing an ever-multiplying array of entitlements.

---

86. Alexis de Tocqueville, *Democracy in America,* ed. J. P. Mayer, trans. George Lawrence (New York: Harper and Row, 1969), 2:672.

87. Ibid., 2:672, 515.

88. George Sabine, cited in Canavan, *Pluralist Game,* 135.

On the other hand, there is the inner dynamism of the liberal idea of freedom itself. As Nisbet remarks, "Individual autonomy is the transcending goal of historic liberalism."[89] It is this commitment to the maximization of individual autonomy that drives liberal rights doctrines. This commitment, in turn, demands the emancipation of individuals from any ties incompatible with the autonomy of the individual (as liberalism understands it), from any institution organized on principles incompatible with the individual's right to self-definition and self-determination. In this view, the state is hardly the only threat to individual freedom; on the contrary, strong, solidaristic institutions threaten it just as profoundly, perhaps even more so. From the viewpoint of Enlightenment liberalism, "groups that threaten to close off full and complete individuality"—that threaten the sovereignty of the individual—"must be regulated or banned."[90]

When it captures the state, therefore, the inner dynamism of liberalism's commitment to the sovereignty of the individual over his or her values and way of life impels it to employ government to refashion other social institutions in accordance with its atomistic vision of social relations, in accordance with its commitment to the maximization of individual autonomy. The rights of the individual, in other words, do not merely "limit" the liberal state, they simultaneously empower it. Indeed, given their far-ranging character, they effectively confer upon the state an essentially open-ended mandate to reorder all of social life in accordance with their demands. The result is what Nisbet describes as "a revolutionary liaison between the individual and the omnipotent state" in which the liberal state is charged with responsibility for liberating individuals "from the toils of society," for emancipating individuals from the claims of "other institutions." Far from being responsible for protecting and fostering the institutions of civil society, the state becomes "the agency of emancipation" by which "the individual can be freed from the restrictive tyrannies that compose society."[91]

The essential point is that, as Bruce Frohnen has remarked, "liberalism's true goal is not limited government per se; it is liberty," understood as the maximization of individual autonomy.[92] Thus, its commitment to individual rights (as it conceives them) trumps its commitment to limited

---

89. Nisbet, *Twilight of Authority*, 42.
90. Phillip Abbott, "Liberalism and Social Invention," in *The Liberal Future*, ed. Abbott and Levy, 70.
91. Nisbet, *Quest for Community*, 126, 129, 139, 128.
92. Bruce Frohnen, *The New Communitarianism and the Crisis of Modern Liberalism* (Lawrence: University Press of Kansas, 1996), 33.

government and underwrites a massive expansion in state power and a massive invasion of the institutions of civil society in the name of vindicating the rights of the individual. Ironically, when all is said and done, the very individual rights employed by liberalism to circumscribe the power of the state prove to be almost as destructive of limited government as they are of the institutions of civil society. The end result toward which liberal rights doctrines tend in practice is a massive, omnicompetent state presiding over an atomized mass of individuals inhabiting a monistic society in which the whole of social life is ordered in accordance with the liberal vision of the sovereignty of the individual.

Now, it is certainly true that liberal rights doctrines have resulted in an expansion of the freedom of the individual (as liberalism understands this freedom). But it is also true that the ascendancy of these doctrines has been accompanied by a marked reduction in the corporate freedom of groups; a growing homogenization of social life as one institution after another is reconfigured in accordance with liberal social morality; a far-reaching erosion of the institutions and groups composing civil society; the emergence of an increasingly atomistic social world; and a dramatic expansion in the power and scope of government. The resemblance to the social world so vividly evoked by Tocqueville in his discussion of democratic despotism in the concluding chapters of *Democracy in America* is both striking and disconcerting.

Rights and the Goods of Persons in Community

Although the idea of rights has figured prominently in Catholic thought since the writing of *Rerum Novarum*, it would be an exaggeration to claim that Catholic social thought contains a finished, comprehensive theory of rights.[93] Nevertheless, as even my cursory survey above suggests, a rights doctrine rooted in Catholic social thought would differ in important respects from those that issue from the intellectual universe of Enlightenment liberalism. Perhaps the most obvious difference concerns the rights of corporate groups. As we have seen, in contrast to liberalism, Catholic social thought insists that as "corporate" or "juridical" persons, the institutions and groups that issue from our nature as social beings are subjects of rights just as individuals are, rights that are more than "the sum total" of the rights of the individuals that compose them.

---

93. For a helpful compendium of recent Church statements on the subject of human rights, see Giorgio Filibeck, ed., *Human Rights and the Teaching of the Church: From John XXIII to John Paul II* (Vatican City: Libreria Editrice Vaticana, 1994).

The differences between the two traditions regarding the content of the order of rights, however, become intelligible only in light of the starting point from which each tradition's thinking about the whole subject of rights begins. While Enlightenment liberalism frequently appeals to human dignity and the affirmation of "the sublime dignity of the human person" (*GS*, 927 [sec. 26]) lies at the very heart of Catholic social thought, the fact is that the two traditions understand this dignity in fundamentally different ways because they disagree fundamentally about what a human being is. In sharp contrast to liberalism, for Catholic social thought, a human being is neither a monad nor an unencumbered self free to make of itself and the world whatever it chooses. On the contrary, Catholic thought maintains the existence of an order of human and social ends inscribed on the very structure of human nature that obligates the person prior to, and independently of, his or her consent, an order of ends inscribed on the very structure of human freedom and in which this freedom finds its fulfillment.[94] Indeed, our very "dignity consists in observing this law" (*GS*, 916 [sec. 16]). Simultaneously, it affirms that "the nature of man . . . is as essentially social as it is individual," and thus "regards the community as 'given' equally with the person."[95] The "community" here, of course, encompasses the whole complicated matrix of diverse and interrelated groups and institutions that flow from our nature as social beings.

Catholic social thought thus rejects both liberalism's atomism and its collapse of the world of civil society into the world of the market. It insists, in other words, that an adequate ontology of social life must reckon with the full depth of human sociality, and include an appreciation of the distinctive nature and roles of nonstate, nonmarket institutions. Insofar as our nature is as essentially social as it is individual, moreover, Catholic social thought insists that our obligation to create and sustain the institutions necessary to human flourishing is fundamental and unconditional, rather than derivative and secondary. Thus, the juridical order must take into account these institutions, the conditions of their flourishing, and the legitimate claims they make upon individuals and society as a whole.

Catholicism's thinking about rights begins not with the abstract, isolated individual, but, as Lisa Sowle Cahill asserts, with the idea of "a universal order inclusive of the human community within which the individual functions." Rights, therefore, "are woven into a concept of community" and

94. For an in-depth discussion of the Catholic understanding of freedom and how it differs from the understanding that what I have called Enlightenment liberalism inherited from medieval nominalism, see Pinckaers's *Sources of Christian Ethics*.

95. Murray, *We Hold These Truths*, 293.

"exist within . . . a social context," within the context of a wide array of social relations that are constitutive rather than external, artificial, and contractual, relations that flow from the very nature of the human person.[96]

For Catholic social thought the structure of social relations that flows from human nature and the goods that these relations instantiate enter into the very constitution of the order of rights. These relations and goods "are the foundation of both rights and obligations that are prior to and independent of consent."[97] Accordingly, these relations and goods act to give form to particular rights, to specify their nature and scope, as well as those of the responsibilities that attach to them. The claims of "society" here are not something external that limit and threaten rights from without, but are internal to the rights themselves, as it were, and order them from within. They are internal to these rights because rights are understood as representing, in Elshtain's apt phrase, "the goods of persons in community."[98]

Understanding the rights of the person as the rights of the person in community, as the rights of the person existing not in isolation but enmeshed in a complicated web of diverse social relations, Catholic social thought points us toward a type of "rights discourse" significantly more complex and less individualistic than that which emerges under the auspices of liberalism. It is more complex because it incorporates into its conception of the juridical order a host of actors and goods that liberal rights talk, with its single-minded focus on the isolated, abstract individual and the good of choice, completely ignores. It is less individualistic because it understands human beings as intrinsically social creatures, because the subjects of rights include not just individuals but a wide array of diverse social groups and institutions, and because the goods in which rights are rooted include the full range of diverse goods instantiated by these institutions individually and collectively. All of these goods bear on the juridical order; all of them enter into the determination of the nature and scope of rights both individual and corporate.

Catholic social thought thus conceptualizes rights in a broader, more complex framework than does liberalism: it integrates its thinking about the foundation, nature, and scope of rights into a framework that encompasses the demands of social life, the claims of the institutions and groups in which our nature as fundamentally social beings finds expression. In this understanding, rights claims develop "alongside, in the context of,

---

96. Lisa Sowle Cahill, "Toward a Christian Theory of Human Rights," *Journal of Religious Ethics* 8 (Fall 1980): 285, 284.

97. Canavan, *Pluralist Game*, 131.

98. Elshtain, "Catholic Social Thought," 105.

and often subject to, other political norms, rather than by transcending or . . . 'trumping' such norms."[99] Indeed, Catholicism maintains neither that all political issues can be adequately conceptualized as simple clashes of rights nor that all social and political goods can be adequately articulated in the language of rights. If liberalism tends to reduce the language of politics to the language of rights, in Catholic thought rights language is but one element in a richer, more subtle vocabulary that brings into play concepts such as the common good, solidarity, subsidiarity, the public order and welfare, obligation, social ecology, and so on.

As this suggests, the differences between the two traditions are not limited to questions of the rights of corporate groups, but extend to the nature, scope, and rights of individuals as well. By virtue of their different starting points, even when Catholicism and liberalism affirm the existence of the same rights, they understand their content, their nature and scope, differently. While Catholic social thought emphatically affirms that individuals possess a series of rights that together afford them a broad sphere of freedom (such as freedom of religion, speech, etc.), for example, this affirmation is not to be equated with the liberal claim that the individual's right to act on his or her preferences trumps all human and social goods save the right of other individuals to that same autonomy. In the Catholic understanding, the freedom of the individual is circumscribed by the whole ensemble of social goods that collectively constitute the public order and welfare, including the social ecology required for human flourishing, the demands of public morality, and the claims of social groups to institutional autonomy and integrity. In the Catholic understanding, moreover, these rights do not necessitate the privatization either of religion or, more generally, of substantive conceptions of the human good. On the contrary, they presuppose a particular understanding of this good.[100]

Likewise, while Catholic thought affirms the existence of rights to private property and economic initiative, its understanding of the nature and scope of these rights differs from those characteristic of the liberal tradition. Here again, in Catholic thought these rights have a social dimension and reflect a body of social goods (for example, the universal destination of material goods, the demands of social ecology, the "social function" of

99. Paul Marshall, "Two Types of Rights," *Canadian Journal of Political Science* 25 (December 1992): 674.

100. For the Catholic understanding of the nature, scope, and foundation of the human right to religious liberty, see Kenneth L. Grasso and Robert P. Hunt, eds., *Catholicism and Religious Freedom: Contemporary Reflections on Vatican II's Declaration on Religious Liberty* (Lanham, MD: Rowman and Littlefield, 2006).

private property, etc.) largely absent in the intellectual universe of liberal rights discourse. The "limits" that Catholic thought imposes on these rights flow from their "very nature," from the very goods in which they are rooted and that give them their form. In the Catholic understanding, far from being "absolute" rights, the rights to "private property" (*CA*, 43 [sec. 30]) and "free human creativity in the economic sector" are "circumscribed within a . . . framework" (*CA*, 60 [sec. 42]) that places them "at the service of human freedom in its totality" and orients them "toward the common good" (*CA*, 61 [sec. 43]).

Rights, Social Life, and the Subsidiary State

Incorporating a range of goods foreign to the hyperindividualistic anthropology that undergirds so much of contemporary rights talk, Catholic social thought points us toward a more balanced form of rights discourse, a form of rights discourse that provides for the claims of "individuality . . . together with the claims of social obligation."[101] Indeed, it points us toward a theory of rights consistent with our nature as intrinsically social beings, and thus with the demands of social life. In contrast to those spawned by liberalism, the rights doctrine toward which Catholic social thought points is not corrosive of solidaristic institutions; the rights it affirms do not undermine the ability of these institutions to maintain their distinctive characters, impinge upon their legitimate autonomy, or subvert the social ecology on which they depend.

Unlike liberal rights doctrines, furthermore, this doctrine does not require the remaking of all social institutions in keeping with a single model. Whereas the inner logic of liberal rights doctrines tends to demand the reconstruction of all social institutions along atomist lines, a rights doctrine grounded in the Catholic model of human nature and society would allow for the existence of diverse types of social institutions. Consistent with the full range of social institutions and groups in which our nature as social beings finds expression, it would allow for the existence of both the utilitarian and nonutilitarian forms of community, for both solidaristic and voluntaristic forms of social relations.

Catholic social thought, furthermore, points toward an approach to the whole question of the limits of state power that differs fundamentally from that which informs liberal rights doctrines, an approach that avoids placing individual rights on a collision course with limited government. As we have

101. Elshtain, "Catholic Social Thought," 105.

seen, it is no accident that modern liberal rights doctrines are associated with a massive expansion in the scope of government. An omnicompetent state is the inevitable result of liberal rights doctrines' combination of an expansive view of the scope of individual rights and insistence on the priority of individual autonomy over all other human goods with a social ontology that makes the state responsible for the vindication of all rights claims.

Like modern liberalism, Catholic social thought has tended toward an expansive view of the order of human rights. In contrast to liberal rights doctrines that tend to reduce the powers and limits of the state to the implications of antecedent rights claims, Catholic social thought understands these powers and limits against the backdrop of a complex account of the nature and mission of the state as a distinctive social institution. And, in contrast to liberal rights doctrines that tend to unfold against the backdrop of a social ontology that, in Bertrand de Jouvenel's apt phrase, refuses "to see in society anything but the state and the individual,"[102] Catholic thinking about rights unfolds against the backdrop of a pluralist understanding of the proper organization of social life. In this view, a society is not a collection of atomized individuals, but a *communitatis communitatum*. Precisely for this reason, the responsibility for common good—for the totality of social goods (moral, spiritual, intellectual, and material) necessary for human flourishing—is shared by the whole range of institutions that collectively constitute society.

What this means, in turn, is that, as Murray notes, "the purposes of the state are not coextensive with the purposes of [human] society,"[103] much less with the overall purposes of human life. Insofar as this means that the state must be understood as a limited order of action for limited purposes, moreover, this means that there exists "a whole wide area of human concerns . . . remote from the competence of government,"[104] a whole body of important social goods whose primary care is entrusted to institutions other than the state. Responsibility for securing the totality of goods constitutive of the common good does not rest with the state alone: government's mandate is limited to the protection of the limited ensemble of goods constitutive of the public order and welfare. An adequate understanding of the powers and limits of the state thus requires more than a

---

102. Bertrand de Jouvenel, *On Power: Its Nature and the History of Its Growth*, trans. J. F. Huntington (1948; reprint, Indianapolis: Liberty Fund, 1993), 417.

103. John Courtney Murray, "The Problem of Religious Liberty," in *Religious Liberty: Catholic Struggles with Pluralism/John Courtney Murray*, ed. J. Leon Hooper, SJ (Louisville: Westminster/John Knox Press, 1993), 145.

104. Murray, *We Hold These Truths*, 76–77.

doctrine of rights—it requires an adequate grasp of what John Paul II terms "the tasks proper to the state" (*CA*, 18 [sec. 11]) in the overall economy of social life. From the perspective of Catholic social thought the limits of the jurisdiction of government are thus "inherent in the nature of the State" itself (*CA*, 69 [sec. 48]).

The implications of all this for the whole subject of rights and the limits of government are profound. The state's mission does not extend to a responsibility for protecting and promoting the whole order of human rights, and government does not possess an open-ended mandate to vindicate the full range of rights proper to the human person. On the contrary, precisely because government shares the responsibility for protecting and promoting this order with a wide array of other groups and institutions, precisely because the care of the order of rights "devolves" not only on the state but also upon the full range of "social groups" in which our nature as social beings finds expression,[105] government's responsibilities vis-à-vis this order are limited. As John Paul II contends, for example, although the state plays an essential role in "overseeing and directing the exercise of human rights in the economic sector," "the primary responsibility" for the protection and promotion of human rights in this area "belongs not to the State but to individuals and to the various groups and associations which make up society" (*CA*, 68 [sec. 48]).

If, in contrast to liberalism, Catholic social thought's commitment to limited government is not in tension with its commitment to individual rights, this is not only because of its different understanding of the content of the order of rights, but also because of its less open-ended conception of the role of government. If Catholicism can combine a commitment to limited government with an expansive view of the scope of human rights, this is because for it government is limited not merely from "without" by rights, as it were, but from "within" by the limited character of the functions proper to it as a distinctive social institution.

Conclusion

By providing us with a "thick" conception of social life that does not absorb society into the state and the individual into the social whole, Catholic social thought lays the groundwork for a way of thinking about rights that is decisively richer than the flawed and corrosive doctrines that

---

105. Pope Paul VI, *Dignitatis Humanae*, 173 (sec. 6).

dominate the contemporary scene, for a theory of rights that reintegrates our thinking about rights with the demands of social life (and thus with the demands of the full range of diverse social relations in which our nature as intrinsically social beings finds expression), as well as with the principle of limited government.

Contemporary abuses to the contrary notwithstanding, the idea of rights represents one of the most important political achievements of Western civilization. By laying the foundation for a theory of rights untainted by the shallow, atomistic model of social life that undergirds contemporary rights talk, Catholic social thought can help assure that this idea continues to bear good fruit, that it continues in the new millennium, as it did in the last, to contribute to the improvement of the human condition.

Toward a Social Pluralist Theory of Institutional Rights

Jonathan Chaplin

The American dialect of rights talk disserves public deliberation not only through affirmatively promoting an image of the rights-bearer as a radically autonomous individual, but through its corresponding neglect of the social dimensions of personhood. Just as our stark rights vocabulary receives subtle amplification from its encoded image of the lone rights-bearer, our weak vocabulary of responsibility is rendered fainter still by our undeveloped notion of human sociality.

—Mary Ann Glendon, *Rights Talk: The Impoverishment of Political Discourse*

Those who argue that corporations have a social responsibility . . . assume that corporations are capable of having social or moral obligations. This is a fundamental error. A corporation . . . is nothing more than a legal fiction that serves as a nexus for a mass of contracts which various individuals have voluntarily entered into for their mutual benefit. Since it is a legal fiction, a corporation is incapable of having social or moral obligations much in the same way that inanimate objects are incapable of having these obligations.

—Daniel R. Fischel, "The Corporate Governance Movement"

One of the principal deficiencies of the dominant liberal individualist understanding of rights is its inability properly to do justice to the rights of institutions.[1] This inability is a telling instance of what Mary Ann Glendon terms "the missing dimension of sociality" in contemporary liberal-rights discourse. Because contemporary liberalism lacks an adequate notion of "sociality," liberal legal, constitutional, and political theory have proved unable to generate a convincing account of the reality and character of the legal rights of institutions.[2] Such rights are actually and legitimately possessed by many social institutions. I shall call them "institutional rights." Insofar as liberal theorists reflect on the phenomenon of institutional rights and the responsibilities corresponding to and balancing them, they tend to construe them merely as derivative from the rights of associating, self-interested individuals rather than as having some independent foundation and status not finally reducible to individual rights—a construal precisely reflected in the quotation from Daniel R. Fischel above.[3] The empirical observation that many social institutions themselves do have positive legal rights seems indisputable. Yet liberal indi-

I am grateful to Stephen Safranek from Ave Maria School of Law for his response to an earlier version of this paper delivered at the conference "Rethinking Rights: Historical, Political, and Theological Perspectives," held at Ave Maria School of Law on November 19–20, 2004; and to the editorial team of *Ave Maria Law Review* for editorial work on and bibliographical suggestions for an earlier, abridged version of this paper published under the same title in the *Review*. Any shortcomings in this version are, of course, my own. Research for this paper has been assisted in part by my participation in the research project "Politics and the Problem of Human Nature," funded by The Pew Charitable Trusts.

1. I will not here detail the problems of "liberal individualism." The essays in this volume by Kenneth Grasso and Kenneth Schmitz state these well. I stress, however, that the version of social pluralism I want to commend presupposes the high importance of individuality, individual freedom, and individual rights. See n. 63 below.

2. For brief standard surveys of the legal status of what I am calling "institutions," see R. W. M. Dias, *Jurisprudence,* 5th ed. (London: Butterworth, 1985), 250–71; and Dennis Lloyd, *The Idea of Law* (1964; reprint, New York: Penguin, 1991), 300–309. On nineteenth-century English law, see the classic statement by Frederic William Maitland, "Trust and Corporation," in *Group Rights: Perspectives Since 1900,* ed. Julia Stapleton (Bristol: Thoemmes Press, 1995), 1–37. See also Frederic William Maitland, "Moral Personality and Legal Personality," in *The Pluralist State,* ed. David Nicholls, 2nd ed. (1975; reprint, New York: St. Martin's Press, 1994), app. D. See also Robert F. Cochran Jr. et al., *Law and Intermediate Communities: The Case of Torts* (Lanham, MD: Rowman and Littlefield, 2004). I regret that this volume came to my attention too late to be discussed in this paper.

3. For one account of this distortion in American legal history, see Rockne McCarthy et al., *Society, State, and Schools: A Case for Structural and Confessional Pluralism* (Grand Rapids, MI: Eerdmans, 1981), 51–78. Daniel R. Fischel, "The Corporate Governance Movement," *Vanderbilt Law Review* 35 (1982): 1259, 1273 (I am grateful to Christopher Topa from Ave Maria School of Law for supplying this citation).

vidualism seems unable to offer much beyond an implausible contractualist explanation of their origin and status.

The aim of this paper is programmatic: to point to the need for and the possibility of an account of institutional rights that grounds them in a plurality of social institutions widely experienced as vital to human flourishing. I shall call this a "social pluralist" account of institutional rights. I do so by retrieving some promising conceptual resources from two earlier pluralist thinkers and indicating some directions in which such resources require critical development. A social pluralist account affirms the indispensable social, political, and legal significance of the multiple institutions subsisting in the space between the state and the individual. Social pluralism, in the sense intended here, regards itself, if not as a comprehensive social theory, at least as an essential corrective to the individualist theories—and their collectivist and statist alter-egos—that have exercised such a pervasive and damaging hold over modern social theorizing. It thrusts to the foreground of our attention those "intermediate bodies"—now often termed "civil society institutions"[4]—that these reductionist theories have typically left languishing on the margins of theoretical reflection.

The term *institutional rights* requires preliminary clarification. When I use the word *rights* I have positive legal rights principally in mind, though I also consider the view that institutions also possess "natural rights." I intend the term *institution* as a broad category embracing most organized and relatively enduring social bodies, corporations, communities, or associations—such as marriages, families, religious organizations, business corporations, trade unions, and voluntary associations. I exclude consideration of two types of social forms that lack "institutional" properties: first, amorphous or unorganized groups like informal social clubs (as distinct from those deemed in law to be "corporations" or "unincorporated societies"), neighborhoods or larger geographical communities (as distinct from municipal councils), ethnic or linguistic communities (as distinct from the organized interest groups representing them), social movements (as distinct from formal associations spawned by them), nations (as distinct from states), and virtual networks; second, complex webs of interaction that may wield substantial power but lack formal organization, notably markets (as distinct from stock exchanges). A full account of institutional rights would, of course, require attention to these wider social contexts that substantially shape the definition and exercise of such rights.

---

4. These terms have their limitations as descriptors of the "institutions" I have in mind, but I will not pursue this point here.

Institutions so defined, I shall claim, possess "agency" and are thereby capable of what I call "legal subjectivity" (I intend this term to be taken more widely than *legal personality,* which refers essentially to the capacity of an entity to be recognized by the state as a bearer of legal rights and duties).[5] By that I mean that they can exercise legal rights, discharge legal duties, and wield legal powers,[6] including the power to establish valid jural norms within their own "spheres of justice" (to employ Michael Walzer's term).[7] I shall call the spheres within which institutions can establish such norms their "jural spheres." The contents of such jural spheres, I shall also suggest, are determined by the defining normative purposes of the institution possessing them. I wish, then, to explore two propositions regarding the importance of "contextualizing" rights. In the first place, an account of institutional rights will be one component of a wider account of institutional jural spheres: we need to contextualize both rights in relation to institutions and also institutional rights in relation to institutional duties and powers. In the second place, an adequate theory of institutional jural spheres requires an account of the defining institutional purposes that give legitimacy and point to the content of the jural spheres they possess.

A social pluralist theory of institutional rights will, perforce, need to proceed by way of three important negations. In the first place, it will need to

---

5. See Dias, *Jurisprudence;* and Maitland, "Moral Personality."

6. My threefold distinction between rights, duties, and powers (or competencies) may be compared to Wesley Hohfeld's famous fourfold classification of distinct types of "jural relation" that, he observes, are often unhelpfully lumped together simply as *rights,* namely, claim-rights, liberty-rights, powers, and immunities. Hohfeld's attempt to specify and relativize rights in relation to other types of jural relation to which they should not be assimilated—including, of course, "duties"—is salutary. See Wesley Hohfeld, *Fundamental Legal Conceptions as Applied in Judicial Reasoning* (New Haven: Yale University Press, 1919); and the account of Hohfeld's scheme in Peter Jones, *Rights* (London: Macmillan, 1994), 12–25. My classification is drawn instead from the legal theory of the twentieth-century Dutch Neo-Calvinist philosopher Herman Dooyeweerd. Among Dooyeweerd's works see *A New Critique of Theoretical Thought* (Nutley, NJ: Presbyterian and Reformed, 1953–1958; Lewiston, NY: Mellen Press, 1997); *Essays in Legal, Social, and Political Philosophy* (Lewiston, NY: Mellen Press, 1997); *Encyclopedia of the Science of Law,* vol. 1 (Lewiston, NY: Mellen Press, 2002); and *Political Philosophy* (Lewiston, NY: Mellen Press, 2004). For a statement of the wider social and cultural theory in which he grounds his legal theory, see Dooyeweerd, *Roots of Western Culture* (Toronto: Wedge, 1979). For overviews of Dooyeweerd's political and legal thought, see James W. Skillen, "Philosophy of the Cosmonomic Idea: Herman Dooyeweerd's Political and Legal Thought," *Political Science Reviewer* 32 (2003): 318–80; and Alan Cameron, "Dooyeweerd on Law and Morality: Legal Ethics—A Test Case," *Victoria University of Wellington Law Review* 28 (1998): 263–81.

7. Michael Walzer, *Spheres of Justice: A Defense of Pluralism and Equality* (Oxford: Blackwell, 1983). Walzer does not construe such spheres in exactly the same way that I use the term *jural spheres.*

challenge the pervasive individualist premise that institutions are merely contingent creations of the contracting wills or pooled rights of morally autonomous and self-constituting individuals, lacking any inherent properties of their own.[8] It will also need to challenge two influential legal positivist assumptions: that institutions possess no original competence to make valid jural norms and—its corollary—that institutional rights are ultimately legal "fictions" merely delegated or "conceded" by the state.[9] The individualist and legal positivist propositions against which such a pluralist theory pits itself are rarely defended with much philosophical vigor today, at least not in the bald form in which I have just summarized them. Yet their cumulative influence still shapes much contemporary social, political, and legal thinking and decision making and continues to shore up substantial barriers to the reception—even the comprehension— of a social pluralist account of institutional rights.

In the next two sections, I revisit the work of two theorists whose insights merit critical retrieval and elaboration by those committed to the project of "rethinking rights": first, the distinctive theory of associational law and legal pluralism[10] proposed by the influential nineteenth-century German legal historian Otto von Gierke; second, the conception of a natural teleology of plural social bodies formulated by the twentieth-century Thomist Heinrich Rommen (which, I shall venture, provides a better theoretical grounding for legal pluralism than that offered by Gierke).[11] In the

8. See Henry N. Butler and Larry E. Ribstein, "Opting Out of Fiduciary Duties: A Response to the Anti-Contractarians," *Washington Law Review* 65 (1990): 1, 3 ("Contractarians view the corporation as a set of private contractual relationships among providers of capital and services"); Frank H. Easterbrook and Daniel R. Fischel, "The Corporate Contract," *Columbia Law Review* 89 (1989): 1416, 1418 ("The corporation is a complex set of explicit and implicit contracts").

9. Maitland states the link bluntly: "If the personality of the corporation is a legal fiction, it is the gift of the prince." "Moral Personality," 175.

10. The term *legal pluralism* is typically used to refer to a constitutional arrangement in which different ethnic or religious communities within a state are governed, in limited areas of civil law such as family and property, by distinct legal norms adjudicated by special (often religious) courts or tribunals. I am using it instead to refer to a theory that affirms that many nongovernmental institutions (in the sense I have defined that term) possess original jural spheres. Of course, an affirmation of the latter can be used to defend the former. See, for example, Ayelet Shachar, *Multicultural Jurisdictions: Cultural Differences and Women's Rights* (New York: Cambridge University Press, 2001). Shachar's notion of "jurisdictional sub-matters" has some parallels with my notion of "jural spheres." For a wider discussion of the term *legal pluralism*, see Nancy L. Rosenblum, ed., *Obligations of Citizenship and Demands of Faith: Religious Accommodation in Pluralist Democracies* (Princeton: Princeton University Press, 2000), 5–8.

11. There are, of course, many other schools of social pluralist theorizing being utilized in contemporary debates (such as the Tocquevillian or the Hegelian). I choose

final section, I suggest some of the ways in which these insights need to be refined and elaborated.

Otto Von Gierke: Associational Law

Gierke's writings contain a forceful affirmation of the reality and ubiquity of plural human associations and of their possession of distinct jural spheres. His accounts are grounded in a broad understanding of association, the fruit of his immense scholarly excavations in German legal history.[12] Modern individualist and contractualist legal and political theory, he judges, is inadequate to the task of coming to terms with the myriad associations that have come to populate and animate Western—especially "Germanic"—history. These continually proliferating associations testify to a deep human impulse toward organic interaction. Such associations had proved themselves leading historical actors but were routinely neglected in the standard legal history and legal theory of his day. Gierke proposes as "firmly-established historical fact" a fundamental duality in human nature: not only do human beings exist, will, and act as individuals, they also manifest an irrepressible associative inclination the expression of which is equally important for human flourishing. There is "a twofold tendency of human consciousness and instinct"; self-consciousness cannot exist without the simultaneous presence of group-consciousness.[13] Organic integration in a social whole is an undeniable

---

these two thinkers both because they have proved influential in important twentieth-century schools of pluralist thought and because they address more explicitly than many other pluralists the notion of institutional jural spheres.

12. Gierke's magnum opus is *Das deutsche Genossenschaftsrecht*, 4 vols. (Berlin: Weidmann, 1868–1913). Substantial parts of this work have been translated into English, as cited in subsequent notes. The Germanic Fellowship (*Genossenschaft*) is, he claims, the most adequate example of human association.

13. Otto von Gierke, "The Basic Concepts of State Law and the Most Recent State-Law Theories," in John D. Lewis, *The Genossenschaft-Theory of Otto von Gierke: A Study in Political Thought*, University of Wisconsin Studies in the Social Sciences and History 25 (Madison: University of Wisconsin Press, 1932), app. D, 169–70 (an abridged translation by Lewis of "Die Grundbegriffe des Staatsrechts und die neuesten staatsrechts-theorien," *Zeitschrift fur die gesamte Staatswissenschaft* 30 [1874]: 153–98, 265–335). Gierke's robust associationism leads him to reject two principal rival social theories: "universalism," according to which the individual lacks full reality and exists only for the political community; and "individualism," which recognizes only individuals as real, denies the reality of group-life, and holds that the state exists merely to allow individuals to pursue their own ends (Gierke, "Basic Concepts," 166–68, 179).

datum of our subjective experience, and to attempt to think it away leaves human existence miserably impoverished: "What man is, he owes to the association of man with man."[14]

An association is formed by the transfer of a part of the essence and will of each individual member to the social whole. It is not simply an aggregate of externally related individual wills, but a real, organic unity constituting an independent communal whole. Such a whole possesses a reality distinct from and transcending the separate wills of its individual members and capable of willing and acting on its own account. It possesses personality; it is a "group-person."[15] I note straight away that this Romantic-idealist notion was roundly (and rightly) criticized by many commentators, including some of those who otherwise appreciated Gierke's associational theory.[16] The postulation of a real group-personality supposedly transcending the personality of its members was seen as an illegitimate reification. Yet that theory and the theory of legal pluralism built on it can survive quite well without such a notion. In any case, it was not intended to imply the subsumption of individual into associational existence. Gierke is clear that no association can ever absorb the entirety of a member's will. Only part of that will is transferred in joining any group. Members still retain a sphere of private will independent of any group; and since will always establishes legal right, a sphere of individual rights is guaranteed.[17] Further, since individuals are members of several groups, their associative activities and loyalties will be dispersed in a variety of complementary and mutually limiting associational contexts.

A distinctive theory of law flows from this theory of association. In developing it, Gierke aligns himself with the "Germanist" wing of the nineteenth-century Historical School of law against its "Romanist"

---

14. Gierke, introduction to *Das deutsche Genossenscahftsrecht*, vol. 1, *Rechtsgeschichte der deutschen Genossenschaft*, in John D. Lewis, *The Genossenschaft-Theory of Otto von Gierke*, app. A, 113 (abridged translation by Lewis of *Rechtsgeschichte der deutschen Genossenschaft* [1868], 1–4).

15. The idea that human collectivities possess a "group-personality" derives from Romantic thinkers, who initially applied it to the nation and, in some cases, to the state. But, as Anthony Black points out, Gierke was the first to extend the idea to human groups in general, including the wide variety of associations arising in modern industrial society, such as trade unions, credit and insurance societies, and producer and consumer cooperatives. Anthony Black, *Guilds and Civil Society in European Political Thought from the Twelfth Century to the Present* (London: Methuen, 1984), 211–12.

16. Compare Maitland, "Moral Personality," 173–79; Nicholls, ed., *The Pluralist State*, chap. 4; Paul Q. Hirst, introduction to *The Pluralist Theory of the State*, ed. Hirst (London: Routledge, 1989), 1–47.

17. Lewis, *Genossenschaft-Theory*, 71–72.

rivals.[18] Just as law unproblematically recognizes the legal personality of individual human beings, so it must acknowledge the legal personality of groups. The reality, unity, and agency of the group are prior to any positive legal ordering. For Gierke, as George Heiman puts it, "Law arranges and penetrates this inner unity and hence the inner structure of the group, but it does not serve as its source." Rather, law must "accept the existence of a force, an urge, a stream of consciousness that has to be placed in a legal context."[19] Groups of any kind, possessing a unified and living will, ought to be recognized as independent agents capable of legal personality.[20] Group-persons should, like individuals, be recognized as capable of possessing rights, and this legal capacity does not depend on recognition by the state, even though the state supplies the legal *form* for group-rights.

This argument was deployed against the influential "Romanist" corporationist theory of Friedrich Carl von Savigny. Savigny did not deny that groups could be recognized as "legal persons," but, following a certain interpretation of Roman law, he held that this personality was "fictitious" rather than real. According to the "fiction theory" of corporations, as Gierke characterizes it, "the personality of an association comes into existence only by a juristic artificiality, by virtue of which the association assumes in law an attribute that it lacks in reality."[21] A legal person was simply an artificially conceived subject, lacking any independent life or will and therefore having no independent standing from which to claim legal recognition by the state. Such recognition was a grant or "concession" from the state, not an acknowledgment of a previously existing right.[22] But the fiction theory founders on the rock of social reality: "to achieve it is historically impossible . . . corporate persons will not yield."[23]

Savigny's theory of the fictitious personality of groups depended on his acceptance of the fundamental Roman-law distinction between private

18. Ibid., 44–48.

19. George Heiman, introduction to Otto von Gierke, *Associations and Law: The Classical and Early Christian Stages*, trans., ed., and intro. by George Heiman (Toronto: University of Toronto Press, 1977), 7, 10 (a translation of sections 3–5 of *Das deutsche Genossenschaftsrecht*, vol. 3 [Berlin, 1881]).

20. Gierke, "The Nature of Human Associations," in Lewis, *Genossenschaft-Theory*, app. C, 143 (an abridged translation by Lewis of "Das Wesen der menschlichen Verbände" [Leipzig, 1902]).

21. Gierke, introduction to *Rechtsgeschichte*, 141.

22. Gierke judges that the ultimate logical conclusion of the fiction theory was that the state itself was no more than a legal fiction, so that the subject of state authority was deemed to be simply the ruler (or ruling organ) alone rather than the political community as a whole, a development in which he discerns the seeds of absolutism.

23. Gierke, introduction to *Rechtsgeschichte*, 142–43.

and public law and its assumption that the individual is sovereign in the former while the state is sovereign in the latter. Since an individual is sovereign in his private sphere, his personality is regarded as indivisible. Transferring part of one's personality into a group—a process at the heart of Gierke's conception of the reality of group life—was therefore impossible given the terms of Roman law. It was not possible, Savigny thought, to make the process of concession depend on the wills of private individuals because such wills were arbitrary, and legal uncertainty would thereby be created. Only the state could concede legal personality to groups.[24]

Against this conception, Gierke proposes a "Germanic" understanding of group-personality, which, he maintains, represents the most profound realization of that organic social theory that was already present in classical and medieval thought. It had been temporarily undermined in the modern period as a result of the dominance of the individualistic theory of natural law, but was undergoing a revival, initiated by Fichte and advanced in Hegel, among others, and manifested in a wide variety of social scientific theories.[25] In Germanic legal theory, he claims, groups are accorded legal recognition as real personalities. Germanic law had not been encumbered with the stark Roman-law separation between private and public law. A sphere of individual will is always recognized, but seen as being balanced by the requirements of communal life. In the Germanic conception, personality is not seen as indivisible. The possibility exists of transferring part of one's will to a group-person and thereby establishing an entirely new and distinct personality endowed with rights and duties of its own.[26] Once a group is organized as a collective person with a unified will, there exists a presumption that it will be recognized in law as possessing legal personality.[27]

24. Gierke holds that this theory amounted to the denial of the natural right of individuals to freely associate (compare Heiman, introduction to *Associations and Law,* 30–32, 35, 41; and Lewis, *Genossenschaft-Theory,* 45–47).

25. Gierke, introduction to *Rechtsgeschichte,* 143–44; Gierke, "Nature of Human Associations," 114.

26. Heiman, introduction to *Associations and Law,* 36–37, 40.

27. Not all social unities possess such a unified will. Gierke distinguishes between those that, although real unities, have not yet constituted themselves as organized bodies and those that are so organized and have thereby become collective persons with their own will. (This distinction does not correspond exactly to the one I drew earlier between institutions and other social groupings.) Gierke held that any of the following can exist in the first, preorganized condition before acquiring the second: *Volk,* religious community, class, profession, interest group, and political party. His inclusion of the nation is noteworthy. In his view the nation only becomes a collective person when it is organized as a state; a nation that lacks a state or that spans more than one state thus has no claim to legal recognition (Gierke, introduction to *Rechtsgeschichte,* 151).

Law is in essence "an ordering of spheres of will," and it must take account of will wherever it manifests itself in society. Since there exist two distinct kinds of will, that of the individual and that of the group, there are therefore two quite different kinds of law, "individual law" and "social law."[28] The first operates externally upon people or associations and treats them in their separate individuality, apart from any incorporation into a higher association. It establishes a "free sphere of activity in which the individual through his own free act of will creates legal relations." Social law by contrast engages with the associative side of personality and includes all the law that orders the internal life of associations, whether that of the state or of other associations. It does not *create* the organic unity of such associations, but only declares and so publicly verifies it. Social law governs the relations between individual wills insofar as these are governed by organic, associational relations.[29] It is not concerned with the rights of individual members against the group, for these fall within individual law, but rather with the role of the individual within the group as a part to a whole.

Social law therefore contains concepts that are entirely absent in individual law and that the individualistic contract theory of associations is incapable of generating, for example, the concept of the constitution, that is, the legal determination of the internal structure of a social whole and the various relationships among its members; and related concepts of membership, organ, election, and so on.[30] The content of an association's legal sphere will therefore include such things as associational purpose, criteria for membership, office holding, decision procedures, rules for the administration of property, and so on. None of these are derivable from the content of individual rights. While all such elements will display some common features arising from the general principle of "organic association," each will take on a different character according to the specific nature of the association in which it is found. There is within every organic group "a special law corresponding to its concrete individuality."[31] Thus,

---

28. Gierke, "Basic Concepts," 180, 152. In this article he distinguishes between "private law" and "public law" (179), elsewhere employing the term *public law* in a more restricted sense (e.g., Gierke, introduction to *Rechtsgeschichte*, 152; compare Heiman, introduction to *Associations and Law*, 10–14, 46–47; and Lewis, *Genossenschaft-Theory*, 71–72). I confine myself here to the wider distinction between individual and social law.

29. Gierke, "Basic Concepts," 180; Gierke, introduction to *Rechtsgeschichte*, 152.

30. Gierke, introduction to *Rechtsgeschichte*, 152–54; Gierke, "Basic Concepts," 184–85.

31. Gierke, introduction to *Rechtsgeschichte*, 156. This seems to be a modern rendering of Althusius's concept of the unique "symbiotic right" of each kind of association.

for example, office holding within a workers' cooperative will be governed by principles different from those applicable to office holding within a church.

Social law is also concerned with ordering some of the relations *between* groups. Some such relations will fall under the category of individual law, as in the case of private contracts between business corporations; no organic link is involved here. Organic links are involved whenever lesser groups are united into higher, more inclusive ones as parts to a whole[32]— when, for example, a number of trade unions combine to form a confederation. The most inclusive group is the state, and thus a major part of social law will be concerned with ordering the relations between the state and its constituent members. This branch of social law Gierke calls "state law."

Like many other associations, the state has an "original, real essence," possessing a "unitary collective life distinct from the life of its members."[33] As John D. Lewis puts it, for Gierke, the state is "but the last link in the chain of collective units developed into persons."[34] Yet while the state is a "general" association, it is certainly not identical to human society as such. The state is "only one among the associational organisms of mankind and only one definite side of human social life is represented by it. . . . [I]t is only with part of his being that the single man belongs to the state as a member." The state is simply incapable of satisfying all our associational inclinations. Nonpolitical aspects of associational life are expressed in specific "functional" associations, such as social, religious, artistic, economic, and other groups. These are in no sense created by the state, and each of them can claim a certain independence over against the state. Indeed, especially in a modern, differentiated society, "the non-political sides of human associational life find expression in special institutions which are in no way to be confused with the state-organization."[35]

Gierke's depiction of the state as simply *one among many* associations in society was taken up enthusiastically by the English pluralists writing at the beginning of the twentieth century such as Frederic William Maitland,

---

Compare Johannes Althusius, *The Politics of Johannes Althusius,* trans. and intro. by F. S. Carney (Boston: Beacon Press, 1964), 14. This concept is theorized in highly complex and sophisticated fashion in the social and legal philosophy of Herman Dooyeweerd (see esp. *New Critique,* vol. 3, 379–620, 664–92). See also Paul Marshall, "Dooyeweerd's Empirical Theory of Rights," in *The Legacy of Herman Dooyeweerd,* ed. C. T. McIntire (Lanham, MD: University Press of America, 1985), 119–42.

32. Gierke, introduction to *Rechtsgeschichte,* 155.
33. Gierke, "Basic Concepts," 172.
34. Lewis, *Genossenschaft-Theory,* 63.
35. Gierke, "Basic Concepts," 173–74.

J. N. Figgis, and the early Harold Laski.[36] They seized on Gierke to buttress their essentially constitutionalist argument against the doctrine of legally unlimited state sovereignty that they saw being deployed to justify excessive state control over other associations. It has to be admitted, however, that in doing so they were reading Gierke selectively.[37] For while this constitutional-pluralist argument certainly finds plenty of textual support in Gierke's work, it must be read alongside his wider view of the nature and role of the state, a view in which some interpreters (such as Lewis) see potentially monistic tendencies.

For Gierke the state is unique by virtue of its being a comprehensive, inclusive association. While it does not create other associations, it alone can bind all its citizens into a unified organic whole. The state alone is able to embody the unified general will of the entire community, formed by a union of the associated wills of its members; hence (at least in its modern constitutional form) it embodies an element of fellowship (*Genossenschaft*). On the other hand, it alone is the bearer of sovereignty, by which Gierke means both comprehensiveness and monopoly of coercive power; and thus it displays the element of hierarchical authority (*Obrigkeit*). While subordinate political associations are "state-like," the state's authority stands above theirs; it is "an authoritative union whose authority from above is limited by no similar authority and from below is superior to all similar authority." Its authority is likewise higher than any of the nonpolitical associations within its territory. While such associations retain their independent sphere of existence, they nevertheless have a political aspect insofar as they require authoritative regulation by the state.[38]

Worries about Gierke's monism are not unfounded; the fusion in his later writings of organicist with German nationalist motifs certainly does nothing to allay them. Yet such worries should not be allowed to overshadow his achievement of formulating an original theory of legal pluralism. This emerges with particular clarity from his view of the contentious jurisprudential problem of the "sources of law." Gierke insisted that, while in modern society the body normally responsible for *promulgating* social

---

36. Compare Nicholls, ed., *The Pluralist State;* and Hirst, ed., *The Pluralist Theory of the State.*

37. Maitland, for example, was interested mainly in the consequences of Gierke's theory for private law. Compare Lewis, *Genossenschaft-Theory,* 64.

38. Gierke, "Basic Concepts," 172–73, 171. This political aspect of other associations "finds its final definition of purpose and definitive boundary in the state, which, as the sovereign organism of social authority, alone among all organisms has no institution above it to limit its power" (Ibid., 174).

law is the state,[39] this emphatically does not mean that the state is the *sole source of* valid law. On the contrary, he held that "the final source of all law remains the social consciousness of *any social institution whatever.*" This affirmation of sources of valid positive law other than the state is the core of his theory of legal pluralism and sets him firmly against the legal positivist dictum that the state alone can claim this prerogative by virtue of its unique capacity for coercive enforcement. He asserts:

> The social conviction that something is right needs, to be sure, embodiment through a social declaration in order to come into objective existence as a principle of law. But this declaration can take place in different ways. Usually, of course, it takes place through the state; it is a chief function of the *Kulturstaat* to formulate as law the consciousness of right of the people. Still, beside the state operate in a similar and at times very far-reaching fashion other social organisms—for example, church, family, *Gemeinde* and so forth—as formative organs of law.[40]

Yet, in Gierke's mind, an emphatic assertion of legal pluralism is not at all incompatible with recognizing a wide-ranging integrative ("organic") role for the state. These complementary emphases come together in his account of how state law relates to associational law. For Gierke, law is an irreducible aspect of social life, present in many associations, and the state has no monopoly on it. State and law have quite different tasks: "[W]hile the state should advance the social purpose of humankind in every sphere of social life, law has only to mark off the boundaries within which the free pursuit by all existing will of individual as of associational goals may take place."[41] Law nevertheless is linked in a unique way to the state; law and state are "equally original" with humankind.[42] Although enforceability is not a necessary part of the definition of law, law cannot properly realize its purpose of ordering wills without the backing of state power. Although law without enforcement still counts as law, it is nevertheless "incomplete."[43] The sovereignty of the state is therefore a necessary con-

---

39. Otto von Gierke, *The Development of Political Theory,* trans. Bernard Freyd (London: George Allen and Unwin, 1939), 329–330 (a translation of *Johannes Althusius und die Entwicklung der naturrechtlichen Staatstheorien,* 4th ed. [Breslau, 1929]. 1st ed. pub. 1880).
40. Gierke, "Basic Concepts," 176 (my emphasis).
41. Ibid., 177–78.
42. Gierke, *Development,* 328.
43. Gierke, "Basic Concepts," 178; compare Gierke, *Development,* 329–31.

dition for the law of any other association to realize its purpose. The state gives legal effect to its comprehensive responsibility to sustain an organically articulated society in which each part both comes into its own as a unique whole with its distinctive, nonderived purpose and sphere of conduct and at the same time contributes insofar as it is required to the life of the whole.[44] This includes the centrally important task of recognizing associations as legal persons, specifying their rights and duties, safeguarding their independence, and regulating their activity. The protection of associational independence and the legal definition of its character and boundaries are essential not only for the associations but also for the state itself, since its healthy functioning is inextricably bound to theirs. A strong state can only be sustained by a vigorous associational life in civil society.

In addition to these functional associations standing in a horizontal relationship to each other under the supervisory role of the state, there are also subordinate political associations—municipalities, provinces, or other territorial units—that are vertically integrated into the state. Gierke holds that these are based on the same legal principles as the state (except that they lack sovereignty),[45] implying thereby a general qualitative difference between political associations, at any level, and the many nonpolitical functional associations. The former are inclusive public bodies, while the latter are exclusive functional bodies.[46]

The state also has the role of determining which associations are to be designated as "public establishments" empowered to exercise political functions.[47] At this point the influence of Hegelian corporatism does become evident. Gierke draws a distinction between associations viewed

44. So far as the state-individual relationship is concerned, state law deals with issues such as citizenship and civil rights. In addition, state law also apportions the respective powers and duties of the various organs of government itself.

45. Gierke, "Basic Concepts," 184.

46. While Gierke did not believe that his organic theory of associations necessarily implied political federalism—for this would entail the notion of divided sovereignty that he rejected—he did nevertheless recommend that the newly established German state be modeled on the organic idea (Lewis, *Genossenschaft-Theory*, 79–87; compare Rupert Emerson, *State and Sovereignty in Modern Germany* [New Haven: Yale University Press, 1929], chap. 4). He advocated not a federal state, but a decentralized state in which the relative autonomy of subordinate political units would be preserved in recognition of the independent source of their rights (Lewis, *Genossenschaft-Theory*, 193, 85). Thus not only do nonpolitical associations retain their independence by virtue of their intrinsic, nonderived rights, but subordinate political bodies do also, even though they are (decentralized) parts of the same state structure.

47. Gierke, "Basic Concepts," 155–56, 181–85; compare Heiman, introduction to *Associations and Law*, 47–48.

in terms of their specific functional role (as "particulars," as Hegel would put it),[48] possessing legal status analogous to the private citizen's, and corporations as members of the state, as "intermediate organisms" between state and citizen.[49] In this latter capacity they fall within the scope of state law, as well as possessing their own internal social law pertaining to their specific function. The boundary between these two jural spheres will be a variable one, according as the specific interests of the corporation impinge upon the general interest:

> So far as the member-position of the narrower association reaches, the state will possess a more or less extended right over not only the external, but also the internal life of the organism attached to it. The rise and modification, composition, business, content and compass of membership, its organization and activity in general, will not be determined for the narrower community by its will alone, but to some degree or other by the will of the state.[50]

It is apparent, then, that Gierke envisages a potentially wide measure of state intervention affecting the activities of associations, especially those he calls "intermediate organisms." Yet, as I noted, he still wishes to attribute to associations other than the state something approximating a "natural right" to establish valid jural norms within their own sphere, norms deriving their authority not from the will of the state but from the intrinsic associational right of self-government. This right constitutes an external barrier to state authority.[51] His overall position, in my view, seems to imply a clear presumption in favor of associational autonomy, with the onus resting on the state to defend its interventions on specific public-interest grounds, rather than on the association to defend itself against the putative claims of the public interest. It suggests that when the state wishes to intervene in an association, the internal laws of an association and the decisions made in accordance with them have a prima facie right to be acknowledged by the state.

---

48. Georg Friedrich Wilhelm Hegel, *The Philosophy of Right*, trans. T. M. Knox (Oxford: Oxford University Press, 1952), 152 (para. 251).

49. Compare George Heiman, "The Sources and Significance of Hegel's Corporate Doctrine," in *Hegel's Political Philosophy*, ed Z. A. Pelczynksi (Cambridge: Cambridge University Press, 1971), 111–35.

50. Gierke, "Basic Concepts," 183–84.

51. Ibid., 182.

I have already alluded to one significant problem in Gierke's account. This is the implausible notion of a "group-personality." I noted the objection to the apparent reification to which he seems to fall victim here, namely, the supposition that a group-personality somehow transcends the personalities of its members. But there is a deeper objection. This reification seems to be the outcome of an illicit reductive move: an excessive *psychologizing* of associational bonds. The danger here is of reducing what holds an association together and sustains its capacity for agency to a supposed psychological fusion of the subjective "wills" of the associating individuals. Institutional agency clearly includes a social-psychological element; hence we may rightly speak, for instance, of a "corporate ethos." Nevertheless, such agency cannot be reduced to, or explained primarily in terms of, that element alone.

If this problem reveals the adverse influence of idealism, a second arises from the ambiguities of historicism. In addition to affirming that law can be validly promulgated by the "social consciousness of any social institution whatever," Gierke also endorses the notion advanced by the Historical School that law is the outcome of a continuously evolving and organically founded national spirit (*Volksgeist*).[52] It appears that the national spirit is itself an example—the most capacious—of a "social consciousness" capable of generating valid law (it does so via the organ of the state). This raises the question whether, when the various nonstate associations are creating law, they are formulating their *own* unique kind of law or simply serving as decentralized conduits for the formulation of an all-embracing *national* law that pervades them all. Gierke's "pluralist" proposition regarding the multiple sources of law appears facially at odds with his "historicist" assumption that law in general is ultimately the expression of the spirit of one particular community, the nation.

This historicist presupposition gives rise to a related problem. Gierke sometimes appears to imply that the Germanic law of associations is *itself* a unique historical product of the Germanic national spirit. Its ultimate foundation, it seems, is not a transhistorical natural law; indeed, Gierke specifically rejects this notion.[53] Yet he also holds that the associational inclination and the reality of organic association are *founded in human nature*. The Historical School, he concludes, had shown that there could be no going back to a universality based in an "abstract" natural law; all law is positive law, and such law is the expression of a particular national

---

52. Gierke, *Development*, 328.
53. Ibid., 338.

spirit.[54] Yet he also affirms that the abiding insight of the natural law theory must be preserved, namely, that law must reflect the *idea of justice*, which is innate in humanity and thus of universal significance and appeal.[55]

There is, then, a residual ambiguity in Gierke's theory of legal pluralism. He seems ambivalent over whether associational rights are grounded ultimately in the authority of a particular historical tradition or in universal features of human nature. Anthony Black suggests, perhaps generously, that this apparent tension can be reconciled by observing that Gierke regards the German *Genossenschaft* tradition as but a pioneer in discovering what is in fact a universal truth.[56] That is, Gierke seeks to approach a universal norm (the plurality of associational jural spheres) via an examination of one of its most advanced historical manifestations. Heinrich Rommen's variant of legal pluralism, by contrast, may be said to move in the other direction: proceeding on the assumption of a substantive conception of universal human nature, rooted in Thomist natural law theory, it explores the shape of the historical manifestation of such human nature in the plural institutions of the modern West.

Heinrich Rommen: Social Teleology

Thomism and pluralism are not typically thought to belong together. I cannot explore here the question whether St. Thomas Aquinas's social thought might be seen as anticipating what I am calling "social pluralism."[57] It is clear, however, that official Catholic social teaching since Pope

54. Insofar as Gierke's critique was directed at eighteenth-century rationalistic theories of natural law, it certainly has merit. Such a charge of "abstractness" does not, I think, apply in the same way to premodern conceptions of natural law. On this see Heinrich Rommen, *The Natural Law* (St. Louis, MO: B. Herder, 1947; reprint, Indianapolis: Liberty Fund, 1995.)

55. Gierke, *Development*, 328–29.

56. Black, *Guilds and Civil Society*, xvi, xx–xxi.

57. On this, see Russell Hittinger, "The Plural Nature of Society in Leo XIII: Response to J. D. van der Vyver" (Conference on the Legacy of Abraham Kuyper and Leo XIII, Calvin College, Grand Rapids, MI, October 31, 1998). Hittinger identifies in Thomas's *Contra impugnantes* a "natural law" defense of the corporate rights of the Dominican order; see also John E. Kelly, "The Influence of Aquinas' Natural Law Theory on the Principle of 'Corporatism' in the Thought of Leo XIII and Pius XI," in *Things Old and New: Catholic Social Teaching Revisited,* ed. Francis P. McHugh and Samuel M. Natale (Lanham, MD: University Press of America, 1993), 104–43; and Nicholas Aroney, "Subsidiarity, Federalism and the Best Constitution: Thomas Aquinas on City, Province and Empire" (2005; unpublished paper, on file with the author).

Leo XIII qualifies as a distinct variant of this approach.[58] In the writings of Heinrich Rommen this social pluralist theme is especially pronounced.[59]

Rommen's social and political theory is elaborated on the basis of a Thomistic metaphysics. Central to that metaphysics is a conception of a teleological and hierarchical order of natural and supernatural ends. Social bodies, Rommen holds, can be understood as compounds of form and matter.[60] Their form or essence operates internally and is given with their end, toward which they naturally tend and which secures their unity (*SCT,* 39–40, 43; compare 77–78). Such bodies do not form a "substantial unity" like the human body, but rather a "unity of order" (*unitas ordinis*). A "unity of order" is not a thing, but an enduring coordination of discrete substances that, while lacking substantiality itself, nevertheless exists as a real communal whole. Social bodies originate in "nature." This term is not to be understood in a biological sense, but in the sense that each social body promotes purposes that are rooted in human social nature and are necessary for human flourishing. A social body is "a teleological, intentional form of human existence morally necessary for the realization of the idea of man" (*SCT,* 136–37). They are "intentional wholes," which means that they are brought into being by the intentional human realization of naturally given ends (and so are not merely the product of pooled subjective wills, as Gierke suggests). The concrete design of social bodies clearly bears the stamp of their particular historical context and, yet, is not wholly a product of historical contingency. That design is conditioned by ends arising from the recurring inclinations and imperatives of universal human nature. When established, such bodies do not acquire an independent existence over and above the existence of the persons who make them up. While Rommen speaks of social bodies as "moral" and sometimes "organic" communities, he does not construe them as reified "group-personalities." Social being cannot be reduced to individual persons, but yet exists solely for and

58. See my "Subsidiarity and Sphere Sovereignty: Catholic and Reformed Conceptions of the Role of the State," in *Things Old and New,* 175–202.

59. Given an indirect influence of Gierke on Rommen, this is not surprising. Rommen wrote after the appearance of the influential "pluralist" social encyclical of Pius XI, *Quadragesimo Anno* (1931) (reprinted in *Two Basic Social Encyclicals* [Washington, DC: Catholic University Press, 1943]). Pius XI had commissioned the young social theorist Oswald von Nell-Breuning to prepare a first draft and advised him to turn for guidance to the "solidarist" school of Catholic social thought associated with the German economist Heinrich Pesch, who had been influenced by Gierke. See Nell-Breuning's own account of the writing and (controversial) reception of the encyclical, in "50 Jaar 'Quadragesimo Anno,'" *Christen-democratische verkenningen* 12 (The Hague, 1981): 599–606.

60. Heinrich Rommen, *The State in Catholic Thought* (St. Louis, MO, and London: B. Herder, 1945), 34. Hereafter this work will be cited parenthetically in the text as *SCT.*

through persons (*SCT,* 43, 124–27, 131–32). A social body "enlarges, exalts and perfects the individual person and cures the shortcomings and wants that are connected with mere individuality and isolation" (*SCT,* 136).

The order of ends is the basis for a hierarchy of communities or associations,[61] the spiritual ranking higher than the temporal and the more inclusive temporal ends ranking above the less. "The hierarchy of ends is mirrored in a hierarchy of functional associations designed, directed and measured as to efficiency and goodness by their objective ends" (*SCT,* 303). The temporal communities include family; vocational, professional, and educational organizations; neighborhood; town; and nation (*SCT,* 301). They come into existence through the course of history as expressions of particular, partial aspects of human social nature (*SCT,* 302). While man's supernatural end is his highest, he can move toward it only through this plurality of natural communities. Each of them is directed to fulfilling one partial end, for the essences of all things are defined by their ends (*SCT,* 269). Since these ends are rooted in human nature, humans have a responsibility and a capacity to realize them through free rational initiative by creating communities appropriate to their fulfillment.

It is this responsibility and capacity to pursue objective moral ends that is the fundamental basis for a natural right to self-government through those associations necessary to pursue them (*SCT,* 303). Here Rommen follows Leo XIII's view that, since to join an association or "private society" is an individual's natural right, the associations themselves have a natural right to exist that must be upheld by the state.[62] He thus presents a complex social landscape in which, as he puts it, a "plurality of social forms and of cooperative spheres that proceed from the person, serve independent particular ends in the order of the common good and therefore

---

61. For the purposes of this paper the significance of the distinction between *community* and *association* need not be elaborated.

62. J.-Y. Calvez and Jacques Perrin, *The Church and Social Justice,* trans. J. R. Kirwan (Chicago: Henry Regnery, 1961), 316. The authors observe that Leo looked to associations of many kinds—including workers' associations, vocational bodies, mutual aid societies, and charitable trusts—to "help to re-knit the connecting tissues of a society which individualism had reduced to isolated units," to act as shields between individual and state and contribute to the realization of social justice; "the principle of association lay at the centre of the pope's thought" (408; compare 411, 382). Leo held that such associations should be left free by the state to adopt their own internal rules. On the other hand these rules must be conducive to the associations' realizing their natural moral purpose. The freedom of association is more than the individual's right to join an association. It also carries with it the duty to see that the association fulfils its morally legitimate purpose (384) and so is limited by the requirements of the common good.

have their own rights and duties." Because the ends such forms serve are not created by the legal enactments of the state, their rights and duties derive from a source independent of and prior to it. The state certainly affords them the necessary legal recognition, but (as Gierke also insisted) "it is their essence, their ends, that control the legal forms, not vice versa" (*SCT*, 143).

This philosophical account of social bodies is reinforced by an empirical argument concerning the conditions for human liberty. Like many pluralists (including Gierke), Rommen holds that the protection of intermediate social bodies is necessary to safeguard the individual from the likely encroachments of a burgeoning centralized state.[63] Individual freedom is extended by safeguarding associational freedom: "[T]he greater his freedom to form associations and the greater the freedom of the associations themselves in self-initiative and self-government, the freer, actually, is the person, although his bonds and ties increase in these associations" (*SCT*, 145). Alongside a space for individual existence the human person also fulfills many functional roles within specific communities— as family member, resident, professional, believer, and so forth, and "[t]hese qualifications constitute his social life" (*SCT*, 300). To abolish such communities would be "to rob the persons of a protective shield and to transform them into social atoms," each facing a centralized state yet deprived of intrinsic rights and liberties: "Such a power [would substitute] its commands for the ordered activities and free initiative of the persons, families and groups therein governed. Such absolute sovereignty . . . is opposed to the Christian idea of the state" (*SCT*, 256). Threats to such bodies can come not only overtly from totalitarianism, which seeks to eliminate all loyalties other than that to the state (*SCT*, 144–45), but also imperceptibly from an individualism that dissolves the essentially communal values of family, marriage, profession, or citizenship into mere aggregations of individual interest.

Rommen's theory of plural social bodies is an innovative elaboration of Aquinas's philosophical account of natural communities. That account

63. Successive popes expressed a similar concern at any threat to the vitality of intermediate bodies. Compare Calvez and Perrin, *Church and Social Justice*, 416. At the "Rethinking Rights" conference at Ave Maria School of Law on November 19–20, 2004, Stephen Safranek rightly observed that the expansion of individual freedom can serve to empower resistance, on the part of various "intermediate bodies" formed by free individuals, to excessive statism and corporate power. He noted, *inter alia*, developments in the law of contract facilitating alternate forms of dispute resolution outside state courts, the emergence of townships and "new communities" situated beyond the clutches of bureaucratized metropoles, and the growth of voluntary associations in general.

primarily has in view domestic and political communities.[64] Rommen, however, extends Aquinas's Aristotelian argument for the organic evolution of state from household, to embrace the full range of nonpolitical bodies typical of modern industrial, differentiated society, thereby achieving for Catholicism what Gierke had achieved for organicism.[65] The social process develops in different stages, from individual to family; to lesser territorial groupings, professional and vocational organizations, and religious, national, cultural, and educational bodies; and finally to the state and the community of states (*SCT,* 301).[66] Each of these is rooted in a natural process and each possesses a unique character and range of rights, duties, and powers determined objectively by rational human nature. That is, they have what I am calling an original "jural sphere."[67]

The various qualitatively different functional groups, associations, and communities belong to the realm of "society." Rommen's definition of society contrasts sharply both with the classical liberal notion of society as an autonomous, self-regulating system of individual interactions and with the Hegelian notion of "civil society" as an unstable system of self-interested competition.[68] Society is a "multitude," lacking the "unity of order" displayed by the state. But its members are linked in a dense network of free, cooperative relationships, maintaining a looser kind of order sustained by a multiplicity of associative and solidaristic social ties. These can range from informal ties of friendship to legally enforceable contracts, to organized cooperation in permanent institutions and corporate bodies

64. But see Hittinger, "Plural Nature of Society."

65. See n. 15 above.

66. Developing a contrast found in Pius XI's writings (compare Calvez and Perrin, *Church and Social Justice,* 423, 431), Rommen distinguishes between two kinds of natural association: those that contribute "directly and immediately" to the perfection of social life (family and state) (*SCT,* 136, 227) and those that, while also classed as "natural," nevertheless have fewer fundamental purposes and thus only transient existence (unions, voluntary associations, and so on). The family has primary significance: it is "a genuine and necessary community with specific and non-transferable ends" (*SCT,* 249); it has a certain self-sufficiency, appropriate for its particular ends, namely, propagation, cooperation, and education; and it has a specific kind of authority—paternal—which has a "kind of sovereignty." This means that while civil law rightly regulates the family in accordance with the requirements of the common good and to prevent the abuse of paternal authority, it must do so assuming and respecting this paternal authority, which it cannot replace (*SCT,* 269).

67. Rommen, however, does not speak, as Gierke does, of lesser associations' having genuine "law-making" capacity. They have rights, duties, and powers, but the *rules* they formulate to govern their internal affairs are not, strictly, *laws*. On this point, Dooyeweerd agrees with Gierke rather than Rommen.

68. Compare John Ehrenberg, *Civil Society: The Critical History of an Idea* (New York: New York University Press, 1999).

such as territorial units; educational, business, or labor organizations; or voluntary associations of numerous kinds. This complex of interlinkages that comprises "society" must never be confused with the state (*SCT,* 274). Such interlinkages are created by the initiative of individuals and free associations, for which the state provides the external framework and support. "The state affords legal hulls, formal standards, and prevents violation of the public order, the common good and its basic moral values. The state does not create them nor has the state a right to destroy or confiscate them without due process of law" (*SCT,* 274).

This is the sense in which society as a whole can be construed as the "matter" of which the state is the "form." The state's form-giving activity is indispensable. As with Gierke, therefore, Rommen's vigorous assertion of social pluralism is far from implying a classical-liberal minimal state, existing merely to adjudicate conflicts of individual wills and interests. While nonpolitical bodies are natural, essential, and the bearers of original rights and powers, they nevertheless satisfy no more than a part of human social nature (*SCT,* 269–70). The limited goods that each secure point to the necessity for a higher body to secure the comprehensive requirements of the whole community and possessed of sufficient authority to realize this end. The fullest development of human nature is attained only in the state. The state is the teleological culmination of a natural social process proceeding "by inner moral necessity from the social nature of man for the sake of the more perfect life" and leading to "the fullest realization of personality for all its members in a working sovereign order of mutual assistance and mutual cooperation." Rommen can thus characterize the state as an "order of solidaristic responsibility" and as "a cooperative whole of mutually complementary functions," whose members, though "substantially" equal, are nevertheless "functionally" unequal (*SCT,* 137, 299–300). It is a "moral organism" whose purpose includes both the provision of material conditions and also the fostering of social and political virtues (*SCT,* 286). Like all social bodies, it is a "unity of order," not a "substantial unity."

As a Thomist, Rommen holds that the state's purpose is, finally, religiously founded: "It is inserted into the universal order of human ends, into the order of creation, therefore subordinated to the supreme end of all creation, the glory of God" (*SCT,* 307). Proximately, however, the state belongs to the natural realm, within which it can be described as the "perfect" community by virtue of its possession of "self-sufficiency," and this in a threefold sense: economically, in its capacity to meet all material needs; politically, in its creation and sustenance of a unified, ordered community of individuals, families, and intermediate bodies; and legally, in its possession of sovereign authority (*SCT,* 223–24, 250, 253–54).

The third sense is especially germane here. The state's self-sufficiency acquires *legal* expression "inasmuch as the state reveals itself as an order with all the original rights, competences and powers that are necessary to produce the secular sufficiency of community life" (*SCT,* 255). This is the sense in which the state, too, has a unique "jural sphere." The legal self-sufficiency, or "sovereignty," of the state is necessary if the state is to fulfill its unique role as guardian of the common good. The need for a final, unappealable decision is inescapable if order and security among the various individuals and groups within the state are to be established, and this competence must belong uniquely to the state (*SCT,* 400–402, 254). Because the state possesses sovereignty, intermediate associations, while they retain their own original jural spheres, may not also presume to claim it (*SCT,* 271).[69] The state's possession of sovereignty means that state law is common to all within its territory and that no other state's law applies. Such law is "supreme and universal"; in relation to it, the "laws" of other social bodies (such as a collegiate constitution or municipal charter) are "particular and subordinate" (*SCT,* 254, 258–59).

But the jural sphere of the state can never be all-inclusive precisely because that sphere is circumscribed by those of many other social bodies. Sovereignty is essentially the supreme responsibility for pursuing a specific moral end, the common good of the whole society, and, in the case of the state as with all other social bodies, such an end simultaneously directs, empowers, *and delimits* the state, because it transcends it (*SCT,* 404). The state is sovereign only "in its own order" (*in suo ordine*). "The spheres of the individual, of the family and of the cultural and economic organization (society), represent genuine limits to sovereignty" (*SCT,* 400).[70]

In its most general terms the common good touches everything concerning "external secular felicity," all that promotes a condition of public peace and justice (*SCT,* 311, 329). Concretely, it embraces social, economic, technical, legal, intellectual, and cultural aspects of life (*SCT,* 255) and also

69. The Church, by contrast, does possess "sovereignty" within the *spiritual* realm because it too is a perfect and self-sufficient community within that sphere (*SCT,* 261). The church is subordinate to the state in matters affecting the temporal common good, while the state is subordinate to the church in matters affecting the supernatural common good. Further, since the church possesses sovereignty, it also wields genuine "law-making" power. Thus canon law is real law, whereas the jural norms of, e.g., a trade union, remain "rules."

70. Sovereignty is also limited externally by the rights of other sovereign states that collectively constitute a higher community of nations, and these rights are defined in international law (*SCT,* 256–57). The state's law is in fact only one order of law among four irreducible types, each pertaining to its own sphere: the positive law of the state, the positive law of the church, positive international law, and, transcending and judging them all, natural law (*SCT,* 262).

public virtue (that is, that virtue necessary for the promotion of the common good) (*SCT,* 311; compare 330). The common good is the "final cause"
of the state, the end to which it is teleologically directed. It is the object of
the state's activities, the source of its legitimacy, and the norm that governs
the purpose of law and the principle that prevails over any other claim
made upon the state (*SCT,* 139, 142). The common good is "the creative
principle and conserving power of the body politic," transforming an
"external amorphous mass of individuals" into "a solidarist body of
mutual help and interest, into an organically united nation" (*SCT,* 310–11).
It is not simply the sum of private individual goods, but is qualitatively
different from and morally "prior to" the sum of private goods (compare
SCT, 386). The common good is a criterion against which the practices of
all actual states must be continually tested by their rational citizens, especially since their scope necessarily expands or contracts historically
according to changing circumstantial imperatives (*SCT,* 306, 401).

Rommen's claim regarding the "priority" of the common good of the
whole community must be understood in terms of a careful grasp of the
Thomistic conception of the whole-part relationship. This is not a zero-
sum conception according to which what accrues to one detracts from the
other. Rather, the common good cannot be realized at the expense of the
good of its parts, but only through the attainment of their particular goods
(*SCT,* 307). While the common good is morally prior to the partial goods
of individuals or associations, if the parts are harmed the common good is
to that extent not attained (*SCT,* 317–18).[71] Thus integral to the common
good is the provision of the security and peaceful functioning of nonpolitical bodies and their protection from both internal disruption and external disturbance (*SCT,* 138). Moreover, the basic rights of nonpolitical
bodies constitute a major limit to the degree of sacrifice legitimately
demanded of individuals (*SCT,* 308–9). While they may need to make sacrifices on behalf of the common good and come under the overall regulation of the state, their realization of their own partial goods is a necessary
part of the realization of the common good of the whole. A crucial responsibility of the state is thus to ensure "that none of the endeavours of human
social nature prevail hypertrophically over the others, but that all grow as
balanced parts of a well-organized order in unity" (*SCT,* 253). The state

71. The priority of the common good means that individuals may be obliged to make
specific sacrifices on its behalf, perhaps of property but including the extreme case of
losing their lives in the event of a (just) war. Yet even such sacrifices, while harming the
interests of individuals, are to their ultimate good, since in obeying a moral obligation
deriving from God's law they contribute to the realization of his higher spiritual end.
Thus while the common good does not absorb the individual's good, from the point of
view of the individual's final end, they ultimately coincide (*SCT,* 138–39, 326, 333).

supplies for other social bodies merely a "sovereign unity of order" maintaining conditions for balanced public interaction among social bodies each with its own irreplaceable ends. Yet—as Gierke also recognizes—preserving such order will require various kinds of intervention in the internal activities and structures of social bodies. While nonpolitical bodies possess a protected jural sphere, they may as a result of ignorance or self-interest prove incapable of ordering their internal affairs rightly or act so as to harm the interests of other bodies. Such intervention as is called for must, however, conform to the principle of subsidiarity (*SCT,* 303), which Rommen summarizes thus: "Any task that free (private) cultural or economic or educational organizations and institutions can perform, in the framework of the public order of law, by their own initiative or by their own service to ideals which often transcend those of the state, should be left to their discretion and competency" (*SCT,* 280).

Toward a Critical Elaboration

I have attempted to show how Gierke and Rommen provide valuable theoretical resources for rebutting the three assumptions that I suggested were still significant obstacles to the development of a social pluralist theory of institutional rights. First, both reject the individualist premise that institutions are merely contingent creations of the contracting wills or pooled rights of morally autonomous and self-constituting individuals. Against this premise Gierke advances the historically grounded insight that participation in multiple organic associations is as fundamental to human flourishing as individual freedom, while Rommen proposes a metaphysically grounded account of the plural social bodies arising from human nature and furnishing necessary contexts for the rational exercise of individual freedom and responsibility.[72] In my view, while Gierke's historical retrieval of an associationist legal pluralism is rightly regarded as a monumental scholarly achievement, it is inadequately grounded in a rudimentary and ambiguous synthesis of historical and psychological generalization. By contrast, Rommen's theoretical grounding of social pluralism in a rich notion of distinct and complementary institutional purposes arising from irreducible human inclinations seems more promising.[73]

72. These, of course, are two variants of a now-familiar "communitiarian" argument about the necessary social embeddedness of the self.
73. I do not have space here to consider the possible shortcomings of the Thomistic metaphysics underlying Rommen's social theory. For brief reflections, see my "Subsidiarity and Sphere Sovereignty."

Yet, even on these quite different grounds, both affirm that institutions possess inherent structural capacities not derived from those of the individuals who establish or compose them, including the capacity for institutional "agency." Thus, for example, when the board of directors of a business corporation approves a resolution, that decision is not explicable as a mere aggregation or convergence of simultaneous and contiguous acts of the individual board members.[74] Upon the establishment of a corporation (family, university, state, etc.), a new locus of intentional action ("will," for Gierke; "intentionality," for Rommen) is generated that is more than the sum of the successive individual acts that continue to be necessary to sustain its existence. A new structural reality—an institution equipped with legal subjectivity and possessed of its own jural sphere— has been brought into being.[75]

Both thinkers also pointedly reject the two related legal positivist doctrines I earlier placed in my sights: that only the state can generate valid jural norms and that institutional rights are mere "concessions" from the state. Yet their accounts point to the need for a fuller articulation of the complex *contents* of the original jural spheres possessed by diverse institutions. They suggest the need to move beyond Gierke's legal history to legal doctrine and beyond Rommen's social philosophy to jurisprudence. This would involve developing more sophisticated theoretical accounts of what is undeniable (if often very imperfectly encoded) in legal practice, namely, that institutions do indeed possess legal rights, fulfill legal duties, and exercise legal powers. The questions at stake are: Why do these institutions display the jural spheres that they do? And are these spheres adequately constituted internally and protected externally, given the normative purposes such institutions legitimately pursue? Let me list some specific examples now undergoing fierce contestation: Do parents currently possess too many or too few powers over their children? Can any two (or more) individuals enter the institution historically known as "marriage"? Do business corporations wield rights over their property that undermine states' capacity to advance the common good? Why should the institutions of

74. To employ Maitland's hypothetical example: if we find ourselves owed money by a state—"Nusquamania"—we know this does not mean we are owed money by a collection of individual citizens of that state. You may not "convert the proposition that Nusquamania owes you money into a series of propositions imposing duties on certain human beings that are now in existence" ("Moral Personality," 178).

75. Even a legal positivist like A. V. Dicey had to recognize that "[w]hen a body of . . . men bind themselves together to act in a particular way for some common purpose, they create a body, which by no fiction of law, but by the very nature of things, differs from the individuals of whom it is constituted." Quoted in Maitland, "Moral Personality," 173–74.

health care, education, and social services be subject to such extensive legal control or even ownership by public authorities? The claim to jural "originality" is central to all these examples. This is a claim regarding the distinctiveness of the contents of the jural spheres of diverse types of social institutions. To sustain it, even perhaps to make it intelligible, would require an argument from the assertion of institutional agency (that institutions can act pursuant to some normative purpose) to that of institutional legal subjectivity (that institutions can act *jurally* on account of an inherent capacity to pursue that purpose). Equally contested, of course, is the question of how one identifies the "normative institutional purposes" in which claims to institutional agency and legal subjectivity are grounded, or even whether one can do so at all.[76]

Yet if at least some clarity on the question of jural originality can be obtained, we will be in a position to approach another crucial question that surfaced in both Gierke's and Rommen's accounts of legal pluralism. This is the question of how to identify the boundaries between the distinctive rights, duties, and powers of diverse social institutions, on the one hand, and on the other, those necessarily inhering in the state pursuant to its discharge of its responsibility toward the public good. Both thinkers claim that state law does not itself create the legal subjectivity of associations, or the numerous interlinkages between them (and individuals), but only recognizes them in law and coordinates them in policy. But these processes of legal recognition and political coordination have come to be both extensive and intensive, penetrating deep into the core of what formerly were thought to be the exclusive internal affairs of an institution. One needs to note only the fact that what counts as a "marriage" for public policy purposes has in recent centuries come to be defined by the state, not by the parties to the marriage or by their (religious or other) communities.[77] Or think of the way that the "law of contracts," originally emerg-

---

76. For an attempt to lay out a possible approach rooted in natural law thinking, see Michael Pakaluk, "Natural Law and Civil Society," in *Alternative Conceptions of Civil Society*, ed. Simone Chambers and Will Kymlicka (Princeton: Princeton University Press, 2002). An application of Jacques Maritain's social pluralism to American legal practice is Larry May, *The Morality of Groups: Collective Responsibility, Group-Based Harm and Corporate Rights* (Notre Dame, IN: University of Notre Dame Press, 1987). For a comparison of Catholic social pluralism with parallel Calvinist and historicist traditions, see *Political Order and the Plural Structure of Society*, ed. James W. Skillen and Rockne M. McCarthy (Atlanta: Scholars' Press, 1991).

77. Concern that the long-standing political consensus over what counts as marriage is no longer sustainable in secularized liberal democracies has led some to argue for a universal "civil unions" regime in which the definition of marriage is left to nongovernmental institutions like churches, so acquiring a standing similar to baptism. Compare

ing out of private interlinkages between free economic agents, is now so extensive that it is widely believed that contracts themselves are really the creation and province of the state.[78] Or, consider the extent to which the content of corporate law has come to be determined by statute rather than by private agreements between businesses and employees or other businesses.[79] Indeed, even the institutions seemingly most independent of the state—charities, including religious bodies—are increasingly being brought under detailed statutory regulations that seem to hem them in at every turn.[80] In brief, legal pluralism needs to develop an argument whereby plausible criteria can be identified for distinguishing *in a nonarbitrary fashion*, yet also through appropriate democratic deliberation, between the jural spheres of the state and those of nonstate institutions.

I will not attempt even to sketch such arguments here; however, let me conclude by recording an observation about the character of such arguments, which may perhaps guide those tempted to construct them. It appears that legal practice has often recognized the reality of legal pluralism much better than has (modern liberal) legal philosophy, sometimes even in the face of overt hostility from that quarter. Maitland, for example, famously showed how, for much of the nineteenth century, the English law of trusts served to protect unincorporated societies (that is, those lacking the formal status of a "corporation") tolerably well in spite of its ramshackle and

---

Iain Benson, "The Future of Marriage in Canada: Is It Time to Consider 'Civil Unions'?" *Centrepoints* (Winter–Spring 2003–2004): 5–7. Available at www.culturalrenewal.ca.

78. I am grateful to Alan Cameron for clarification on this point. John D. Calamari and Joseph M. Perillo point out that, while originally the law of contract was formed in the context of a Judeo-Christian theory of natural law in which the sanctity of a promise was central, this natural law theory of contract eventually gave way to the theory of private autonomy, construed as a concession by the state. Such a theory, they suggest, "sees the foundation of contract law as a sort of delegation of power by the State to its inhabitants." *The Law of Contracts*, 4th ed., 8 (Eagan, MN: West, 1998).

79. Kent Greenfield summarizes the formerly dominant view thus: "There is little question that the dominant view of corporate law for at least the past century has been that it is private law. The early twentieth century view of the corporation was that it was defined by agency relationships and that the obligations of the management were dictated by fiduciary duties akin to those present in private principal/agent relationships such as those of trustee and beneficiary." "Using Behavioral Economics to Show the Power and Efficiency of Corporate Law as a Regulatory Tool," *University of California-Davis Law Review* 35 (2002): 581, 591–92.

80. Leslie G. Espinoza, "The Quality of Mercy: Abandoning the Quest for Informed Charitable Giving," *South Carolina Law Review* 64 (1991): 605, 642. See also Charles Nave, "Charitable State Registration and the Dormant Commerce Clause," *William Mitchell Law Review* 31 (2004): "The states retain the general police power to regulate the solicitation of charitable contributions from their residents and within their jurisdictions. Forty-three states and the District of Columbia have exercised this power by enacting statutes regulating charitable solicitations" (227).

theoretically incoherent nature. If legal practice sometimes does better than legal theory (it does not always), it will thus be necessary to seek to elicit our philosophical concepts from critical reflection on legal practice, rather than to work deductively from a series of a priori, abstract, and putatively "universal" concepts, which we then attempt to "apply" to the crooked timber of legal reality. In fact, both Gierke and Rommen, in their different ways, seem to proceed in something like this manner. Gierke seeks to discern the "universal" reality of plural jural institutional spheres primarily from critical reflection on legal and political history. And even the universal metaphysical concepts from which Rommen in the first instance proceeds are selected in virtue of their supposedly superior capacity to shed light on those historically developed social and political forms that best accord with the empirical realities of human nature. If this methodological observation is correct, then we are indeed well-advised to attend simultaneously to "historical, political, and philosophical perspectives" as we engage in "rethinking rights."

Epilogue

Toward an Integrative Vision

Bruce P. Frohnen

This volume reaches toward an integrative vision of rights as essential to social relations serving the good of society and its members—both groups and individual persons. Central elements of this vision are an understanding of human sociability, the instantiation and specification of certain essential moral truths within concrete historical practices, and the purposive nature of the person and social life. I cannot hope to flesh out this integrative vision in a brief epilogue. Indeed, such a task could take many years and many works to complete. What I intend here is more modest: to piece together notes toward a synthesis of the perspectives offered in this volume. To do so I begin by pointing out some differences in viewpoint among the authors to preclude too facile an identification of perspective and intention. This done, I proceed to draw some conclusions from the perspectives presented here, with which the authors in this volume may or may not agree, either in general or in detail. To protect the authors' deniability regarding complicity in my conclusions, I avoid reference to particular essays, though my reliance on their insights should be clear.

First to the differences: specific terminology and the general tenor of some of the essays might lead one to classify this as a book centered on a vision of reality dictated by adherence to a specifically Christian and perhaps Roman Catholic doctrine. Yet several of the authors are not members of the Catholic Church; indeed, more than one are members of no religion of any kind. What does this mean? Certainly not that any appearance of connection with ideas commonly identified with the Catholic intellectual tradition is accidental, nor that there would be no substantive difference in this volume were its authors predominantly Buddhists, Muslims, Hindus, or atheists. The essays, like the problem they address (the increasingly conflicted and underdefended state of rights), clearly are of the Western or North Atlantic world. But, as Charles Taylor has pointed out, the age in which we live makes it impossible (were it even desirable) to simply point toward a set of religious dogmas as the answer to any question of existential importance. We must seek answers "on the ground" in historical experience, political conduct, and, in part from these, philosophical understanding and build on whatever common ground we may find if we are to make greater sense of rights and their role in our common lives.

As such it is important to note that there are many languages in which one might express the fundamental convictions emanating from these essays. The language of Calvinist sphere sovereignty expresses crucial insights into the social nature of the person and the requirements of a decent public life. At a more basic level, the ordered universe at the center of both the ancient thought of Cicero and the modern Enlightenment form of Deism provides a relevant, essential grounding to human rights. The "lowest-common-denominator theology" on which these essays seem to me to be based is low indeed, though still liable to challenge. That "theology," however, is no bowdlerized set of general assumptions. Rather, it consists merely of those convictions allowing for belief in an objective moral order in which the person has inherent dignity. It is possible to argue whether one theology or another is sufficient to maintain or even consistent with belief in this moral order; but such arguments, while of great importance, are not those with which this volume or the examination of rights *qua* rights are concerned. Rather, we must look to the perspectives explicitly embodied in the essays presented here to see what if any coherent vision they produce.

The "perspectives" announced in this volume's title are historical, political, and philosophical. As such the intention is not to present a coherent theological perspective. Moreover, to the extent such a perspective is relevant it is at the level of derivations embodied in history, politics, and understandings of the nature of existence. Thus, while it may be the case that I or another author believe that rights, like all other forms of human construct, are best understood in light of their relationship with a transcendent goal and order of existence, this is not the level of discourse in which we currently are engaged, and opinions on this issue are not currently relevant. Moreover, it clearly is the case that adherents to markedly differing religions and theological beliefs have accepted and continue to accept a view of the nature of reality similar to the one that, in my view, emanates from these essays.

A second point of differentiation concerns political policy preferences. There is a very real danger that this volume will be seen as attempting to justify a set of policies deemed to belong to the political Right. Yet several of the authors would actively resist any conservative label, and the variety of policy positions represented here should give pause to anyone considering the view of rights herein presented as inherently "right wing." Several of the authors (including this one) would distance themselves in particular from an activist American foreign policy they see as bound up with the attempt to make over the world and in effect stamp out competing cultures and ways of life. Several authors (including this one) also would seek to distance themselves from economic policies and political cronyism they see as enabling economic predators. One of the benefits of modernity is that we seldom are expected any longer simply to accept the words and conduct of persons who happen to be in positions of power. One of its less successful results has been the transfer of a kind of moral authority to the most economically successful on the mistaken grounds that such success is rooted in merit, and a merit that translates beyond the money-making sphere.

In brief, this volume presents and seeks to present no specific theology or political ideology.

Perspectives

What, then, can one synthesize from the historical, political, and philosophical perspectives presented here? To begin, history is both contingent and purposive. The past need not have happened the way that it did, but what did happen (and how) has shaped events, beliefs, and the character of societies and persons to the present and will continue to do so into the future. History also is both empirical and normative. We know about what happened through factual inquiry as to events, institutional developments, and changes in social understandings. And these changes, because they alter people's expectations, should alter the manner in which people are dealt with. Historical experience changes institutions, beliefs, and practices and so ought to change laws and other prescriptive understandings of appropriate human conduct. Finally, history is both timeless and timebound; we can come to understand the things that have happened in history and to judge them good or bad according to objective moral criteria that transcend the particular convictions of any particular people or background understanding. By the same token, however, not only is no society a perfect instantiation of timeless principles, but the instantiation of these principles in one place and time, even if appropriate there and then, may be wildly inappropriate elsewhere and at another time.

This, of course, is a natural law understanding of history. It has been worked out over time in facing the necessity of condemning evil practices (for example, chattel slavery or suttee) while respecting differences of culture and avoiding the mistake (and near occasion of oppression and other evils) of assuming all societies must look and act alike. Whether rooted in religious doctrine, aesthetic appreciation for the order of existence, or empirical study of consistencies and inconsistencies in social structures, recognition of both timeless standards of good and evil and the differentiation of general precepts through historical experience is essential to a proper understanding of history.

In relation to rights, this historical perspective provides both specific and general guidance. Specifically, a review of the history of rights within the North Atlantic civilization, and in the Anglo-American context in particular, shows them to have a longer pedigree than is generally allowed. This history shows that the rights we deem universal have been fundamentally shaped in their particulars by historical circumstances, including the medieval multiplicity of jurisdictions, the English monarchs' desire for a means of overseeing local administrations, the relative strength of the English barons, and the relative vigor of the canon law. It also shows the purposive, transformative role of these rights over time. The conception of rights dominant at the American Revolution was no mere ideology spun out of the mind of John Locke, but a vibrant practice rooted in centuries of conflict and consensus on the ground, each influencing the other in both idea and conduct.

Moreover, these rights have changed in both theory and practice over time. From their beginnings rights have been spurred in their development by the drive for individual freedom from feudal ties and duties and the drive for self-government on the part of a variety of groups. Rooted from their beginnings in theological conceptions of the dignity of the person, rights also were rooted in conceptions of the inherent limits of political, and particularly royal, power. Finally, rights have been shaped by a set of structural and ideological changes emphasizing the splintering of wholes into their parts (groups into individuals and societies into strictly controlled spheres, such as public and private) and an increasingly prevalent analytic reductionism. The disintegration of real groups—by their nature greater than the sums of their parts—into smaller elements has helped produce our current, impoverished conception of rights as individual trumps for use in marking off our separations from the nation-state and from other individuals.

The historical perspective allows us to see that rights in significant measure are the product of events and expectations that combine the particular (for example, the barons' victory at Runnymede) with the more general (for example, conditions in England during the Middle Ages) and the universal (for example, the human drive for personal flourishing and community). This is not the whole story, and does not in itself present a coherent vision of rights. It is only one perspective, and one that, properly understood, points to the need for integration with others.

Because methodological perspectives are not hermetically sealed, the historical perspective throws light on the political, in particular by showing the limits of a purely ideological reading of rights. Because rights are not mere ideological constructs but products of social interaction, they are implicated and shaped by political institutions and practices as well as political beliefs. In particular, the development of rights has been shaped fundamentally by the distribution of political power. Rights developed in an era during which a multiplicity of authorities wielded juridical and in important senses explicitly political power. Kings, clerics, barons, boroughs, and so on competed during the Middle Ages for power, control, and space for self-government.

From a political perspective, the modern concentration of power in the nation-state has emptied out the realm of intermediary communities and institutions once claiming and exercising rights of their own. The result has been increasing focus on the individual as the sole bearer of rights. And the recent multicultural turn has not altered this concentration, instead demanding from the state increased recognition of the claims of certain groups to a greater share of political power in shaping the public sphere.

Some genuine and important goods inevitably have resulted from the reduction of powers in the various loci of authority once highly active in society. In the contemporary North Atlantic civilization we have no religious Inquisition. We have no murderous barons wielding power over peasants required to remain on lands not their own. We have no chattel slavery. These clear advances in human well-being can be seen in terms of advances in human rights. Individuals in the North Atlantic now have a recognized right to freedom of religious expression; they have the right to own property and to protection, through court action where necessary, from various impositions on their persons, property, and dignity; and they have the right to move as they see fit, answering to no master save laws protecting the rights of others.

But need these individual rights have been purchased at the cost of other, more socially integrative rights? Are even purely individual rights secure in a political milieu dominated by one centralized power? Concentration of power at the center leads to a concentration of attention on, loyalty to, and demands for benefits from that center. And such a focus weakens checks on those who wield power as it enervates realms in which people learn to recognize, respect, and practice rights. Valuable as the rule of law clearly is, if the only place one can vindicate (indeed the only place one can think of vindicating) one's rights is in the court system, itself an instrumentality of the nation-state, one will lose the habits and practical understandings necessary to exercise even those juridical rights.

As rights become more a matter of individual versus individual and, especially, individual versus government, the practices of self-government increasingly fall into disuse or are reduced to the abstract and nonformative casting of ballots. Rights then become objects, valued as possessions more than exercised as social habits, too self-directed to protect communities and too brittle to survive the rough and tumble of political life over the long haul. Moreover, as rights come to be defined in purely juridical terms (as tools for court or the threat of court), they lose their efficacy in social life. The too-common spectacle of those possessed with economic power forcing the less powerful to bow to their will because they can outspend them in court (or before ever getting to court) shows clearly the limits of contemporary rights in defending people from indecent treatment at the hands of those who fail to recognize the existence and importance of human dignity and their duties to their fellows. Reducing social life to a centralized political sphere tends to reduce rights to juridical rights. And such rights are irrelevant to much of actual life and incapable of sustaining themselves over time in the face of increasingly unchecked power.

A central concept lost in contemporary political discourse is that of the common good. Historically central to political life, this concept today is seen as disruptive and likely to produce conflict and even oppression if allowed to develop beyond the notion of mutual tolerance and material benefit. And this attitude makes a certain sense given the current concentration of power at the political center. Unitary power in pursuit of a unitary goal is properly a frightening prospect.

But institutional autonomy and variety are crucial to the development and protection of rights. Each of the groups constituting society has its own common good, embodied in relations and practices aimed at, for example, holiness, the making of shoes, or, at the more general, political level, nurturing the political friendship integral to vibrant social relations. What joins a society's constituent groups and enables them to cooperate is a shared recognition of and commitment to the common good. Within a context of multiple authorities the common good—mutual respect and support as people pursue the goods of their particular lives and groups—allows us to accept limits on our own wants and desires and to negotiate mutually acceptable limits to the rights of ourselves and the groups that constitute much of our lives. The daily effort to get along in community, when accepted as a good for all, is an essential spur to the development of habits that make rights matters of normative practice rather than mere paper barriers to be given lip service but little substantive defense when threatened.

A truly political perspective begins from an understanding of that narrow sphere of governmental and juridical action as rooted in culture rather than ideology. Such a perspective resists the flattening and disintegration of the public sphere, recognizing the state as properly one among many loci of authority. In this context one can recognize more rather than fewer rights than at present. But these rights are not necessarily juridical. And the rights depend for their character as well as their vindication on a consensus according to which they and those who bear them (whether individual persons or groups) have inherent dignity, purpose, and important roles within society.

Such political conceptions clearly rest in their turn on philosophical understandings of the nature of the person and the place of that person in the order of being. Of course even to assert the existence of an order of being today is to set oneself outside the mainstream of academic discourse. But this presumption is a historical fact on which contemporary rights were developed and an integral part of a conception of rights according to which they are social realities rather than mere possessions.

Contemporary legal philosophers like John Rawls and Ronald Dworkin attempt to construct theories of rights presuming near universal agreement that the person is a decontextualized choice maker. But such theories fail to capture even current understandings. It may or may not be true that the vast majority of Americans operate within a background understanding according to which their individual dignity and worth are bound up with the capacity to make rational choices and in which rights are strong claims to those things necessary for maximizing individual choice. But, while such a background understanding may exert influence on our practice of rights, there is a deeper background that is more fundamental.

Because rights, like all social constructs, exist and develop through time, this deeper background shapes the actual practices, customs, and normative force of even contemporary liberal democratic rights. What we mean by and what we practice in furtherance of, for example, the right to free speech is historically framed. Contemporary rights are fundamentally anchored in words in our (over two-hundred-year-old) Constitution, in our centuries-old tradition of political discourse, and in a view of what is due citizens from their government that is traceable to medieval canon law and, through that, to Christian understandings of the nature of the person and the universe.

Contemporary rights have deep roots in religious symbols. Central among these symbols are that of the creation, by which God gave each person inherent dignity by creating him and her in his own image and likeness, and that of the handing down of the Ten Commandments by God to Moses (rather than by a king to his subjects), thus instituting the higher-law tradition. Western civilization may have excluded such symbols from contemporary discourse. It may even have constructed, as Taylor argues, an alternative ethic of buffered individual authenticity. But our rights not only grew up within but remain in large measure shaped by a conception of the person as occupying a place within an ordered universe that both accords him or her a particular kind of dignity and places on him or her both rights and duties in accordance with that dignity, in its particular form.

I am here attempting to synthesize arguments already made, not to justify all their assumptions. Nonetheless it is important to point out that, even if Christianity as a theology has been removed from public discourse, certain key Christian symbols remain central to rights as actually practiced in the North Atlantic civilization. Whatever the state of ideological debate, the deeper background remains that of an ordered universe with moral purpose. Moreover, behind the deeper background is an existential reality, or at least what we can glean of that reality—that is, what we can learn of our condition from a philosophical perspective.

Philosophy builds on certain existential facts to produce a view of the person as inherently social, purposeful, and possessed of dignity. Those facts, which a natural law understanding insists any person who reasons carefully can know, can be encapsulated in brief form as the inevitability of social interaction that constitutes much of our character, the inevitability of actions aimed at some good, and the worthiness of our existence as social, purposeful beings. From this we can discern a number of things. Here I would point to two. First we can discern that the groups we form have their own history, purpose, and goods. They exist and develop over time, pursue goods as more or less self-governing units, and are existentially greater than the sum of their parts in that they act in ways and toward ends unachievable by their members alone and have an existence and importance as groups; thus, if organized for ends in keeping with the common good (for example, shoemaking, holiness, or many other ends not including, for example, murder or extortion), they have their own rights. Second, as to rights themselves, these, like all other social constructs, are (among other things) inherently purposive. And their purpose is to serve human dignity in its constitutive social relations.

Integration

Taken together, the perspectives of history, politics, and philosophy show rights to be integral to that which they by nature serve: social relations. Because persons are by nature social and purposive, they are born into and form purposive associations or communities. Rights are the more or less formalized means by which persons and groups negotiate the terms of their participation within larger groups. Rights change noticeably over time and with changes in circumstances because, like all permanent goods, they must be instantiated in history and because justice requires that social norms move toward approximating people's rational expectations. But rights have an abiding character rooted in their purpose of enabling social interaction that accords dignity to the person. They are essential claims to respect.

Rights are not so much claims to things in themselves, such as free speech or even life, as claims to respectful treatment—they are more about process than substance. One's freedom of speech is limited by its purposive nature, to enable civil discourse, and so does not include the right to libel. By the same token, in social practice the right to speak freely actually entitles one to respectful procedures regarding any challenge to one's particular speech acts; one has the right to a fair legal proceeding if charged with libel. It is the social interaction that is being regulated, much as the medieval right to sustenance entitled one to a fair procedure determining whether one properly demanded food from a person with surplus food.

Such a procedural understanding of more or less juridical rights adds credence to a whole host of currently contested rights, showing their real but primarily social rather than juridical nature. Rights such as that to work or that to health care are very real in the sense that decent work and health care are crucial to a life of dignity. But whether one has a right to them in the contemporary, narrow sense of having a claim to demand them from the government, or from others through the court system, is a separate matter that neither must nor can be decided in the abstract. Such rights entail or require respectful treatment in social pursuit of these goods—to open discussion of the best means of securing them and decent conduct in dealing with people seeking employment or health care. The attitude of mutual respect is objective and timeless, the particular policy or remedy is time-bound and contingent.

In terms of politics, we can glean certain prudential norms in dealing with rights, though no blueprint guaranteeing them. Indeed, such blueprints appear downright dangerous to the rights of persons because they emphasize substantive results over procedural respect. Thus in politics it would seem crucial for there to be a combination of settled procedures (a rule of law) and splitting up of loci of power—what today we call checks and balances and separation of powers, but which can more usefully be termed a multiplicity of authorities. In social terms this multiplicity of authorities would serve rights by providing many self-governing groups within which persons could negotiate social relations with mutual respect. The goal, for groups as well as individual persons, would be self-government within respectful communities.

Conclusion

Some readers may be frustrated by this search for an integrative vision of rights, not least because it seems far removed from specific issues of contemporary debate. In particular, here, I note debates over the proper manner in which rights theory should address issues relating to race, sex, and sexual orientation. Scant attention is paid to such contemporary issues in this volume. There can be no credible claim that these issues are not highly salient to public policy and human dignity today, or that they do not implicate rights thinking in important ways. But if we are to address these issues usefully, in a manner likely to produce actual improvements to the dignity and well-being of those involved, we must begin by rethinking what it is we mean by *rights*.

Rights today are so often seen in terms of claims to specific goods, whether they be valued as things in themselves or as necessities for lives of dignity, that it is difficult to see debates regarding the rights of minorities, women, or homosexuals as anything other than conflicts waged by each side over the distribution of power. As has been argued here, political power is one relevant element in any coherent vision of rights. But, because rights in their inherent purpose are claims to respectful treatment, power itself cannot bring rights (though it certainly may help). Moreover, the conflict over rights actually may undermine the bases of mutual respect integral to rights as battle follows battle and feelings of resentment and betrayal mount on both sides.

What we have here, I submit, is an invitation to rethink the terms of our debates over issues ranging from free speech to homosexual unions such that we can place them in a context of mutual respect. And that respect must be rooted in an understanding of our commonality as well as our differences and in our dependence on one another so that we may pursue the goods of our own lives, of the groups that constitute so much of those lives, and of the society through which we share our lives. Some concrete injustices have been eliminated or at least ameliorated. But there is much work left to be done. I submit that a good deal more consideration of the way in which we are working and the tools we are using is called for so that the work itself may improve us and our lives as persons and communities.

Notes on the Contributors

George W. Carey is Professor of Government at Georgetown University and author of numerous books and essays on American political thought, including *In Defense of the Constitution.*

Jonathan Chaplin is Director of the Kirby Laing Institute for Christian Ethics and former Dooyeweerd Chair in Social and Political Philosophy at the Institute for Christian Studies, Toronto.

Bruce P. Frohnen is Visiting Associate Professor at Ohio Northern University's Pettit College of Law, Editor of the *Political Science Reviewer,* and author of, among other works, *The New Communitarians and the Crisis of Modern Liberalism.*

Gary D. Glenn is Distinguished Teaching Professor of Political Science Emeritus at Northern Illinois University and a member of the National Council for the Humanities.

Paul Gottfried is Raffensperger Professor of Humanities at Elizabethtown College and author of, among other works, *The Strange Death of Marxism: The European Left in the New Millennium.*

Kenneth L. Grasso is Professor of Political Science and Director of the Project on American Constitutionalism at Texas State University, San Marcos, and editor of several volumes, including *Catholicism and Religious Freedom: Contemporary Reflections on Vatican II's Declaration of Religious Liberty* (with Robert P. Hunt).

Kenneth L. Schmitz is Professor of Philosophy Emeritus and Fellow of Trinity College at the University of Toronto, Associate Fellow of the Pontifical Institute of Mediaeval Studies, Toronto, and author of, among other works, *The Recovery of Wonder: The New Freedom and the Asceticism of Power.*

Brian Tierney is Bryce and Edith M. Bowmar Professor of Humanistic Studies Emeritus at Cornell University and author of numerous works in intellectual history, including *The Idea of Natural Rights: Studies on Natural Rights, Natural Law, and Church Law, 1150–1625.*

Index

Abbott, Phillip, 203n90
Abelard, Peter, 67
Abortion, 104n52, 158
Abrams, Kathryn, 131n87
Acquired rights, 91, 97
Adair, Douglass, 100n44
Adam, 73
Adaptability of idea of rights, 181
Addis, Adeno, 25n67
Aegidius Romanus, 42n15
Africa: ethnic politics in sub-Saharan
    Africa, 12–16; genocide in, 2, 15;
    minority languages in, 13; one-
    nation model in, 14; Tutu in South
    Africa, 54; U.S. foreign policy on, 1
Agency of institutions, 215, 237–38
Alienable rights, 88, 91, 93, 95
Althusius, Johannes, 221–22n31
America: Articles of Confederation in,
    100; business corporations in, 123–
    28, 129, 130; civil rights movement
    in, 166, 173; class action suits in,
    168; conservative movement in,
    172–73; foreign policy of, 1, 243;
    immigration issues in, 172–73;
    Locke's influence in colonial
    America, 51–52, 53; municipal
    rights in, 119–23, 129, 130; rights
    dialect in, 102, 179–80, 212; sermons
    and political essays leading up to
    Revolution in, 96; social contract

mode of thinking in founding era
    of, 83–85. See also Constitution, U.S.;
    Declaration of Independence;
    Jefferson, Thomas; Massachusetts
    Constitution (1780); Paine, Thomas
American Enterprise Institute for
    Public Policy Research, 172
American Indians, 45, 46
*American Political Writings during the
    Founding Era, 1760–1805,* 83–84
American Revolution. *See* Declaration
    of Independence
Analogy, 148n30
Andreae, Johannes, 49
Anthropological relativism, 54
Antidiscrimination laws, 7–9
Aquinas, Thomas. *See* Thomas
    Aquinas, Saint
Areté, 160
Aristotle: on analogy, 148n30; on *areté,*
    160; Bellarmine on, 68, 73, 74, 78; on
    energeia, 137; on *ethé* (custom), 160;
    on *ethos tés politeias,* 160; on
    evolution of the state, 232; Filmer
    on, 66, 66n28; on human nature, 73,
    159–60; influence of, on Declaration
    of Independence, 82; on law, 159;
    Millar on, 63; political philosophy
    of, 41, 42, 59, 67–68; rights theories
    based on, 54; on slaves, 46; on
    virtues of social life, 145

255